LONG TIME GONE

To
Brian, Carolyn, Karen, & Russell

LONG TIME GONE
The Years of Turmoil Remembered

Curt Smith

Icarus Press

South Bend, Indiana
1982

LONG TIME GONE
Copyright © 1982 by Curt Smith

Icarus Press, Inc.
Post Office Box 1225
South Bend, Indiana 46624

1 2 3 4 5 86 85 84 83 82

Library of Congress Cataloging in Publication Data

Smith, Curt.
  Long time gone.

  Includes index.
  1. United States—History—1969—   . 2. United
States—History—1969—   —Biography. 3. United
States—Biography. 4. Smith, Curt. I. Title.
E855.S64   1982   973.92   82-12043
ISBN 0-89651-425-0

Contents

An Acknowledgment

This book owes its origins to men and women of uncommon bent—and I want to thank those who assisted with their yarns and memories. From John Mitchell to John Chancellor, the figures who appear in these pages were generous with their time and care—and I cannot help but be generous in my gratitude toward them.

Thanks too to John K. Hutchens, former book critic of the *New York Herald-Tribune*, who was kind enough to review my manuscript and make comments. Michele Davis was first to insist that a retrospective of the early 1970s warranted (and could become) a book. David Parker, Linda Stillabower, and Maynard Good Stoddard lent grace to their counsel, as is their wont, and Elizabeth Smith and Helen Wehrnle read and assisted in editing the book with intelligence and tenderness. Finally, Bruce Fingerhut, President of Icarus Press, nursed the manuscript toward completion. To all I am deeply appreciative.

Curt Smith

Book One

Now for ten years we've been on our own,
And moss grows fat on a rolling stone,
But that's not the way it used to be. *

*"American Pie"

1
Crossroads

I BELONGED TO THE MOST TUMULTUOUS FRESHMAN CLASS in the history of American education. We entered college in the fall of 1969, our debut marked by Woodstock, moratoriums, and talk of "impudent snobs." We left in the spring of 1973, with the Viet Nam conflict ending, our prisoners of war at home, and the era's central figure (thoroughly modern Milhous) engulfed in a "third-rate burglary" which would later sear his presidency—the then-inexplicable Watergate affair. Amid our fear that nothing had remained unaltered, we looked in vain for contrary proof.

During those four years we perhaps matured—indeed, were forced to mature—more than most freshman classes in fourfold that time. With constants uprooted, we groped for courage and reassurance, for wistful ventures that might speak of impossible dreams. In the cultural collision that marked the decade's beginnings, the college campus was its spiritual crucible. It was a grand and awful, stirring and infuriating, lyrical and barbaric age.

The early 1970s once meant a call to freedom and adventure; now they evoked a strangely haunting sadness that came unsummoned, like a sirensweet postcard from the past. In this, exactly a decade after my freshman class witnessed a

3

spring of Cambodia and September at Attica, of turbulence abroad and near insurrection at home, I felt myself drawn back to college—for me, tiny Allegheny College in Meadville, Pennsylvania, and Geneseo State University in upstate New York—where during my years as an undergraduate, civility and madness grappled, each bidding for the other's soul.

So much had happened since then, so little of it calm and resolute. Memories came flooding into consciousness; for my friends and me, the era had left us both ennobled and marred. How were the years with them—and with those who gave the period its indelibly polarized tinge? What had happened to our New Jerusalem, the dream to save the land? Only by returning *now* to college, I thought, might one understand what had changed and what remained and where the dream went wrong. Here, at last, one might come at length to realize what we had.

2
Sunset At Dawn

NEEDING, HOPING FOR, BUT BEING UNSETTLED BY A VOYAGE back to the America of my youth, I drove north to western Pennsylvania, there to seek again a confused and crowded time.

Meadville (population 18,500) had changed little in the intervening years. Overwhelmingly traditional, predominantly Republican, conservative in style and substance, it epitomized the "Silent Majority" many public figures chose to prize and cultivate, then proceeded to betray.

Even as a student, I had identified more with its residents than with many of my peers. Now, as a decade before, they attended church suppers and school board meetings; gravitated more toward Henry Fonda than to Jane; viewed the Eastern Seaboard as injurious to the moral values and social decencies of an earlier, more ordered age. Middle aged, largely middle class, they were much like my parents—the sturdy image of America's old-style stock. These people had been natural allies; their idiom was my idiom, their culture my culture, and more perhaps than most students, they felt toward me a trust.

They had watched incredulously, I recalled, as the politics of confrontation entrapped my freshman year: violence, coercion, and terror assumed proportions undreamt of when the 1960s dawned. Across the nation, including Allegheny College, bombings, sit-ins, and vandalism besieged campuses where beer blasts and panty raids had once been labeled daring. During the 1969–70 academic year there were 1,792 demonstrations and 7,561 arrests; 8 people killed and 462 injured; 247 cases of campus arson and 282 attacks on ROTC facilities; an innocent mathematician blown to death at the University of Wisconsin, a university building burned at Harvard, fires at Stanford that did over $100,000 damage and destroyed the work of ten visiting scholars.

The turmoil was wild, unprecedented, and left Meadville's populace aghast. It scorned giant moratorium rallies led by antiwar forces in the fall of 1969; cheered Spiro Agnew in November when he excoriated the national press; applauded President Nixon earlier that month when he asked "for your support" to stabilize South Viet Nam; reacted bitterly when in May of 1970, following the murder of four students at Kent State University and two more at Jackson State College, hundreds of colleges and universities closed or went on strike, their classes suspended and examinations canceled. Thousands of students had left school to march on Washington, where events seemed unalterably beyond control.

Roaming Meadville streets, I felt old wounds and pleasures reemerge. I could not forget the anger that prompted me, a freshman of fewer than three weeks standing, to write a column in the college paper labeling the October 15, 1969, moratorium "a monument to well-intentioned but manipulated minds"; the rancor on both sides, understandable yet self-defeating, which made compromise impossible and discussion moot; the April 30, 1970, Nixon address announcing the invasion of Cambodia, a speech proclaiming that the United States would never become "a pitiful, helpless giant"; or the firestorm of protests that followed, passion so wide and deep-rooted that by the middle of June—for the only time before or since—a Gallup Poll showed that most Americans considered campus unrest to be the nation's greatest problem. It was a time one might not want to relive, but would not for the world have missed living.

If Meadville had changed little, Allegheny had changed

much. Where once students gathered to canvass homes and churches, they scurried now to find and compete for jobs. Where once the Freshman Class Council debated whether American society was "repressive" and its leaders "immoral" (my view that they were not was conspicuously alone), the debate revolved instead around fraternities, seniority, and grades. Ten years earlier the editors of eleven major Eastern college newspapers had run a joint editorial urging "the entire academic community of this country to engage in a nationwide university strike" in protest against the Viet Nam War. Today that community lay splintered and inward-looking—and the only strike being talked about concerned major league baseball and whether its athletes would picket or play ball.

All this, I supposed, was largely for the good. After all, students of the 1980s resembled their counterparts of several decades ago—serious, industrious, yearning for security and employment. For generations these had been the tenets around which American education thrived. What was absent, though, and what made the early 1970s so unique, was students' belief—indeed, their steadfast *conviction*—that college currents could affect the nation's course; that we could shape things, mold things, alter for the better the land in which we lived. In sum, make a *difference*. In short, change the world.

The events of 1969–73 both enriched and afflicted, almost like a behavior-transforming drug, and of all their attributes, perhaps emotion was the most intense. For me, as for most freshmen I knew, feelings ran raw and unmitigated through all of the years' unrest—in love found and love discarded; in the causes one adopted and the villains one despised; in the romantic vision that every side claimed as its exclusive domain.

How, today, could students raised on Jimmy Carter, Charles Percy, and other bland brethren understand the passion—the surging torrents of admiration and disgust—that exploded whenever Richard Nixon delivered a nationally televised address, held a prime-time press conference, or otherwise made his presence known? How could freshmen raised on disco and Andy Gibb understand the impact—the bittersweet sense of loss—created by the moving melodies of Crosby, Stills, Nash, & Young? How could a later generation of *Jaws* and *Star Wars* understand the unparalleled extent to which movies, sport, art, and music not only influenced the ferment of the early 1970s—but mirrored it as well?

Because truth was intuitively *felt*, not arrived at by logic, even the probing so characteristic of the times—the debate over values and morality, the demand that grades be abolished and students allowed more participation in university decision-making, the doubt surrounding America's mission and responsibility in the world—acquired an instinctual, overtly emotional hue.

Ironically, this emotion served as both cross and shield. Ten years ago, like many of my friends, I had taken pride in independent, unconciliatory ways: poor once ourselves, we would not submit our future to the care and dependence of others. By the 1980s independence lingered but pride had fled. One could not be proud of what the last decade had done to America. One could not be confident, as I once so adamantly was, that courage and self-sacrifice would weather any hardship—that one need not bow and compromise to make one's own way in the world.

"For many of your generation," George Christian, former press secretary to Lyndon Johnson, told me, "your lives have been an act of defiance." Yes, but what had defiance won, and at what cost? Those who clashed in the great battles of the early 1970s—those who hated the war and those who supported it; those who hated the Nixon administration and those who respected it; those who marched in candlelight peace processions and those who despised them—all of us harbored hopes, fears, hostilities, beliefs. Among our feelings, many were vengeful, many hard and intolerant. But they were real. Passionate. Certain. Alive. Truths to shield the intellectual insecurity virtually every student feels.

The inflammation of 1969–73 touched even those not drawn to politics and debate. For those more actively involved, our values, convictions, even sense of self, were affected equally by Americans we detested as by the men and women we endorsed. The left-wing underground gained relevance as much by its hatred of John Mitchell as by its advocacy of Bobby Seale; defenders of traditional mores were often moved more by the fervor of Janis Joplin than by the lyrics of Johnny Cash; while most of academia denounced J. Edgar Hoover, Middle America delighted in deriding Ramsey Clark.

Such conflicts reinforced one's differing identity and purpose. Students thought of themselves as crusaders for ideals, causes, entire ways of being. In the short run, then, we felt morally uplifted—but as the 1970s faded, taking with them the clashes that defined our views (and in many cases, ourselves), we saw much of what gave life meaning almost wholly disappear. The shield had departed. Only the cross remained.

During the 1980 campaign, serving as speechwriter for a presidential candidate, I drafted several addresses that prompted one syndicated columnist to label John Connally "unafraid—in fact, eager—to renew the emotional political rhetoric so familiar a decade ago." They produced, the columnist continued, "a cold sense of deja vu." Deja vu. Yes, perhaps that term put it best.

For decades teachers had complained that college left its students unaltered, little different after graduation from the way they were before their initial first-year exam. "Whether in the early 1960s or the early eighties," said my favorite teacher, Jeanne Braham of Allegheny's English Department, "students came hoping for a job and security, spent much of their time preparing for a job and security, and left with the hope of attaining those goals."

Not so with the freshman class of 1969–70. Its members had long ago left that calendar year, but the year would not, *could* not, leave them. For many, its effect was such that even as Gerald Ford gave way to Jimmy Carter, and Carter to Ronald Reagan, as Miss Vicki gave way to Miss Piggy, as Jay Silverheels died and Bert Parks was fired, they remained transfixed in an earlier, more kaleidoscopic time. They could not understand the 1980s because their emotions would not let them.

In college we had challenged, queried, marched, protested, picketed and counterpicketed, above all, cared. We lived now in a nation with leaders who spoke of limitations; with voters, regardless of party or ideology, who agreed only that things would not get better; with students whose priorities so differed from ours that comparison might have resembled a dialogue of the deaf. Our vision resided in a time capsule—lilting and elevated, but ultimately, a prisoner of the past. The world we now encountered was not the world we knew.

Strangely, none of this had eroded my classmates' post-graduate success. Of the five freshmen I had known best, one had become a senior counselor for underprivileged youth; another a teacher for the mentally retarded; the third an officer in the Air Force; two more earned their doctoral degrees in medicine.

To employment, as to school, they brought intensity. In all, of the freshman class's 473 students, 335 graduated in 1973. Sixty would become teachers, seventy-two doctors, lawyers, or government employees; sixty-three would enter business. By society's long-accepted yardsticks (work hard, study, reap thy just rewards), they had done battle in the marketplace; they had competed and won.

Why, then, I wondered, had so many spent the last decade seeking empathy and trust? During the past few weeks I had talked with nearly two dozen of my freshman colleagues; most of them remained troubled and troubling figures, ones who wanted in the worst way to amount to something, and did—but not quite in the way they had expected, or hoped. Many had asked, as I did now, why professionally we had started with so little and gained so much—why personally we had begun with so many assets, only to lose and abuse them along the way.

Time, thus, for ripe conjecture. What, sweet Moses, had caused such cleavage? What in the early 1970s, which was not so very long ago, had left us so divided, a generation at once emboldened and unsure? To relive the era's meaning, I decided, I would have to meet again the men and women who gave it form. Nixon and Reagan. Hesburgh and Graham. Friedan and Rubin. Wallace and Clark.

The names unleashed a torrent of recollections. How was *their* alliance with the years? How had *they* dealt with the unflinching enemy, time? They had inspired us, chastened us, indeed, helped to crystallize our views. Until we could understand them, we could not understand ourselves.

I drove south to Pittsburgh, then swept east on I-76 toward a cleaner, better-lighted place. Washington, home of John Newton Mitchell, lay six hours away.

3
The Squire of Rye

THREE HUNDRED MILES SOUTHEAST OF MEADVILLE, AN elevator climbed to the fourth floor. Inside the building at 2550 M Street, gray-haired John Mitchell spoke serenely with visitors. An odd vignette, I reasoned, for one whose public posture approached half-curse and half-command. Mitchell stood and thrust his hand forward. "How are you?" he said. "I don't envy the age you have to write about."

From 1969 to 1972, John Mitchell served as attorney general of the United States. Midwestern by birth, Victorian by nature, he was a stern, almost autocratic fixture. His bent was conservative; he dealt with colleagues on a no-nonsense basis founded on authority and respect. Some called it fear, or complexity, or the resultant stirrings of a troubled man. Few doubted that Mitchell was hard or that he commanded the grudging notice of underlings, peers, and presidents.

To government he brought the same demeanor that marked his approach to life: deference seldom graced Mitchell's repertoire, but a gruff, almost endearing candor did. "Watch what we do," he often told reporters, "not what we say." He seemed to treasure his image as an aging yet stalwart figure, severe and tart-tongued and unyielding. My grandfather would have called him "crankified."

11

Mitchell motioned me toward his desk. "Coffee?" he said.

"Love some," I responded. The man was an impeccable host.

"So you want to talk about ten years ago?" he asked, amusedly. "I would have to say that for me, at least, it was a time not wholly unfamiliar. And not unduly dull." His gestures were slow and steady, his speech direct. When the need demanded, I concluded, John Mitchell could still author a virtuoso ad-lib.

"What I remember most vividly," he started, "are the decisions faced by the Nixon administration. You know, for most of us—the president, his cabinet, his attorney general—it was an extraordinarily remarkable time."

Only eight months younger than the future president; like him, a World War II veteran of the South Pacific (where he commanded the PT squadron on which John F. Kennedy served), Mitchell was early bequeathed with Richard Nixon's favor. In 1963, following his defeat for governor of California, Nixon moved east to New York City, there to join the law firm of Mudge, Stern, Baldwin, and Todd. Lonely in new environs, Nixon found in John Mitchell, his fellow senior partner, a confidant and friend. They struck an immediate affinity, these products of an old culture seeking desperately to make good. Both valued work—for Nixon, politics; for Mitchell, law—as a means of upward mobility and social ascent, of escaping the past and its inflamed convention. Both needed ordered bearings; life was fraught with danger, even success not absolved of peril.

The two shared many bonds—dignity and decorum, a defensive mistrust of the outside world, a pragmatic, coldly efficient view of life, an abiding love of America for what it had brought. They also shared a common loyalty to family and close friends, a knowledge that their profiles lacked the elegance—"in that fashionable word," Mitchell huffed, "*charisma*"—which drew plaudits to the Kennedys and Adlai Stevenson and Martin Luther King. For Mitchell, like the president, the public often masked the private. Even as a youth, a friend related, Mitchell had decided he must suppress real emotions; almost invariably, his front was calculated, facade. Yet around Nixon, the acquaintance said, "John seemed to relax, to unwind, to be real. They were like two pieces cut from the same American pie."

To Mitchell, Rye, New York was home country, effete (exquisite irony) yet reposed. There, on summer evenings, would Nixon retreat, and while Mitchell's second wife, Martha, played Scarlett O'Hara, his law partners entertained. Leonard Garment coaxed a clarinet. Nixon preferred piano. "We never had the wild, swinging times many trendies think of," the former president later told me. "What we *did* have, of course, was a lot of fun. I, for example, and depending on the season, naturally, loved to sit down and belt out some Christmas carols."

Bound by friendship and vocation, Nixon and Mitchell encountered 1968. Chosen as the Republican nominee in 1960, bowing narrowly to Kennedy; humiliated in California two years hence by Edmund G. (Pat) Brown, Nixon—in this, his last chance for the presidency—sought a man to whom he could entrust the campaign's organization. His preference for manager, not surprisingly, was John Mitchell.

Encamped in headquarters at 445 Park Avenue, and the candidate's liaison to local, state, and national party operations, Mitchell performed superbly—the campaign's major figure, and some said, asset too. "Unlike previous Nixon campaigns," he said, "whenever we got a problem, we didn't push it on the candidate. We solved it ourselves." I remembered an anecdote from 1960: Leonard Hall—the former Republican national chairman—saying of Nixon in flight, "Where's Dick? Oh, he's up in the front of the plane, whittling pencils." Mitchell would prevent such obscenities; Nixon must husband his energy and strength.

To secure the peripheral South, its electoral votes threatened by the third-party candidacy of George Wallace, Mitchell proposed the name of Spiro T. Agnew, governor of Maryland. To check any hemorrhage of conservative support, he urged that Nixon score Lyndon Johnson's softspoken, left-leaning attorney general, Ramsey Clark, as being soft on crime. "When I am elected," Nixon pledged at almost every stop, "we're going to have a new attorney general of the United States." When Nixon *was* elected on November 5, climaxing the sun-dazzled autumn in which his image as a two-time loser was finally, implausibly obscured, he chose as Clark's successor, "the man who, as much as anyone alive, is responsible for my victory." The Squire of Rye.

Inaugurated on January 20, 1969, Nixon lunched two days later with his new attorney general. They talked of crime and judges, of safety in the nation's capital and vacancies on the Supreme Court. The president admonished Mitchell to rigidly limit wiretapping. "I want no climate of fear in this country," he said. For John Mitchell, glib and brooding, a puzzle even to his aides, the upcoming years would both enlarge and mock him, teasing him with summitry before plunging into night.

Outside July beckoned, warm and bright. The blocks around the White House sparkled in the sun. The man behind his desk, now talking on the phone, had once cascaded across the nation's press. Profiles chronicled him as a man inclined to labor and disinclined to smile; hilarity, one sensed, was alien.

He was a serious man, I decided, as his chin jutted forward and his eyes grew tense.

"What was the situation in our first few years?" he asked, the phone conversation done. "When we came in, vices that had been confined to the back streets were now flaunted openly." Judges, Mitchell said, hesitated to enforce laws against prostitution, gambling, homosexuality, and illegal strikes against the public. The affluent and fashionable either ignored existing laws or repealed them altogether, declaring the act a victory for enlightened thought. "And nobody said anything in a position of power. Nobody showed any guts. When people looted Washington in April 1968—following King's assassination—the federal government made no arrests, just stood there in fear and trepidation. There was no law and order. The country had gone to hell."

An unforgiving man.

"When Nixon came in, just remember the conflicts we had. The riots. The urban violence. We spent most of our first term just trying to clean up the mess we inherited." America, said Mitchell, was tinged by malice ("some of which you caused," I suggested), a victim of self-inflicted harm. Main Street had yielded to burning streets, civil liberty to civil license. Restraint was labeled vulgar, religion gauche, patriotism a refuge for rustic boors. "We didn't have to try and reverse these trends," he said. "We could have floated with the tides. But that's not what government is all about. Nor our administration either."

And reflective, too, beneath the rhetoric that bordered on excessive and made diplomacy foreign.

"Sure, I think about the early 1970s. Who wouldn't? I imagine some people think about the moratoriums. Kent State. Bobby Seale. Agnew. McGovern. You know what I remember? November the third," the date of Nixon's "Silent Majority" address in 1969. "That and days like it, with the president speaking as a president should.

"This was the first time in years," he insisted, "that working-class people in this country made their voices heard." Disdain encircled Mitchell's face. "The leaders before us—they were too busy pandering to the crazies, the kooks trying for a counterrevolution. But we thought it was time to speak for people who weren't kooks, who weren't vitriolic. It's ludicrous no one hadn't done so before."

"But how do you know who's a 'kook' and who's vitriolic?" I wondered. "Those who criticize you say that by labels like these, by dividing America into white and black hats, you polarized the country."

"It may have been polarized," he countered, "but not by us."

"Shouldn't you have been concerned, though, about *all* Americans—not just those who got you elected? After all, you weren't just representing sleepy towns in New Hampshire. Your arena was the nation." I hesitated. "Even Watts."

"Look around you," he counseled. "People who want reverse discrimination had leaders. Opponents of the military had leaders. The bureaucracy had leaders. Business and labor had leaders too." Everyone had spokesmen, Mitchell said, except the people who deserved them most—the millions of Americans who worked and saved and paid their taxes; who were content with being overlooked but not with being neglected; who asked their government neither to bless nor subsidize their lives, only for respect and dignity.

"These are the people we tried to help," he said softly, "and those are the people, I suppose, we let down." Mitchell smiled, sadly, as he rose from the desk. Reaching for a pipe, he sought his tobacco reserve.

The early 1970s, I started; turbulence had become wedded to discontent. What, in retrospect, had the dance of dreams and fury meant?

Mitchell scowled, his profile marked by creases. His face grew pensive, his nature dark. "Not that we'll ever be given credit for them, especially by the press, but I think we made advancements at home," he retorted, "and in foreign policy, there's no question but that Nixon was superb." But progress, I protested, was hardly the period's exclusive province; intertwined also were crudity and compassion, the flights of meanness and pervasive good. He agreed; the age *had* been insufferably complex. "Even now," he allowed, "I don't know wholly what it was all about," and shaking his head, he sat in his chair, unable to define further its duality or ideals.

"What, then," I probed, "do you *remember* about the early 1970s?"

Mitchell paused and gestured, then began to attack his pipe. "We thought of ourselves as Americans," he responded, "not as a member of separate racial or ethnic groups. I'm talking about our administration—and about most members of my generation. A lot of that, I think, came from our backgrounds. Remember, we'd ousted depression, lessened famine, even triumphed"—the PT 109—"at war. No task was too demanding, no effort too extreme." His America was cloaked in a mythic mold, divinely created, liturgically acclaimed.

"Is that vision of America even relevant today?" I asked. "There's no Pearl Harbor now to unite the nation."

"No, but that doesn't mean American unity is irrelevant."

"But isn't pluralism a fact? I mean, you sort of ignored that fact in the early 1970s, some say. The nation had changed—it wasn't all white faces and a white picket fence. Identity meant more now to divergent groups."

"What about their identity as Americans?"

"That's not how some minorities saw it," I said. "And by trying, they suggest, to implant your vision of America on a nation that no longer was, you divided the country."

"Not true," he objected. "Our vision was fine." Had not Watergate exploded, Mitchell said, the Nixon administration might have become America's high solstice of the twentieth century. Nixon, he said, was beholden to no special interests.

"His only special interest was America. And that's what people wanted, at least the majority—the old-fashioned, the disciplined, the unstylish, if you will. They wanted a no-nonsense man. They felt ignored by the big shots in Washington. They felt ridiculed by the nation's press. And Nixon challenged the press outright."

A laugh burst forward from Mitchell's chest. "I'm even now amazed," he confided, "at the hypocrites who could have helped us—the institutions which could have stood for reason and order, and turned into fountains of irrationality, of opposing for opposition's sake." Pipe billows clouded the air. "The universities. The savants. The think tanks and foundations. The very people who liked to think of themselves as the best and the brightest. Turns out they were nothing more than the shrillest and the worst. Look at the Johnson administration, with holdovers from Kennedy. They helped bring Johnson down from within and then when we came in, they took off the wraps altogether. No restraints to stop them. All they wanted was to hate."

"Maybe," I said, "but you weren't exactly seen as an apostle of love and brotherhood."

Self-wonderment pierced the former attorney general. "A man in my office couldn't afford to be," he said.

As attorney general, Mitchell proposed that less sympathy be extended to the perpetrators of crime and more to its victims; demanded that police departments be respected, not made hostage to ideological inquisitions and civilian review; insisted that America would not be a safe place for *any* of us to live in until it became a safe place for *all* of us to live in; and (with words that later cursed him) vowed that "given the choice between the law forces and the criminal forces, I'll take the law forces every time."

He authorized wiretaps on newsmen and government officials, supported the president's 1970 invasion of Cambodia, led the assault in court on the privacy of reporters' sources, and as director of research for Supreme Court nominees, sent Nixon the names of Clement F. Haynsworth and G. Harrold Carswell, both of whose appointments were rejected by the Senate. Mitchell thrived on turbulence, associates agreed; bulky, alternately cold and charming, he was a man around whom power fit easily and disquiet raged.

"Did I jar a few nests?" Mitchell said. "Yes, especially in those first few years. I guessed right. I guessed wrong. But we had to move quickly; we had a lot to overcome."

Mitchell stared for a blank instant. "The country was coming apart," he said of the late 1960s. "You had bomb-throwers on campus, their gutless teachers egging them on. College administrators wouldn't do anything about it—they were afraid of the reaction at their schools. So guess who had to quell the violence and disorder? We did. The American people expected their government to act." A small, vague smile. "We tried to do as they wished."

Viewing the decade's carnage, I remembered the observation of sociologist Robert A. Nisbet. "I think it would be difficult," he had said, "to find a single decade in the history of Western culture when as much barbarism, as much calculated onslaught against culture and convention in any form, as much sheer degradation of both culture and the individual passed into print, into music, into art, and onto the American stage as the decade of the 1960s." Mitchell, clearly, would endorse those views.

"Look at the record," he exclaimed indignantly. In 1967, Paris reported only twenty armed robberies, London 205, the capital of the United States 2,429. In 1968, with labor unrest peaking, more man-hours were lost through strikes than any previous year. Between November 1968 and May 1969, according to the Center for Research and Education at Columbia University, nearly two thousand high schools in America endured severe disruption, many battered by sit-ins, vandalism, and strikes. Riots savaged Cleveland and Detroit (43 dead in 1967) and Newark and Watts (34 killed, 1,032 injured). "Violence," chortled militant H. Rap Brown, "is necessary. It's as American as cherry pie."

In April of 1968, following the death of Martin Luther King, unrest tormented 168 cities. Snipers fired at police, and stores were looted; smoke swayed over streets ringing grounds around the White House; forty-six people died. I recalled James Baldwin's *The Fire Next Time*: "To be a Negro and to be relatively conscious is to be in rage almost all the time."

Four months later, watching the Democratic Convention

on television, Mitchell saw trained antiwar protesters clash
with club-swinging police—"the shock troops of the Establishment," radical Tom Hayden called them—in Chicago's blood-
swept streets. The following year, Mitchell's Justice Department brought charges against eight men accused of conspiracy
to incite riots. In August of 1969, the bodies of actress Sharon
Tate and four friends were found brutally murdered in her
Hollywood home; within a year nomad Charles Manson, he of
the most wretched side of the decade's darkness, would be
charged with each of the macabre deaths. In Berkeley, students
demanded an autonomous College for Ethnic Studies. In
Philadelphia, the University of Pennsylvania—avoiding a confrontation with student war protesters—removed its American
flags and placed them in storage. At Duke, seizing the
administration building, students insisted upon a nongraded
education program. High above Cayuga's waters, one hundred
black students, all armed with shotguns, captured Cornell
University's Student Union and demanded that disciplinary
reprimands to three black students be revoked (the Cornell
faculty, naturally enough, agreed). Even the golden meridian
of 1969's Woodstock Music Festival, when four hundred
thousand people sat in a rain-drenched field in upstate New
York and listened to the amplified beat of rock, reinforced the
disparity between rectitude and rebellion.

"The problem with all this," said Mitchell, "is the worst
was yet to come." The autumn of 1969 saw nearly five hundred
thousand protesters converge on Washington—their destination, the October and November moratoriums; their tech-
nique, to inflame hostility against the Nixon administration;
their vehicle, national television; their aim, to stop the war.

Six months later, with the trial of Bobby Seale approaching
(he was ultimately acquitted), thousands of students marched
on New Haven, Connecticut, to see the Black Panther leader
freed. Kingman Brewster, the president of Yale, proclaimed his
doubt that "any black revolutionary could get a fair trial
anywhere in the United States." It was a time of chaos; nothing
made sense. "Did we feel ourselves besieged, and with good
reason?" Mitchell asked. "No. We were in power. We controlled the instruments of government. But you could hardly
blame us if we did."

Superlatives, though, I noted, depended upon one's allegiance. Were radical agitators, as Hayden (quoting Fidel Castro) rhapsodized, "guerrillas in the field of culture?" Were they, as Mitchell believed, demagogues bent on base destruction—destruction of the university, of social institutions, of free speech itself—or were they neither, or both?

"I know what I think," Mitchell said, his fingers tapping on the armchair, "but who knows what the truth is, what history will accord? All I know is that you can't act by looking in a rearview mirror. You have to act now."

When crises erupted—"We didn't have many months without them, did we?"—the attorney general would act. He urged that Nixon combat moratorium protesters—and one week later, appearing at a September 26, 1969 press conference, the president said of the demonstrations, "under no circumstances will I be affected whatever by it." In June of 1970, upon learning of a program by White House aide Tom Huston to expand illegal surveillance, Mitchell urged that Nixon cancel the project—and the plan was revoked. Five months later, following midterm elections in which Republicans accented crime in the streets, he said that Nixon, by seeming partisan and vindictive, had resembled a candidate for sheriff. The president, he expounded, should remain aloof and presidential—and two years later Nixon strode, Colossus-like, above the McGovern fray.

Turmoil tore yearly at John Mitchell's calves. In late April of 1971, the May Day movement, part of the radical antiwar People's Coalition, announced that unless Congress mandated total withdrawal from Viet Nam by May 1, it would stage massive rallies in Washington on May 3-4. The stated purpose? To close down the capital; prevent the government from functioning; paralyze its ability to make peace or war. When Congress did not legislate, the demonstrators marched—laying seige to the city, occupying bridges and gutting arteries, keeping thousands of employees from reaching work. Tires were slashed and windows broken; pedestrians knifed and drivers harassed; trash cans overturned and shrubbery damaged; children accosted and intersections blocked.

"Faced with all this," Mitchell said, "we could do one of two things"—incur the invaders' wrath or turn the other cheek. "Needless to say, the choice was relatively apparent."

"Not to a lot of people," I said, recalling how thousands of rioting protesters were herded into Robert F. Kennedy Stadium, placed there by mass arrest.

"When you're charged with protecting tranquility," he said, his eyes ice-blue, "you can't allow self-righteous do-gooders to paralyze the place. The irony is, of course"—here laughter merged with tobacco smoke—"that after the Washington police took them into RFK, we gave the protesters cots, blankets, foodstuffs, and then helped them get out. But if you expect the press to tell that story, Mary Poppins is Martha Raye."

Two months later, when first the *New York Times*, then the *Washington Post*, sought to publish the Pentagon Papers—a secret study of the Viet Nam War stolen from government files by former bureaucrat Daniel Ellsberg—Mitchell's response was clear. The papers were purloined. Their publication could endanger national security. Their release would comprise a breach of law. At Mitchell's request, the Justice Department brought suit to prevent publication. Ruling that newspapers broke no law by printing the study, the Supreme Court disagreed. "The president and John Mitchell? They were furious, incensed," said Bryce Harlow, Nixon's congressional liaison, "but at least it showed how close their minds and instincts were." Mitchell remained, as always, large in the president's councils—the Scourge of Law and Order in an administration that, seemingly, was bent upon and valued both.

By early 1972, Mitchell's fortunes had crested; they were to shatter within a year. What unfolded read like something out of *Lady Chatterley's Lover*. The Squire's name grew dishonored, his honor defaced.

Twilight first beckoned as spring approached. On February 15, Mitchell resigned as attorney general; he would, said Nixon, join the Committee for the Re-Election of the President (CREEP), his title, chairman. Meanwhile, Mitchell became embroiled in conflict, stumbling in lockstep with an unlikely source. For thirty days he testified in open Senate hearings, fending off charges that the International Telegraph and Telephone Corporation had helped finance the upcoming Republican National Convention, in return for which—Democrats claimed—the company received a Justice Department proposal permitting three antitrust cases, then pending, to be concluded discreetly out of court.

The innuendo, never proven, turned Mitchell gray and bitter. The attorney general's hands quivered; the Eastern headlines stabbed. "It was not an easy time," said Mitchell, brusquely. "The charges were outrageous. My veracity was under question. It was an election year. There were a lot of people who wanted to harm the president through me. They had no inhibitions. And they were tough."

"As were you."

"I'd been called worse."

"A fair epitaph, then."

"Epitaph or epithet? I can never keep them straight."

Pale and waxen, Mitchell moved to CREEP. Already accounts existed, later underscored, that among its members were those without respect for law. March 30 saw G. Gordon Liddy, ex-FBI agent and gun-loving zealot, propose that $250,000 in committee funds be allocated for intelligence surveillance, much of it designed for wiretaps, most of it illegal. Jeb Stuart Magruder, Mitchell's deputy at CREEP, would later swear the former attorney general approved Liddy's project; Mitchell disagreed. On June 17, Liddy's centerpiece, the wiretapping of Democratic National Headquarters, exploded— and with it, ultimately, Richard Nixon's presidency.

Five men were arrested that incandescent evening. Who, newsmen wondered, had authorized the break-in? Who would trespass upon accepted law? "Well, what the hell, did Mitchell know about this?" Nixon asked his chief of staff on June 23. "I think so," answered H.R. (Bob) Haldeman. "I don't think he knew the details, but I think he knew." Mitchell resigned as chairman the following week.

His career in purgatory, Mitchell was taunted on another flank. In 1968 his wife, Martha, had spent the campaign's final weeks in a rest home; now, with the ex-attorney general imperiled, her bouts of crying, hysteria, and nocturnal phone calls soared. "I love my husband very much, but I'm not going to stand for all those dirty things going on," she told one writer. "I fear for my husband. They're not going to pin anything on him. I won't let them," was her telephone message to the *New York Times*. Nixon's close friend, Bebe Rebozo, once asked

Mitchell why he suffered Martha's vagaries. "Because," he said softly, "I love her." Amid Watergate, even love did not suffice; Mitchell turned despondent, sullen, lost in this, the worst season of his life.

He was indicted on March 1, 1974, charged with conspiracy, perjury, and obstruction of justice; he and Martha had separated several months before. Mitchell was convicted on New Year's Day, sentenced in February of 1975, then entered Allenwood Institution. His wife died on May 31, 1976, her end slow and anguished and myeloma-induced; burial occurred in Pine Bluff, Arkansas, reporters outnumbering friends. Finally, in early 1979 John Mitchell was freed from prison; disbarred from practicing law, he would (said associates) turn to consulting work in the dual bastions of elitism—New York City and Washington, D.C.

Mitchell would not discuss Watergate: "It's part of the record, the past, part of the history of our times." Instead, he reverted to my born-again question: What had the early 1970s meant?

"Few things in recent years," he said, "show more the importance of timing, of an even break. Had we come along ten years before, or a decade after, with college campuses quiet, with no war going on, what a difference it could all have made. Administrations today or twenty years ago—they make mistakes, they have achievements too, but they never were cursed by something which caused 90 percent of all the problems we ever had."

"But wasn't it within your power to *create* an 'even break?'" I asked. "If you'd have left Viet Nam in '69, '70, college campuses might have been quiet."

"Oh, they probably would have found something else to rant about."

"What could have topped the war?"

"Yes," he said, "it afflicted everyone, affected every corner of the government. We spent so much time trying to end it honorably, to deflect the criticism here at home, that other things went unattended to. Even as we were ending it, the hostility remained. All of the political excesses on *both* sides"— he would never excuse, one knew, Hayden and Fonda and Angela Davis—"where did they come from? The war." Pause.

"And the most disgraceful thing was the way people who got us into the mess—the Ramsey Clarks and Clark Cliffords and so forth—were the most irresponsible in condemning us for not ending it sooner."

Steadfast silence. "Think," Mitchell said, "about what might have happened had we just got out. Just left when we came in. Would there have been a difference? Think of if we'd only had a chance."

"You did," I said. "What if, in 1969, taking office, you did what [Vermont Republican senator] George Aiken suggested—leave Viet Nam and just say you won?"

"We couldn't do it, of course," he stated. "We couldn't just get the hell out of Viet Nam and leave millions of people to be beaten, savaged, murdered in the bloodbath we knew would occur—and which incidentally, *has* occurred. But if we only could have... only could."

I looked at Mitchell's face, strong and hurt and stubborn. A sad man, who changed his country. A decent man, self-destructed by events.

"Without the war," he murmured, "there would have been less hate. With passions cooled, there wouldn't have been the need felt to inflict damage on both sides here at home. And without that need, we wouldn't have had the problems we had later. We might have had tranquility. Peace."

Ten years and a million memories later, my host, belatedly, had reached that goal. Absent, now, were the deeds and longings of his years with Nixon, the crashing tumult that cradled their reign. His manner was, as always, reserved and distant. Yet there was a calmness to his speech, and a sincerity that was real. Repose, that elusive ally, had found John Mitchell at last.

Scandal. Imprisonment. Separation. Death. He had endured all there was and found that one survived.

He smiled wanly, then exclaimed, "Say, I have a meeting." He rose and strode briskly from the door, combative and irascible still.

4
Ramsey Alone

HE MATURED DURING THE GREAT DEPRESSION. LONG, winding breadlines were in pervasive vogue. So were soup kitchens, pleas for one full meal a day, apples for sale on deserted street corners, billboards proclaiming "I Will Share." Herbert Hoover's legacy had already been defined forever; urban shanty towns of the jobless down by rivers bore his name—"Hoovervilles." Men pounded pavement in futile search for employment; winter nights went unmarked by heat. "Happy Days Are Here Again" leaned less to madcap melody than a dirge which sounded daily. The era spoke more of "Brother, Can You Spare a Dime?"

In his native Texas, despair's roots loomed deep. Ignored or exploited since the Civil War, its rich farmlands abused for generations, the rural South saw topsoil crumble and hillsides erode away. Further north and west, out beyond the prairies and Great Plains, winds and drought withered the wheatlands and buried farms in currents of sand. Tenant farmers, both black and white, endured the wreckage. Poverty, it seemed, could eclipse even the barriers of race, a shibboleth which never fled from Ramsey Clark, crusader.

He was a strange man, this loner, pacifist, liberal iconoclast. Where John Mitchell was hard yet malleable, Ramsey

25

Clark was unswerving yet soft. *"Gentle?"* Lyndon Johnson once stormed. "Hell, Ramsey Clark is soft as shit."

Mitchell despised students demanding "peace at any price"; Clark delighted in their probing. Clark's administration began in tragedy—the Bay of Pigs—and ended in an inexplicable war; Mitchell's began in an inherited war and ended with the tragedy of Watergate. Where Mitchell hailed from Wall Street, Clark's companions were avant-garde. Mitchell was sardonic, biting; Clark almost lyrically artless. Both came to Washington proud, substantial men. Each left in ignominy— Mitchell to prison, Clark to New York. They were at once insecure and self-possessed, impressive yet vulnerable—and they presided as attorneys general over six of America's most bedeviled years.

Clark was, one knew, a moralist. Injustice was barbaric, police inequities worse; the war in Viet Nam was a tragedy, an immorality, a sin. Educated at the University of Texas, the son of President Truman's first attorney general, he was met by early comfort. "Like a lot of people who have it fairly easy," a friend of his told me, "Ramsey quickly became a progressive, an apostle of Roosevelt's, something of a do-gooder"—a voice of zealotry and piety, of civil rights in fact and spirit, a flare of liberal conscience in a devoutly conservative state.

"I've never gotten far from those days, really," Clark said, presently, at his offices in Manhattan. "You know, after growing up in Texas we moved a lot before coming home, my father being in the government and all. I remember over a period of a few years returning to Washington four times, going to four different schools.

"You didn't have the chance to get roots, develop friends, or get framed into peer-group values. So I developed my *own* values, and in my home, as I saw a lot of young men in government, idealism, energy, commitment, lose all that"—he halted—"and themselves through compromise and ambition, I decided that if I lost everything else, I wouldn't lose what I believe."

Like Mitchell, Clark was a lawyer. His offices were expansive, informal. Impressionistic paintings jeweled one wall; copies of *District Lawyer* and *The Nation* dotted desks. Four months earlier—seeking the release of fifty-two American hostages—he had returned from Iran, there to denounce

United States-aided "war crimes" committed by its Shah. Defamed by editorialists, scorched by abuse, Clark was a stranger now, even here in New York, seeking home and friendship.

"It hasn't been easy," he said of his fiasco in Tehran, "but I have to say what's inside me. I've always been that way—and I don't think I could change it, even if I wanted to, which I don't. I was that way about civil rights when it wasn't popular, about defense spending when it wasn't the thing to oppose. What would be the use of becoming a liar now? Everything I stood for in the late sixties and early seventies—peace, brotherhood, an end to animosity—would be made a mockery if I did.

"I've seen a lot of people who seemed to stand for something and then didn't, or who had a dream, as we did with gun control in the late sixties, and through compromise let it slip away. You're not going to accomplish anything if your perseverance isn't clear." Rebuffed and solitary, he must seek refuge in the sanctity of his ideals.

Clark entered government in 1961, his title deputy assistant attorney general, his president John F. Kennedy. Four years later, he was elevated to assistant, and succeeded Nicholas Katzenbach as attorney general in 1967.

Shy and deliberate, Clark inherited a Justice Department beset by turmoil. The year before, Richard Speck had murdered eight student nurses on the south side of Chicago; within another three weeks a second madman shot and killed fourteen people at Clark's alma mater. Across America, while intolerance and counterbigotry struggled, urban terror ripped its texture, savaged values, stained its soul.

By June 1968, Robert Kennedy, forty-two, and Martin Luther King, thirty-nine, lay buried, their lives ended by assassin wounds. Students rioted from Stanford to Colorado to Columbia; classrooms were invaded, teachers struck. In Chicago, site of the August Democratic Convention, madness solidified, protesters screaming obscenities as policemen replied with mace. "Whoever tears at the fabric of our lives which another man has painfully and clumsily woven for himself," Bobby Kennedy had said in early May, "then the entire nation is degraded." As 1969 beckoned, Ramsey Clark's America seemed a cruel and degraded place.

"They were terribly difficult years," Clark said, gravely.

"The times were so spiteful. And there was such a horrible reaction in the South, in the Wallace movement, killings, bombings, and so forth, against our struggle for racial principle. In many ways, even though the Depression left a wretched scar, those days were easier to live in." Yes, I allowed silently, perhaps he was right. Even at age thirty, I too often panted for preceding years.

"But they had a marvelous side as well," he noted, his voice rising as the syllables advanced. "We were able to give black people a chance, poor people a chance, the women and minorities, all the people we'd kicked around and abused. We had a belief, a vision almost, that we could bring about profound social change. And with it all an excitement—that we had principle, and that 'We Shall Overcome.'"

The late 1960s, he said, comprised a time of proud achievement, one in which racial pride was encouraged, the dignity of the individual reaffirmed. In the areas of voting rights, jobs, and housing, a multitude of new laws was enacted, old obstacles erased. These laws, Clark insisted, helped to heal, not inflame; to redress old injuries, not inflict future wrongs; to ensure that as all were created equal in dignity before God, all could be viewed as equal in dignity before man.

Yes, I agreed, Americans who had forsaken themselves must be convinced that others had not; the American Dream could not be exclusively a white, or suburban, or upper-class domain.

"But what about the other side?" I asked. "Some charged you were so obsessed with providing equality of results as well as equality of opportunity, that you forgot about your first priority—domestic tranquility. You talked about rights, they said, but you never talked about responsibilities."

Because of men like Clark, critics proclaimed, America had become a splintered society of many conflicting parts. The term *right* itself once meant a legal claim on an area of individual discretion, such as freedom of speech, or a restriction on government's ability to mandate and coerce; today, it was fashionably applied to virtually every demand one group made on another.

"Oh, that's just a lot of right-wing garbage. You know, any time anybody wants to stop progress, they just talk about responsibilities and the need for order," he retorted.

"Those are the same kinds of people who were horrified because I opposed the death penalty. 'How can the country's chief law enforcement officer do that?' they said. Well, the use of force to achieve stability—that's what they wanted—is a violation of constitutional principle. It's more dangerous to freedom and decency than any criminal offense itself."

Pouring coffee, Clark looked past his cup. "These people, the capital punishment crowd, thought you could solve social problems by murdering people. 'Offend me and I'll kill you,' they said. And at the same time they were talking about the need for a stronger, moral America. What a vow for Christ."

I started to respond, then, pausing, shook my head. The man to my left, lithe and tanned and handsome, seemed complex and variable—hesitant at one point, convincing at another, the voice firm and stolid, yet quiet and often melancholy. There was a conviction to his manner, but an element of sorrow too, as if only in the late 1960s—a time that canonized disorder, which made of individualism a shrine—only here could the Solitary Man feel secure. The age had become him; sadly, his role had not.

Clark was miscast—who could not know it?—as attorney general; he might have done better in the Department of Commerce, or in Health, Education, and Welfare, or on the White House garden detail. Sworn to uphold domestic order, he acclaimed the Miranda decision which restricted policemen's methods of apprehending suspects, eschewed legal wiretapping and alibied for criminals, sympathized more with Tom Hayden, who scorned America's "sadistic elements in its police departments," than with J. Edgar Hoover—who later said to Nixon, "That man [Clark] was an impenetrable, blithering boob." Vandals who raped Washington in 1968, he said, were "Americans who deserve our tolerance and compassion"; urging police nonviolence, he nonetheless condoned violence as a recourse for those who felt themselves to have been culturally and materially deprived.

"Remember when Eisenhower said his worst mistake as president was in naming Earl Warren to the Supreme Court as chief justice?" volunteered a cabinet colleague of Clark's. "Well, guess what Johnson thought *his* worst mistake had been?"

No one denied, I proposed to Ramsey Clark, that injustices

lingered or that inequality remained. Had he, though, not confused legitimate dissent with unchecked disorder? Had not his doctrine fostered dependency and social abuse and created needless conflict between progress and order when, in fact, neither could exist without the other? This was not, I could argue, what one of Clark's childhood heroes, Woodrow Wilson, meant by lauding "the real sentiment and purpose of the country." Perhaps the time had come to honor those Americans who *did* uphold the law—those who shared its precepts and understood its ideals and sought the decent stability—the regard for the rights of others—that made progress possible and life worthwhile.

"Oh, yeah," Clark said mildly. "I subscribe to some of that. Did back even in the sixties too. Sure, you enforce laws, but you don't corrupt them. And the way to corrupt them is to say, 'Well, we'll shoot a few looters, knock 'em off, nail 'em in the back, to show how tough we are.' You can't ask law officials to become some sort of Dragnet, Jr. And because I wouldn't, I was looked upon as somehow soft."

"By men," I said, "like Richard Daley?" As mayor of Chicago, Daley had issued an order in 1968 "to shoot to kill any arsonist, to shoot to maim or cripple anyone looting any stores in our city."

"You bet," Clark shot back, smiling. "I mean, the good mayor's philosophy and mine were not exactly one."

"But was yours wrong too? Daley wanted, if need be, to knock criminals off; you sought, some say—especially in '68, when all the fury hit—to let them off. Wasn't there some middle ground, maybe some compromise possible between the poles?"

Clark grimaced; his half-smile went flat. "One radical, Hayden, I think it was," I continued, "said, 'What we are seeking is instability.' The attorney general stands for stability. Some charge you failed that trust."

"No," he declared, a tone of bitter resolution in his voice. "Oh, I know it's easy to say we let the country down, let law and order—whatever that means—disappear, let crooks and hoodlums run wild. Anyone can say that." Leaning forward, Clark tapped his knee, amusement mixed with scorn. "The truth is, I had to look out for those who maybe were abridging rights as well as those who wanted safety in their homes.

"Government's first responsibility is to prevent lawlessness by the government itself. That's the definition of civil rights. If government yields that, it gives up its reason for existing—and that's to uphold the equality of law. The riots of 1968? The threat to the nation's stability was miniscule, really, compared to the dangers of bias and prejudice. Jefferson had a great quote. He said, 'Adopt the most moderate possible reaction to insurgency reflecting social injustice.' That's what I tried to do."

Four years after Clark left office, Herman Kahn of the Hudson Institute addressed a White House meeting. "The strength and weakness of the intellectual," he said, "is that he deals in ideas. The strength and weakness of the average guy is that he can tell black from white—but gets confused in the gray areas." About 20 percent of all Americans, he said, "achieved the ability to confuse night and day in the 1960s." For officials like Ramsey Clark, Kahn maintained, life meant unending dusk.

With Nixon ensconced in the White House, Clark's focus turned to another, more cataclysmic concern. "Before, when he was under Johnson's thumbprint, his hands were tied in the conflict in Southeast Asia," a former associate in the Justice Department said. "After all, how could he attack a war his own commander in chief had started? But when Nixon took over, it was Katie bar the door. There was no need to keep silent, no reason to shut up. He was free; he could say what was gnawing at him. It was time to take off the gloves, time to slug away."

Clark's discontent took root in the early 1960s, long before he felt able publicly to condemn the war. Limited yet expanding, America's involvement in Indo-China had already linked two presidents: Eisenhower and Kennedy sent military advisers to help South Viet Nam repel the Viet Cong, Communist forces abetted by China, the Soviet Union, and the North Vietnamese. Clark motioned to the bookshelf. A tome about John F. Kennedy stood alone. "I remember in the fall of 1963, I think it was, when Kennedy said, 'In the final analysis, it is their war. The Vietnamese are the ones who have to win or lose it.'"

Clark hesitated. "Who knows what would have happened if he'd lived?" he said, finally. "I mean, we tend to reflect what we like to think, and we like to think he'd have kept us out, not escalated the conflict. You just don't know. We had, what, twenty-six thousand advisers there then, and maybe some Pentagon brass would have told Kennedy, 'Double that and we can win.' And maybe he would have agreed. Even principled people can be drawn into quicksand. So you just don't know. Come November 22nd, and it's too late—for him, the country, the war."

Two days after Kennedy's murder, Lyndon Johnson told a visiting diplomat, "I am not going to be the president who saw South Viet Nam go the way China went." Overtly patriotic, a devoted anti-Communist weaned on Alamo mythology and Texas pride, Johnson declined to leave Southeast Asia; the Saigon government must be saved. "What's the use of having friends," said the Father of the Credibility Gap, "if you don't stand up for your allies and stand up to the bastards who want to do us in?"

In August 1964, when two U.S. destroyers were attacked in the Gulf of Tonkin, Johnson ordered a retaliatory assault on North Viet Nam. The crisis prompted a congressional resolution, adopted by the Senate, 88 to 2, and by the House of Representatives, 416 to 0, authorizing the president to repel attacks and "prevent future aggression." Six months later, endowed with an electoral mandate after his pummeling of Barry Goldwater, Johnson ordered an air strike against the North, answering a Viet Cong mortar attack on an air base at Pleiku. March saw the first American combat troops disembark in Viet Nam, the inception of bombing raids up North without any pretense of retaliatory intent, and the debut of strategic sorties that resulted in more United States bombs falling on Viet Nam—North *and* South—than dawned on all enemy targets in World War II.

Americans learned of leech-infested tributaries and steep, careening hills; of casualty rates that, starting in early 1968, eclipsed five hundred a week; of costs exceeding $25 billion in 1967 alone; of troop commitments that soared and multiplied, rising from twenty-six thousand in 1964 to five hundred and forty thousand. One remembered Adlai Stevenson, circa 1953: "The ordeal of the twentieth century—the bloodiest, most turbulent era of the Christian age—is far from over."

Some, like Johnson, presidential-aspirant Richard Nixon,

and Secretary of State Dean Rusk vowed that America must honor its treaty commitments; if not, they said, no nation would ever trust us again. They argued against the desertion of Viet Nam; compared its prospective betrayal with the appeasement of Nazi Germany at Munich thirty years earlier; insisted that, since bombing halts and peace overtures had failed to dim Hanoi's intransigence, only intensified bombing would make the Communists kneel. If South Viet Nam fell, they warned, a chain of sister states would follow. "All of the free countries around Viet Nam," Rusk said years later, "desperately wanted us to see the fight through. Those here at home who dismissed the domino theory, well, they hadn't talked with the dominoes."

Clark's ideological brothers—among them Senate liberals like George McGovern of South Dakota; Majority Leader Mike Mansfield; J. William Fulbright, chairman of the Senate Foreign Relations Committee; and the newly elected Robert Francis Kennedy—scoffed at administration claims, deriding the domino theory, terming the North–South contest essentially a civil war, noting that even if America withdrew from Viet Nam, Communist China—unlike Hitler's Reich—was militarily incapable of expanding the strife. All rejected Johnson's contention that Hanoi was a satellite of Peking. "The pathetic irony," Clark bristled, "is that all our bombing accomplished was the very thing we always wanted to avoid— drive North Viet Nam straight into the camp of Mao Tse-tung."

Enter February 1968, the Lunar New Year in Viet Nam. For months the president had assured Americans that we were slowly, inexorably "winning the war." The Tet offensive made burlesque of Johnson's claim. Assaulting from the North, the Viet Cong ravaged thirty cities, captured the ancient city of Hue, invaded the grounds of the American embassy (supposedly invulnerable), drove three hundred and fifty thousand new refugees into the pockmarked countryside. "The stated purposes," said Lyndon Johnson, "of the general uprising have failed," but few Americans believed him. The Johnson presidency crumbled under the force and presence of Tet.

"As you'll remember, President Johnson withdrew as a candidate for reelection two months later," Clark recollected. "I don't think he ever recovered from what had happened—the way the North Vietnamese rampaged through areas we held. And I think it demonstrated once and for all the bankruptcy of our policy there, of trying to prop up a sleazy, unrepresentative, undemocratic regime in South Viet Nam. You know, Johnson was funny. He had great faith that things would work out if he only persevered. He'd had several heart attacks, recovered from them, and come back. He wasn't one to become discouraged.

"And he had almost a heroic hope in Viet Nam, even after the march on the Pentagon in October of 1967, which I think was the moment that the fever broke in the whole antiwar movement—the time, in other words, when students realized, 'Hey, we're not the only ones who hate this war. Millions out there do, too'—and the contagion spread. And this hope impelled him long after rational analysis told us that things weren't going to work. And then came Tet, and even for Johnson, hope was gone."

The United States, Clark believed, had chosen wrong, supporting a corrupt government in Saigon against peace-loving forces in Hanoi. In 1969, while Nixon unveiled a carefully balanced course of Vietnamization, diplomacy, and phased withdrawals, the former attorney general's antiwar brethren answered with a three-syllable ultimatum—Get Out Now. Clark sought to liquidate the government his own president had helped install; the war, he recited, provoked mindless barbarism, a tragic diversion of resources that could better be used at home.

Now a private citizen, Clark lambasted the Nixon administration, etching its exploits in withering terms—traveling across the country, flailing his way through college campuses, speaking at the Washington moratoriums, challenging the president's right to make (and continue) war. Clark reaffirmed his support for amnesty and abortion, talked of his empathy for busing and civil rights, demanded a curb on penalties for use of marijuana, mocked Pentagon budgets as "heinous and obscene."

Three decades earlier only 1.35 million students had resided on America's colleges and universities. As the 1960s ended, the total soared to nearly 7 million, a surging special-interest group seeking to make known its demands. In them Clark found an audience. In him they found a friend.

"You *were* well received," I said, "whenever you touched down on campus."

"Oh, I suppose so," he conceded. Ardent praise embarrassed Clark, jarred the modesty that cloaked his self-esteem. "You have to recall, though, that any cheers weren't for me but for what I stood for—an end to the destruction, the killing, the incoherence. And they were *ready* to cheer. It was so compelling, the war, overriding emotionally. Most students were prepared to commit themselves and exhaust themselves and ignore all the rest. And why not? Their lives were on the line, that's what."

Clark's revival hour blanketed academia. To students wanting sanctuary from combat and the draft, he emerged as part-prophet, part-statesman, part-spokesman for their fears, and towering above all his roles stood the folkseer, the teller of stories and scenes—of children without limbs and liberty, of napalm-covered villages and mutilated men, of bombers which came in darkness and fled, unmourned, by light.

I recounted Mitchell's acerbity. "Ramsey Clark," he told me, "may have been one bright star on campus—they deserved each other, for sure—but in truth he was a disciple of the Double Standard, one of the clowns who got us into the war and then when we took office, started blaming us for staying in." What would have happened, I wondered, had Nixon acted as Clark's allies asked? What would Clark have done without a president to deplore?

"I would have managed," he explained, and as he spoke I felt that self-pity touched him. "I didn't need to tour this world opposing the war just so I could have a propaganda blast. All I wanted was to stop young boys from being sent to die by old men. Is there anything wrong with *that*? If there is, just tell me."

In retrospect, he said, the war enveloped Nixon. "Actually, you can make a case that by dragging the war out through the 1972 elections, he helped himself politically—playing to patriotism, having people rally 'round the flag. But in the end, the divisions came back to haunt him—and he widened the war as Johnson never did, going into Cambodia and Laos, mining harbors, carpet-bombing Hanoi.

"And the country, what it did to our morality, our sense of decency and mission, what it did to what our young people felt about America—that's what was crippled. That's what we lost." He stopped a long moment. "And what about my successor as attorney general? John Mitchell's life speaks for itself. I can't say more eloquently what the record already shows."

Mitchell was in Florida vacationing in July of 1972. On Thursday the twenty-seventh, Clark left for Hanoi under the auspices of a Swedish group inquiring into "U.S. crimes in Indo-China." Clark had recently been named by George McGovern "perfect for head of the FBI if you could get him," but reviews of his North Viet Nam sojourn proved less sublime.

In Hanoi, he aired a broadcast over government radio asking that America stop its bombing of the North. On August 12, he told reporters of his visit to a prisoner of war camp: "their health is better than mine, and I am a healthy man." Returning to Washington, Clark testified on Capitol Hill about North Vietnamese benevolence. Early the following year, with American prisoners finally home, Hanoi's torture of POWs was recurrently, gruesomely revealed. Men had been clubbed, beaten, held in solitary confinement. Jane Fonda, ever the demagogue, called the prisoners "liars" for making such charges; obviously, she implied, Vietnamese despots were more trustworthy than America's sons. Such venom was foreign to Ramsey Clark; he retreated to Manhattan, silent and alone.

In 1974, Clark tried for the United States Senate, losing narrowly to Republican Jacob Javits, then quickly seized obscurity. Six years later, with Iran in revolution and Americans imprisoned, he again journeyed overseas. Arriving in Tehran, he praised the Ayatollah Khomeini, glorified Muslim culture, attacked United States imperialism, and demanded the return of the former Shah—deposed and exiled, an ally of America for thirty-seven years, and if retrieved by revolutionary leaders, almost certain to die. Patriots thundered. Congressmen urged that Clark be jailed. Admirers called him *principled*. Critics opted for the terms *venal, rancorous*, a *traitor* in a gray pin-striped suit.

"How stupid, how utterly foolish for us to have tried to prop up the Shah," he said, picking at his coffee. "He was a tyrant, a killer; we had no business trying to help him."

"And his successor?"

"Not a saint, but not a Satan, either. We brought a lot of this trouble on ourselves. The rescue operation to free the hostages, to name one instance—how ludicrous of us to think we could fly halfway around the world, transfer to helicopters on a distant desert, and then enter Tehran in the dead of night, seeking out, hoping to somehow find live hostage bodies in a strange, unknown land."

"And the hostages, what of them?"

"It's easy to hate, to raise the American flag and blindly follow it, and to scream foulness at nations like Iran. I only know that hate never solved anything—in war or peace. We'd be better off treating *all* nations with decency, with kindness, and—I know it probably gags you—with love."

In Iran, as in Southeast Asia, Clark's doctrine was clear, courageous, and (many felt) regrettably wrong. He believed— sincerely—that America should be ashamed of its material and economic wealth; that the United States, not the Soviet Union, was the real barrier to world peace; that the weaker we were, the safer we were; that, as Jimmy Carter phrased it in 1977, we have "an inordinate fear of communism." His doctrine rested on the belief that all nations, Communist or otherwise, shared our desire for freedom and liberty; that the concept of human rights would influence power-brokers whose lives were based on tyranny and bondage; that all world leaders, even those in the Kremlin and Peking, would listen to reason if only goodwill prevailed.

Time, I suggested, had fully judged these views; in the real world of geopolitics, love and innocence would not suffice. I reminded Clark of John Connally's testimony: "There were those who said that when the United States left Southeast Asia, there would be no bloodbath, only peace and harmony instead. They were wrong. Dead wrong. And millions of people are dead *because* they were wrong."

Clark's face reddened. "He says there's a bloodbath?" he protested. "What about the bloodbath *before* we left? I guess he subscribes to the psychology that you have to destroy a village to save it. That's what we did in Viet Nam, you know. As far as who's responsible for what deaths, let's let history decide.

"It's a strange, unsettled time today. Many times I think back to the period you're talking about. I don't think there was a greater degree of caring then by people, students especially, than now, but it was easier to channel that caring.

"You knew what you could do as a student—help stop the killing and the death. Today the problems are more diffuse and scattered. What can you do? We wonder. During your time in college, we knew."

The former attorney general was a liberal. I was conservative. Like many of my rightist friends, he too was a true believer, his vision of America unmarred by the complexity that attends our times. "Perspective is all," Jeanne Braham often told me. One could admire Clark's grace and sensitivity, as I did now, and still regard him as misguided and naive.

"You know," I said, "I suppose we don't agree any more now than we did ten or fifteen years ago."

"That's all right," Clark responded. "I imagine we'll both survive."

We trudged toward the eighth floor elevator. "What's on your future agenda?" I inquired.

"Who in the world can say? Wherever I'm needed, I guess." Silence. "There's just one question I want to ask," Clark injected, smiling. "How can anyone who lived through the college era you did come out thinking the way you have?"

He turned and strode toward his office. The elevator closed.

5
Mountain Man

TO FIND MONTREAT, NORTH CAROLINA, YOU DROVE SOUTH and west from Ramsey Clark's Manhattan. Rustic even by mid-South standards, graced by steep passes which beckon to the valleys below, the virgin highlands remained unchanged by time and untamed by man. Through the Appalachian uplands the road climbed and weaved, past farms dotted with share-croppers' cabins; past houses encircled by lumber; past grave-yards and quiet backwaters, artifacts of a slower, less anguished age.

Mailboxes revealed names like *Baker, Nelson, Reed,* and *Weber*—names vaulting back a hundred years earlier, when travelers paused on their sojourn west. Clean and diminutive yards, their grass turning haggard with autumn growth, betrayed the reddish-brown soil that sprawled beneath. Porches were everywhere; most had swings that silently awaited the renewal of companion spring. Already the Blue Ridge hard-woods had yielded color, and in streams that split the forest, blue mixed with rippling white.

Hard by Black Mountain lay Montreat, population 350 and home of an ebullient adopted son. Approaching its heart, I remembered H.R. Haldeman's critique of Richard Nixon. "He doesn't have to establish an identity," the chief of staff said in

1972. "Because of TV and his trip to China, he's probably the best-known human being in the history of the world." Haldeman's belief was understandable, his conclusion askew. For it was the phenomenon moving toward me, his face ageless and aglow, who had been personally beheld by more people than any man or woman in this planet's tide of times. Amid riot and assassination, discord and scandal, he had endured, unmarred and mythic—in Angela Davis's term, "sort of the Lord's American Son."

"Howdy," pronounced my host, "have any problem finding the place?"

"None," I answered. "All I did," alluding to John Winthrop, "was look for the 'Shining City on a Hill'."

The Reverend Billy Graham muffled a yawning grin. "Come on inside," he said.

Born in Charlotte, North Carolina, the son of a dairy farmer, the man at my side was a flawless speaker, at once polished and unchanging, almost electrically pure. At ease in public, at home in crowds, his was a vivid, rapt presence, hosannahs—and a flood of donations—hailing his exuberance and southern-sweet tongue.

He had burst upon America in 1949, when a damnably obscure crusade in Southern California—elevated by the conversion of several entertainers, Graham's anti-Communist pose, and the blessing of publisher William Randolph Hearst—acquired a sweep and following that "I'd never dreamt of, never hoped for, never expected." Within a year he was featured in *TIME* and *Newsweek*, *Life* and *The Saturday Evening Post*. Within a decade he was a global institution, eclipsing even the stature of Norman Vincent Peale.

Beloved by Eisenhower, tolerated by John Kennedy, totally consumed by Lyndon Baines Johnson, Graham emerged as the United States' parish chaplain, a firmament of recognizable talent, respected for the quality of his craft. His being was chaste and sober, his moral vision clinically clean. Those who dismissed him as rural and simplistic, or grew infuriated at his naivete, overlooked Graham's self-assurance—his ingenious likability—which lured grudging envy from even vehement opponents; with the nation his stage and televison his ally, he became an epochal champion of frontier evangelism, a Calvinist's answer to the pope.

"Describe," I began, "your expectations as the sixties ended. You thought, obviously, that Nixon could restore the calm and serenity he had pledged during his campaign—to bring about a resurrection of what America had been a decade and two before."

Graham removed his glasses and released a sigh. "In many ways, yes," he professed. "After all, I knew his family so well—Mrs. Nixon, the girls, David. I knew his mother"—a regular patron at Graham crusades, she was, said Nelson Rockefeller, 'kindly, gentle, almost a saint'—"and, of course, the president and I were friends. I admired his integrity. He had such experience. I thought he could lead us to some of our greatest and most uplifting days, something like the late 1950s," when Ike was the President, Graham the Pastor, and an average of ten thousand letters daily were delivered to his organizational offices in Minneapolis.

"Yes," he allowed, "during the first few years of his presidency I had great hope, great confidence that Nixon could help bring about the spiritual rebirth the country so desperately needs."

The two first met in 1952, Middle American entities from impoverished but prideful homes. Seven autumns later, with Nixon readying to seek the presidency, Graham told an Indiana crusade, "Mr. Nixon is probably the best-trained man for president in American history, and he is certainly every inch a Christian gentleman." The next year, appalled by the prospect of a Kennedy in the White House, Graham offered to write an article for *Life* endorsing Nixon's candidacy (the Republican nominee, urging Graham to stay clear of politics, refused), and in early 1968, Nixon again preparing—tentatively—to run, Graham flew to Key Biscayne, there to counsel the future president, "If you don't run, you'll wonder for the rest of your life whether you should have, won't you?"

Before Nixon's year of celebration ended, Graham introduced the candidate at a western Pennsylvania rally; told an Oregon audience, "There is no American I admire more than Richard Nixon"; visited Nixon's suite in Miami that August evening he gained the GOP nomination; and announced, on November 1st, his support by absentee ballot for—who else—'Nixon's the One.' "In a campaign that relied largely on Nixon's ability to cut down George Wallace's strength in the heavily conservative, heavily Bible Belt South," the Hudson Institute's resident guru, Herman Kahn, explained, "there was no person in the world whose endorsement would be of more help than Billy Graham's."

By 1969, when Nixon assumed the presidency ("I guess," Billy vowed the previous year, "Dick is one of my ten closest friends"), Graham had become—in truth—the nation's spiritual *pere*, the most popular man in America. "I know the idea repels a lot of intellectuals," Kahn continued, "but if you look at the facts, it happens to be true." In 1970 the Gallup Poll named Graham America's second-most-admired man, trailing only Nixon, and through 1978 he never placed lower than fourth. Delivering an invocation at the 1969 inaugural, Graham thanked the Almighty that "Thou hast permitted Richard Nixon to lead us at this momentous hour of our history." With Nixon, he hoped, as under Eisenhower, Main Street would rule America— and Main Street loved Billy Graham.

Graham, like the president, appealed to the earnest, disciplined masses who armed America—the high school teacher, the general druggist, the retired machinist, the men who owned their farms. Yet even in the early 1970s—for Graham, surely, a time of retrospective sheen—his manner spoke more of the Eisenhower years, the good and tranquil years, an age of domesticity and sentimentality and Norman Rockwell nostalgia.

"Eisenhower gave us peace, respect, a moral compass for the nation to follow," Billy Graham said, smiling. "I think if you were to ask Americans what decade they'd most like to relive, the decade when he was president would win overwhelmingly. We had morality then—not the Tower of Babel we have today. And I thought that we had the chance in the early seventies, as we've had on several other occasions, to have that kind of time again. Not necessarily make us a Christian nation—we're too pluralistic, and this country wasn't created to foster any one religion—but to make this a good place for good people to live good and decent lives," and where a man of God might endure.

During 1969–73 his umbrella organization, the Billy Graham Evangelistic Association, ballooned upward yearly—Graham's "Hour of Decision" broadcasts aired on almost nine hundred stations, his crusades televised into three hundred urban areas, his monthly magazine, movie studio, and publishing house proliferating in volume and revenues. He denounced the United Presbyterian Church in 1971 for granting $10,000 to Angela Davis's defense fund; condemned the news media for "imposing a leadership on the American public which they do not want and for making heroes of radicals"; participated in a White House-favored "Honor America Day" on July 4, 1970; made of San Clemente a social meeting place and Key Biscayne a locale to sun. He became almost a cabinet official without portfolio, to Nixon both protector and friend.

"Didn't you really overdo it, go off the deep end, if you will?" I asked. "Where was the separation of church and state—and didn't the linkage hurt your ministry, not to mention yourself?"

The Mountain Man paused. "Oh," he conceded, softly, "maybe in some ways I did." He stared at the cathedral ceiling of his Montreat home. "But you have to remember this. We came from the same backgrounds. Some have said our constituencies were the same. And he did a lot of good as president, helped pave the way to peace." A slight shake of the head. "In retrospect, what happened later was a nightmare. Who could have foreseen it would end the way it did?"

Noon neared. The Carolina woods cried shrilly in the wind. "Was my ministry hurt by the association?" he said, repeating my charge. "No, no, not if you look at what we've been able to accomplish in the past ten years. But I know this—the country was hurt, injured terribly, not by my friendship with the president"—after all, what had *that* meant?—"but by how the country turned on him, and what he did to prompt that turn. I still don't know how to explain it. So much promise. And then so much hurt."

What the early 1970s established, he declared, was that government without morality could not sustain a nation. Religion, argued Graham, determined how well a republic held together, whether it transmitted to its offspring the sources of its inspiration and faith.

"Look at Nixon," he said. "Intelligence. Patriotism. Backbone. But a defect—too much pressure, insecurity, whatever you call it—and poof." Pensively, he gazed out a window. "There is no state religion, nor should there ever be," Graham insisted, "but spiritual principles were rooted in our nation's origins and always *must* be. That's what built this country, made it great. People like my ancestors, my parents, people who knew without God they could do nothing. With Him they could do everything."

Graham's parents, he reminisced, were an old-fashioned couple, their values born in a "time when doing chores meant getting up at 3 A.M. to milk cows, when there was a stigma to divorce, when kids were too respectful to badmouth their parents, and parents—mine, at least—respected their kids too much to swear or even use slang words, and when the national craze wasn't jumping from one bed to another.

"My folks gave me a code of life," he said, "pride in achievement, a belief that America has tasks that need doing, waiting for hands to do them," a conviction that as he followed his principles, he could be lifted by his dreams.

"It was the kind of family where we had Bible reading and prayer after supper each day—without fail—even before my mother cleaned up the kitchen. We got down on our knees and prayed—all of us—sometimes from twenty to thirty minutes. It was the big event in our home, you can be sure of that. Our lives, well, we found it easier to be disciplined than young people today. We were afraid, for one thing, of my father's hand. But now—with all the trash burying teenagers and with parents who don't care enough to interfere—it's harder than when I was young. Those kids who live their lives responsibly, I respect them greatly."

What, I asked, did he want for *his* sons and daughters? A nation with a sense of belonging, he answered, a place where community was prized. "I know something about that kind of country," he said, "and the kind of people who inhabit it. Lacking in material goods? Sure, a lot of them are. But no job is demeaning if it places bread on the table and provides spiritually for one's children." His goal was an uplifted morality, one in which decency and equality could coexist, and where reason could prevail.

How near was America, though, to Graham's elusive and ethereal dream? Sifting through religious clippings, I handed Graham a viewing guide of prime-time television programs, released several months earlier by the Catholic Archdiocese of

New York. "The picture of parents, priests, and teachers delivered by television to this generation of youngsters is very poor indeed," the report read. "We now have evidence that the destructive impact of television and motion pictures on the faith and morals of youngsters is greater than anyone imagined."

Reverend Billy nodded, coughing to concur. For years, he mused, our leaders praised the virtues of rural America—its sober, more deferential, more respectful ways. "But we were more innocent then," he confided, "and television was new."

He recounted a recent report on network television. "Man," a teacher in Louisville had said, "they tell you prayer in the classroom is illegal. Then they say rot and disorder in the classroom are OK." Drugs, Graham mourned, challenged alcohol as the nation's favorite crutch. Decent, law-abiding Americans—"people," he said, "who believe in the flag, who understood what I said in the early 1970s"—were ridiculed by street people who equated law and order with racism and spilt blood. Square seemed evil, he noted, the sardonic good. Security agencies, charged with defending American interests at home and abroad, had become labeled the enemy of a free, informed republic. Work was dismissed as archaic. Disclosure and innuendo, inevitably linked, were excused as aiding citizens' right to know—or at least what the networks *wanted* them to know.

"That's the way it is," said Graham, paraphrasing Walter Cronkite, "but that's not the way it should be. In our media, as in politics, we have to echo American values, not degrade their worth." Softly caustic laughter. "Today, I'm afraid, all we have are jokers who seem oblivious to the moral courage of America's past."

He flung high the hand that often held a Bible. "Without a revival of Christian ideals," Graham declaimed, "American's economic prowess won't matter, American military strength won't count."

Billy Graham endorsed voluntary prayer in public school. "Prayer forced religion on no one," he sniffed, "but lack of prayer has denied many the chance." His long arms framing responses, drinking ice tea as he spoke ("You knew," he confided, "you'd not get stronger here"), Graham said that deeds might prove again that "sheer elemental goodness, that's what God expects," was the thread around which his vision wove. He sought, Graham affirmed, to prohibit the Internal Revenue Service from invoking measures designed to change the tax-exempt status of independent schools; to install Bible-reading in those public schools wishing to restore it voluntarily; to thwart the federal government's censorship of textbooks and its insistence—"enforced with an iron club"—that they be rewritten to expunge any sympathetic portrayal of woman's role as wife and mother.

"If we do this," he announced slowly, "we can begin to stand up to those who vilify the fundamentals in which our crusades believe."

Like Graham, I was a product of small-town, Protestant America and the majority folk-culture that molded its convictions. I understood, I thought, his motives, his principles, his upbringing. What Graham desired, at least as one could tell, was to resurrect the mores he and Nixon once enshrined—the value of family unity and religious fiber; the need for safe streets and social sanity; the virtue of discretion and patriotic pride; the concept that "something for nothing" was a fool's charade.

"What you're saying, then," I proposed, "is that you have no apologies for standing for what you did or for your sanction by the White House. What you regret is that because of Watergate, some of what you represented came to be tarnished. Guilt by association, I suppose."

"It's rather simplistic to put it that way," he objected mildly, "but there's some truth in what you have to say." The reign may endeth, but verily, the cause survives.

Unlike most clergymen, Graham supported America's intervention in Southeast Asia. "I didn't actually support the war," he related. "I didn't say it was morally right or wrong. But because I didn't come out four-square and blast it, I was criticized. And let me tell you, I took a lot of heat." He urged the United States to remain militarily superior ("Here," he remarked disarmingly, "I've done a flip flop since that time. If we don't lessen our dependence on arms, destroying all weapons, if we don't stop this foolish, destructive nuclear race, we're all going to perish, self-destruct, end in a complete catastrophe"); rebuked those pastors who assumed business guilty until proven innocent; called upon the federal government to examine social funding, claiming that sheer praise of financial restraint—without action to attain that goal—was a callow, injurious hoax.

"Those sentiments didn't do much, did they, for your rapport with other religious leaders?"

Graham laughed lightly. "That's not correct with many of them; we got along splendidly. But you mean people, say, like William Sloane Coffin. No, no, but then probably we never had that much in common anyway. You know," he continued, brushing a knee with his forearm, "it was funny. Some have said that the further down we went, the more support we had. And I guess that in the Eastern Establishment, among some of the big-name pastors of the great churches, you're right—they disagreed with what I had to say."

"And in the smaller churches, in the suburbs and hinterlands?"

"Our support there was tremendous. Not for me, of course," he said, quickly amending his priorities, "but for the emphasis we placed on the scheme of things. What I tried to say was that all the peace marches, draft-card demonstrations, antiwar strikes, all these would amount to *nothing*"—a short, abrupt sweep of the hand—"unless we acknowledged our dependence on and love of Christ."

"Was that the reason...?" I said.

"You know," he interrupted, "that was the difference. Some divinity schools, a lot of affluent pastors and their congregations, they got their baskets turned upside down. They stressed earthly matters—poverty, racism, ecology. These are fine, yes, but that's not what a church is there for. Not primarily, anyway. It's to link people with the supremacy of Jesus. And when I kept saying that all over the country, and in conjunction with my ties to Nixon, well, these folks went off the deep end, criticizing me as being an administration toad. But the facts are obvious. Transparently clear."

"What facts?"

"Well," he asserted, "all you have to do is look at membership rolls. The Southern Baptists, the Mormons, some of the more traditional Catholic sects, they're the ones who've grown in the last decade. And what do they talk about? How one can gain eternal life through Christ. Everyone else has lost. And why? Because they became confused in the decade of the 1960s. They forgot what they were founded to do."

Graham rose and ambled to the window, then returned to the table, reclining in his chair. Never, I suggested to him, had this cleavage—"this division between you and some Establishment clergy"—been more apparent than in the springtime of 1970.

"You mean with Kent State, the students, the bombings, and everything?" he inquired. "Lord knows, what a time for penance, a time to forget."

On April 30, vowing that "if, when the chips are down, the United States of America acts like a pitiful, helpless giant, the forces of totalitarianism and anarchy will threaten free nations and free institutions throughout the world," Nixon announced his incursion into Cambodia—the action directed against North Vietnamese-controlled areas, its duration a maximum of sixty days. Campuses exploded, students rebelled. Many envisioned another deathtrap, another conflagration, another—say it—Viet Nam, and in the forefront stood America's upper-class clergy, defaming the war as barbaric, sketching the president as mad. To Coffin, Nixon was "sick, elemental, a killer"; to Father James Groppi of Milwaukee, a prominent Catholic pacifist, the president was "responsible for despair and tragedy"; to Father Hesburgh of Notre Dame, he was "misguided, out of touch, tragically naive."

"These were many of the same people," said Patrick L. Buchanan, Nixon's conservative speechwriter and special assistant, "whose views, when we came into office, had left us with our cities burning, our country in flames. And now, without remorse, with no apology, no shame whatsoever, they savaged us without a pretense of objectivity or of allowing for rational debate."

When four students were fatally shot May 4, killed in a clash at Kent State University between demonstrators and national guardsmen, protest begat hysteria, and hysteria hate. Within ten days, nearly four hundred and fifty colleges closed or went on strike; ROTC facilities were ransacked in a score of cities; Washington became a cynosure of ferment and unrest. Even Nixon's cabinet was not immune from conflict. On May 6, Walter Hickel, strong-willed secretary of the interior, delivered a letter to the president expressing his "hope that we will begin to communicate with young people. They are looking to us for leadership. Too often they are not finding it—nor the willingness to exchange ideas or concerns." Nixon was infuriated, less by the letter's prose than by its timing; Associated Press

published the contents before Hickel's missile even reached his desk.

"I know how it must have looked, like I was deliberately setting him up," Hickel told me. "To the president, it must have appeared as if I was being disloyal by sending the letter in the first place, when he was so under attack. Secondly, that I was being irresponsible by not being part of the team during what can only be called a traumatic and polarizing time. And worst of all, conspiring with the people Nixon hated most—the press—in releasing a letter sent to him before he could even read it.

" 'Course," said Hickel, "what really happened was that I was blocked out from the president by Haldeman and Ehrlichman—they were German and Christian Scientists, and they erected a wall—and I couldn't even get to see him. All this turmoil going on, and what we had to do was communicate, open ourselves to other views, and we weren't doing it. Nixon kept closing himself off—not because he was vindictive, but because he was so insecure. And when my letter hit—leaked by a member of my staff against my orders—well, it was a time of siege panic, remember, and the president really felt, in all honesty, that he couldn't trust anybody—that everyone was out to get him." Writing in *The New Yorker*, Richard Rovere best phrased the fury. "Whirl is King," he said, "and Richard Nixon is First Minister."

Deserted by the nation's elect, Nixon turned for solace to organized labor, whose hardhats marched, one hundred thousand on May 20, down lower Manhattan in support of his foreign policy; to the cherished "Silent Majority," whose members did not begrudge their approval (a *Newsweek* poll in mid-May showed that more than half of all Americans endorsed the Cambodian decision); and to the one eminence whose loyalty was unyielding. "I doubt any but a few of us at the time realized the measure of approval that Billy Graham's friendship brought Richard Nixon," Hickel observed. "He was a signal to every small city and town in America that the president—and what the president did—was all right by God."

In late May, with Nixon still reeling, Graham—at White House request—allowed the president to appear at a crusade in Knoxville, Tennessee. Nixon had not surfaced publicly since Kent State; this, one assumed, would be his "coming out." "The

rally," Graham said, "will show the younger generation that the president is listening to them," his emergence made possible by a Tennessee statute forbidding disruptions at any religious service. Protests transpired, but Nixon appeared, and seventeen months later, his popularity rising, the president was guest of honor at Billy Graham Day in Charlotte, there to honor the righteousness and longevity of the Tar Heel made good.

"It was a glorious day," was Graham's recollection. "John Connally was there. Sam Ervin. Strom Thurmond. The president and his wife. Tributes from around the world. And I guess I'd say it was among the most memorable moments of my life—memorable in not the sense of lionizing me, but what it meant in terms of the potential of an evangelical surge in America, and—as the seventies rolled on—around the world as well."

"How memorable?" I asked.

"Well, during Nixon's time, near the top," he professed. "It's just one of those things you recall with warmth. Like playing golf with Kennedy in Florida a few days after the 1960 election, or all the visits with Johnson—my wife once counted that I'd spent twenty-six separate nights in the White House when he was president—or in 1952, when after the election, I went to the Commodore Hotel in New York to see Eisenhower, and he told me he wanted to inject a moral tone into his Inaugural Address, and I told him, 'General, you can do more to inspire our people to a spiritual way of living than any other man alive,' and then," Graham concluded, "we saw all of that come to pass. That's what the day in Charlotte meant a decade ago. That's what I remember—the chance to turn America around."

The years since 1970, I inquired, what had they wrought? A groping, tentative armistice, or a unity that was real? "Boy," Graham whistled, "I don't know. Understand me, we've had some good men since then. Ford. Carter. And Reagan"—he confided, leaning forward—"well, he's a church-goer, you know. But the country? Sure, I'm delighted about the evangelical revival of the last ten years—but it hasn't touched the nation as a whole. And we don't have much time left. I think we're as divided now as we were back then, and we're more sinful, more strayful from what He expects."

A sad half-smile. "How does it go, 'Of all the words of mouth and pen, these are the saddest, "What might have been?" ' "

Afternoon descended. The sky grew sullen. Our visit over, I made for the door. "You know," Graham said, rising, "I've been thinking about a quote you used a while ago. From Emerson? 'Governments have their origin in the moral identity of men.' Well, that sums it up about today. And it says it all about ten years ago." To make government more responsive, he allowed, to reaffirm America's lost identity and pride, this nation must exist for its *people*—not the other way around.

"Take care of yourself," he called, as my car started forward.

"You bet," I replied, and returning his wave, headed down the hill.

Turning on my car radio, I flew transported back to 1971, when the song now playing, Carole King's "So Far Away," made its debut. I thought of the sounds and profiles that gave the era being—Chicago's clash of brass and cymbals, the understated urgency of Judy Collins, the Carpenters' grace and sensitivity, the poignancy of David Gates & Bread. Graham's bent ran more to Johnny Cash and Waylon Jennings. Gene Autry and Wayne Newton. Donny and Marie. What, after all, did I know of his most sacred memories? And what, Saint Peter, could he know of mine?

"The indestructible American innocent," a biographer once named him. Who, I wondered, leaving Montreat for lower, less rarefied ground, could fully measure the pain and injury, the will and benediction, of the Reverend William (Billy) Graham?

One could be certain only that America had loved his message—its harmony, its calm, its inner charm and sanctity. Perhaps such a nation was great because it too was good. Perhaps there was some of Billy Graham in us all.

6

Interpassage I

DRIVING NORTH TO PENNSYLVANIA, I MUSED ALOUD about Billy Graham and the 1950s; culturally, they were more married than Bogart and Bacall. "Were they a decade?" asked an older friend, who grasped maturity during their somnolent years. "Maybe. And maybe they were more." Indeed, they became a *time frame*, an epoch as indelible as the Roaring Twenties, sane and strange and ingenuously benign. Pinky Lee and Checkers. Elvis and McCarthy. "I Love Lucy" and Uncle Miltie. Edward R. Murrow and rock 'n roll.

Were the 1950s, as Norman Mailer insisted, "one of the worst decades in the history of man?" Were they inadvertently ennobling, an innocence that seems now—after the cataclysms of the past twenty years—almost artlessly kind? Were they neither, I wondered as my car, veering westward, left Harrisburg for Meadville, or were they somewhere in between?

Among my freshman classmates, nearly all had been born in 1951. Thus, half—*exactly*—of our lives elapsed during the 1960s and half in the era of Ike, decades as wildly dissimilar as any the twentieth century might spawn. We entered college weaned on Roy Rogers and upbraided by Mark Rudd, raised on hula hoops and encircled by flower children, stirred by Casey Stengel and benumbed by Tiny Tim—a hybrid of normalcy and abnormality, conformity and revolt. If our composite bayed with conflict, the cleavage exacted its cost.

What we sought, above all, perhaps, was proof of our infallibility, as if the onus of uncertainty could be quelled by shrill vows. Some found meaning in protest, some in introspection, some in a mandate to affront. Even in Meadville, where time seemed bent on retrieving a simpler, more silent poise, combatants trenched themselves in belligerence.

Amid the meanness, the not-so-buried anger, many viewed the 1950s with almost militant nostalgia. Stoicism and humility. Reticence. Reserve. If its disciples wandered from these qualities, at least they understood their worth. The sixties, it seemed to them, had been self-absorbed, intemperate, an age of often mindless candor—of hurting people in the name of honesty—a decade where diplomat Elihu Root might have muttered, as he had sixty-two years before, "I'm a firm believer in democracy, but I do not believe in filth."

At Allegheny too loomed heirs of the 1960s—shaped more by Joe Cocker than Davy Crockett, their lives barely altered by an era Adlai Stevenson called the green fairways of indifference. Born to a time—we know today—of almost unprecedented tranquility, they grew bored with Main Street and condemned the years of their childhood as what John Kenneth Galbraith dubbed the bland leading the bland.

The 1950s, they complained, were hypocritical and authoritative, puritanical and inhibited. They mocked civility, distrusted caution, laughed at television's Andy Griffith counseling son Opie, "Fighting on Sunday, I mean that's disgraceful." One searched vainly for such propriety now.

At Allegheny College, circa 1969-73, where two camps of music, language, values collided, both sought (and seized) a dream to memorialize their cause, but what meant nirvana for one meant nightmare to the other. Neither honored what the other prized. Both denied the diversity of their deeply textured time.

Nearing Bentley Hall, Allegheny College's administrative heart, I glimpsed old, familiar buildings, and as memories merged with symbols, felt almost capable of voiding the intervening years. "At Allegheny College," I once wrote, "I secured new friendships, embarked upon a career, and encountered Jeanne Braham, the most remarkable teacher I ever met."

It seemed, of course, less remarkable at the time. In retrospect, my tenure at Allegheny was etched chiefly by work and study—work to best tuition, study to best my peers. Lonely, I was not alone. Many students, Braham said in a 1977 Baccalaureate address, knew the stillness of "spending four years in a small college in northwestern Pennsylvania where the annual average snowfall is 112 inches, where Saturday tolls the class bell for everyman, where ten-week terms have the ballooning pressure of an inverted bell curve."

Braham and I were both freshmen in 1969. She, however, was a teacher, I a student in the first English class she taught. Twenty-nine, born in Pittsburgh, and educated in Scotland, she had graduated summa cum laude from Wooster, received her M.A. from the University of Pennsylvania and her doctorate in the arts from Carnegie-Mellon University, boasted a certificate from the University of London and other graduate work at Wesleyan University. She was blithe and irreverent, vulnerable and pert. She arrived at Allegheny, Jeanne wrote in 1978, "after a damaging marriage; she was coming home to the world of the living and the loving." She wore black boots, spoke of singer Jim Morrison, and carried a coffee mug atop her papers each morning into class. Did the cup contain coffee? Whimsically, we called her Brandy Braham. The liquid disappeared daily, but the name remained.

By September 21, 1969, our first day at Allegheny College, Brandy Braham and I had already been tinged by news reports that multiplied, proliferated, and ultimately overwhelmed—by the withdrawal in 1968 of Lyndon Johnson as a Democratic candidate ("I shall not seek—and I will not accept—the nomination of my party for another term as your president"); the entrance of Eugene McCarthy, poetic and with a melancholy manner, as a contender for the presidency ("We'll have a short inauguration address and we'll take down the fence around the White House and have a picnic on the lawn"); and the election of Richard Nixon over Hubert Horatio Humphrey, his Democratic opponent ("You young people," barked the combative, irrepressible Minnesotan as the '68 general election crested. "Will you help us now? Do you think we're going to win? Do you want to win? Are you going to help us win? Will you do it this week? All right then, give it to 'em. Rip it to 'em. Sock it to 'em"). Abe Fortas had been nominated and withdrawn as chief justice of the Supreme Court; Mickey Mantle had retired from the New York Yankees, and Theodore Samuel Williams had returned to manage the Washington Senators, they of the "First in War, First in Peace, and Last in the American League."

Striking, too, were the triumphs of pro football's New York Jets (already completed) and baseball's "Amazin' Mets" (who won the World Series on October 17); the deaths, gruesome and inexplicable, of Robert F. Kennedy and Martin Luther King; the transplant to Philip Blaiberg of a dead man's heart; and the marriage of Jacqueline Kennedy, who in marrying Aristotle Onassis, demeaned—to some—a dead man's grave. The Soviets had invaded Czechoslovakia a year earlier, 10 million public servants in France had gone on strike, and since January 1 Everett Dirksen, Judy Garland, John L. Lewis, Boris Karloff, Drew Pearson, Ho Chi Minh, and Dwight David Eisenhower had died. In Northern Ireland, violence erupted, unconscionably abetted by Americans who sold guns to contending forces, and tragedy lurked near Martha's Vineyard, where the names *Kennedy* and *Chappaquiddick* became inextricably linked. Finally, on July 20, 1969, two men first walked on the moon. "Yes," said my favorite teacher, "and in months to come, after we thought we'd seen everything, we found out how wrong we were."

Soft-voiced and introverted, Jeanne Braham was yet animated; her views were often solicited, her convictions appraised. She talked glibly even about matters that troubled her, but underneath her jokes and vigor, one sensed there lay a streak of brooding sadness. She was moved by what she loved—music— and by poetry (which she also wrote) and by spirited, supple art.

Had she forgotten, I asked, how these waves swept 1969? On screen, *Midnight Cowboy,* John Wayne in *True Grit,* and Maggie Smith's *The Prime of Miss Jean Brodie*—all Oscar recipients—buoyed movie theatres, and the next year brought *Patton,* George C. Scott's hard and dazzling portrayal of the European theatre's most full-sized commander. *M*°*A*°*S*°*H*° and *Little Big Man, Carnal Knowledge* and *The Last Picture Show.* Not the most majestic litany, Braham suggested, but hardly the most wretched either.

"Through many of these films," she said, "there was a clear

chasm of difference—on one side, the environment bullying and assaulting the individual; on the other, the individual fighting to make any kind of statement. To evoke dignity, self-respect, friendship, love."

"How about the literature?" I wondered. During 1969-71 major works included *Future Shock* and *The Greening of America*, *Love Story* and *Sexual Politics*, *Stillwell and the American Experience in China*, and *Bury My Heart at Wounded Knee*.

"Sensual, sometimes. Progressive, often. There were themes," she said, "that ran through them—society victimizing its best; in youth lay the potential for change; the ignorance that accepted customs held; the need to understand our past in order not to repeat it. But the sounds, the music. It was memorable. And it meant more to your time—and better reflected its tenor—than perhaps anything else I can think of."

If ours was the youth culture, rock music was its staple. We were bombarded by its exaggerated energy—in dormitories and dining halls, in the college union, in walks along sidewalks where transistor radios leered. During my freshman and sophomore years, popular music slowly, perceptively shifted— from an emphasis on acid rock to a sweeter balladry; from a doctrine electrically amplified to a diversity of sounds and signposts; from a public bent for Jimi Hendrix and Janis Joplin to a nation that could (and did) accept Gordon Lightfoot and Joan Baez, Stevie Wonder and the Beatles.

"We were entering the seventies," Braham said, "and the music couldn't ignore that fact. But the years were an extension—socially—of the sixties, and one couldn't ignore *that* fact.

"So what you got was two worlds, a pair of streams flowing simultaneously—the sheer primal vibrancy of the past decade, the search for purpose in a new and uncharted decade, the political thrusts against intolerance; and another stream, a more private, more inward-looking confessional."

The airwaves echoed with what *TIME* called "a diverse, wonderfully evocative collection of individual balladeers and rock composer-performers," and their most creative themes blended lyricism and personal expression, and an unaffected, often bittersweet perspective. "Joe Hill" and "Rainy Day People." Carly Simon's "Anticipation" and "That's the Way I've

Always Heard it Should Be." "Your Song" by Elton John. "Beginnings" by Chicago. James Taylor's "Fire and Rain." Led Zepellin's medal masterpiece, "Stairway to Heaven." While Cat Stevens, a folk minstrel from London, debuted with "Wild World," Rod Stewart unleashed the classic "Maggie May."

Crosby, Stills, Nash, & Young seduced America with a mixture of often brooding, often literate, always melodic songs—"Suite: Judy Blue Eyes." "Carry On." "The Lee Shore." "Teach Your Children." "Marrakesh Express." "Wooden Ships." "Long Time Gone." And "Woodstock," national anthem of the counterculture. The age's dominant album, Carole King's "Tapestry," was both gentle and activist, communal and private, its songs ("You've Got a Friend," "I Feel The Earth Move," "Natural Woman," and "It's Too Late") reflecting brilliantly the estrangement felt by students who, their protestations notwithstanding, found in the early 1970s a midnight of life's dissolution, an erasure of the verities that lent the sixties worth. "There are teachers here who feel—I think rightly—that the sixties ended in the spring of 1973, when Nixon began to drown and the war ended," Jeanne Braham observed. "When did the sixties end in music? Perhaps in one great blast. I think a case can be made for 'Tapestry.' "

How had *students* changed since the 1960s ended? They were less questioning, less assertive, more patient than a decade earlier, she replied—"in some ways, veritable offspring of the 1950s," Braham quipped. "But more self-satisfied and indulgent too."

"They're concerned about their future, their careers, their place in society, and, quite bluntly," she announced, "as a result, they're more stable than perhaps you and your contemporaries were."

A laugh, partly throttled, ambled across her chest. "Outwardly, they *seem* more stable anyway. The reverse of that is, students are more repressed—and there is a desperation to that reserve. They want to be like members of your generation, maybe, perhaps, even like you," even though, I reminded her, I spent only two years at Allegheny (needing money to pay expenses, I had little; possessing funds for student aid, college officials would give me none) and transferred in August 1971 to Geneseo State University. "You have to remember," Braham said, "there has been a mythology built up around your age.

Students now want to have a stake in that, to have causes like you did, but they don't see one they want badly enough to strike out after. They're empty. So they turn their focus on one thing they know rather well—themselves."

"Offspring of the 1950s?" I said.

"In a way," she countered. "Not so much in manners. Mores haven't changed that much since your colleagues left—let's face it, we're never going to go back to how Fulton Sheen would have us deal with one another. People are just a lot less *nice* than they were twenty years ago."

"But otherwise?"

"There are great similarities. Concerns today are the same as when I was in college [1958-62]. It didn't really matter who was in power—Eisenhower or Carter, or who the big box-office rage was, Elvis Presley or Kiss. It's almost as if the times don't affect the college; we operate in a void. And what are students worried about? Jobs. Affluence. Peer prestige. Fraternities. The same priorities we had before your group came along."

"An anomaly?" I asked.

"The late sixties, early seventies?"

"Yes."

"Oh, I suppose so," Braham said. "But how could it have been otherwise? What was going on in the outside world—the war, the fight against racism, the debate over morality—was so profound, so elemental in its potential to change the nation, that it naturally would do what few eras accomplish: invade and affect the campus. And because much of that potential for change arose *from* the campus in the first place, the influence was magnified. It was in the cards—and it's a miracle, really, that colleges didn't explode even more than they did."

"What do . . . ?" I began.

"I think that perhaps students today will be more successful than your colleagues," she mused. "They'll probably be better trained for jobs they seek. They may know how to manipulate the system more. They won't enter society after graduation with as many hangups about the accepted strata—after all, they want to dominate society, not change it or break it down. They're certainly less sanctimonious, more realistic, their expectations far lower than yours. But as a teacher, I sometimes find them less interesting, more easily cowed—they pass through here with an eye on what they'll do afterward, not on how they can alter the landscape while they're here."

"Is their college important?" I asked.

"In the sense of preparing them, yes," she answered. "In the sense of having college change them, no. They don't probe as much, challenge, entertain rival thoughts." Braham paused for Nescafe, opting for two sips, lightly. "College an ivory tower? It never mattered more than when your contemporaries attended school," she said. "It never affected students more. It never changed the nation more. It was never better, never darker, never louder, never dull."

One year after leaving Allegheny, perusing *Change* magazine, I encountered the Reverend Andrew Greeley—sociologist at the University of Chicago—who scorned "many of my colleagues in the academy who pandered to the worst in the romanticism and irrationality of Movement folk: Kenneth Kenniston, who told them [students] that they were morally superior to previous generations; Margaret Mead, who let them believe they were a whole generation who lived not in the past or the present but in the future.... And Theodore Roszac, who equated irrationality with creative vitality." Did Braham, I asked, recognize Andrew Greeley's foils?

She laughed, rolling her eyes. Present still, I noticed, were the inimitable mannerisms, the buoyancy that marked Braham's veneer—and present, too, several seniors told me, was students' fondness for her, undimmed by the last ten years. "We always have phony-balonies who pander to students," she conceded. "They get their self-esteem by genuflecting before fleeting whims. That, I'm afraid, is not about to change. Today. Twenty years ago. When the twenty-first century dawns.

"But," she continued, "a charge like that vastly overstates the case. Yes, Allegheny was small [enrollment 1,800]. It was traditional. Upper income. Prone to the status quo. Not unlike many other colleges that came apart in the early 1970s.

"Yet I don't remember many teachers—sure, there were some—who told students they were morally superior or possessed of a Christ-like calling. It wasn't the professors—it was the times. If teachers had been the major influence, when you left here, you'd have reverted back to the dreams and values you held before you came. But we weren't—and no one who was on this campus, you and your classmates included, could escape what the times incurred. *Their* impact was *permanent*—the difference between 1960 and ten years later, the difference between now and ten years ago."

Permanent? Yes. Injurious? Perhaps. If we were not endowed with a "Christ-like calling," I suggested, neither were we, as Walter Lippmann wrote in 1932, "a demoralized people, one in which the individual... trusts nobody and nothing, not even himself."

"That's just the point," Braham retorted. "No, you weren't demoralized, but you *were* confused—confused because you were searching; and searching even though you were confident you'd find the truth in the end; and emphatic while you were searching, I think, because you hoped to hide the fact that you were confused. The problem is, though, that all this drive, this emotion, this commitment you had, it all became so out of place as the seventies went by. Not just for you. For many of my colleagues too. Their lives ended when the 1960s ceased."

The woman to my left, alternately assured and tentative, had helped define my life, urging a change in concentration from history to English; demanding an intensity of craft from me that few teachers rivaled; even marking a written exam, as she did during the World Series of 1970, with baseball terminology, i.e., "warm up with a leaded bat...a good solid hit...at least a triple...and a grand slam wrap up."

Emotively, Jeanne Braham was discreet, reflective. But was she right about my classmates? Together, discarding fantasy, we had come upon discontent—the hysteria prompted by the Viet Nam War, epitomized in the trial, abused by mayhem, of Bobby Seale, Jerry Rubin, Abbie Hoffman, and four codefendants accused of crossing state lines to incite rioting at the 1968 Democratic Convention; the desire of migrant workers for equality, and ecologists, rallying on Earth Day, 1970, for clean, unpoisoned climes; the advent of civil war in Pakistan and starvation in Biafra, of cocaine among the middle class and coed dorms among the young; the quandary of a generation that, flushed with material providence, yearned for what Richard Nixon (in one of his instantly dubious assertions) proudly boasted of, the certitude of "inner peace."

Peace at the center, the Quakers phrased it. Who among my

classmates bore that designation? Of my closest friends at Allegheny, each had strayed far from western Pennsylvania— Bill Griffith and Rick Rumbaugh to rural New England; Don Steinweg to the Baltimore suburbs; Doug Pratt, a Presbyterian minister, to a manse in Wichita, Kansas; John Wright, the only freshman I knew who wore a crew cut, assigned as a captain to an air base in Ft. Worth. Already the last decade had judged some fiercely, and although, vocationally, all five sparkled (Rumbaugh and Steinweg were doctors, Griffith a youth counselor), most spoke of separation and common memory and forgotten youth. If they had drifted from each other, I had grown apart from them. One judges time by one's contemporaries. I could not know them fully because, at Allegheny, I did not know myself.

"In a way, that's to be expected," Braham, preparing for a class, professed. "Your bond with your friends was two years of college. When those years disappeared—and the tribulations which united you during their passage—so did the bond. All you had left was the faith that you might have been right—and the memories of your attempts to find your way in life." She left to entertain her students. I left to begin my way home.

Several days later, reading again my former teacher's baccalaureate address, I fastened upon its peroration. The president of Wooster College, Braham said, "liked to tell the graduates of my era that the last word that a college gave to you was your own name. His point was twofold: that the last official act of a college was to announce your name on a diploma; its final wish was for you to discover the true nature of that identity.

"That has happened to me only recently," she related. "Several years ago I returned to a summer home my family had kept during the last years of my childhood. The house was boarded up, and brush had obscured some ambitious bridle paths I had cut with an uncle in two exhausting weekends. But as I walked in the wood I came upon a joltingly familiar chair my father had constructed years earlier to watch the feeding deer he always claimed he intended to stalk but, in fact, never killed.

"It was, for me, a primary discovery. One that bound life into cycles not of endless and futile repetition but of growth. I sat in it and knew my own name."

If I knew my own name, it was partly because of Allegheny

College. If I knew my own identity, it was partly because of Jeanne Braham.

7

Chastened Fall

A PARTIAL HAZE LIFTED AND THE SUN APPEARED. THROUGH the Midwest swept Route 31, past cornfields and high-rise dwellings, leaving tenement slums and blighted factories behind. From Indianapolis, the broad road veered north and west. Ashen skies faded, and South Bend drew near. I left the highway and headed toward the campus. There the Golden Dome towered above its adjacent sites, august and pure and radiant.

"You say you're looking for. Father Hesburgh?" asked a student, wry sarcasm splitting his face. "He should be in the Administration Building. Just make sure you genuflect when you appear."

During the early 1970s, few wove the tenets of religion and academia more tenderly than Father Theodore M. Hesburgh. Articulate and well-spoken, he was among the age's most pivotal figures, a man of loping phrases and subdued yet elegant grace. President of the University of Notre Dame, chairman of Richard Nixon's Commission on Civil Rights, he served as pastor, author, educator, part-politician and part-savant.

"May I help you?" said Hesburgh's secretary, greeting me in the Administration Building's foyer.

"Hope so," I answered. "I'm here to see your boss."

She reached for a telephone, her smile grasping the middle road between bemusement and disdain. As Hesburgh marched toward me, his bearing sturdy and rigorous, memories crested of a decade before, when he fought Viet Nam and racism with a native, pietistic good. "Welcome to Notre Dame," he said, my remembrances yielding to his clasp on the back. "A lot of people before me worked to make it what it is today."

Hesburgh leaned forward and flashed a smile. Entering his office, I motioned to four pictures on the wall, photographs of presidents—Nixon excluded—from John Kennedy to James Earl Carter. Did he remember, I asked, how Franklin Roosevelt, assuming the presidency in 1933, addressed a nation afflicted by the Great Depression and burdened by despair? He could say in viewing the republic's wreckage, "Our problems concern, thank God, only material things." Our crisis today, Hesburgh nodded, was in reverse. Allies and adversaries questioned whether we had the *will* to regain our economic and spiritual vibrancy, whether we could confront the crises of the 1980s with resurgent courage—courage to change, courage to challenge, courage to lead once again.

"What a mess we're in today," he stated, his manner resorting less to pomp than matter of fact. "Just look at the problems we have." Mounting inflation and a plummeting dollar. The duality of recession and rising unemployment. A Byzantine bureaucracy feeding huge federal deficits. The highest interest rates in the memory of man. The loss of respect for conventional values. The loss of respect for America abroad. "Lord knows, we had these problems a decade ago," Hesburgh acknowledged, "but at least we had a hope, a possibility that we could deal with them, even if the solutions proposed by me and the administration, for example, were hundreds of miles apart. At least we had hope. Today"—his frame tightened—"we often don't have that. People are so egocentric. God help the person who goes through life doing nothing for others, like we see so much of now. They're done for. They're doomed."

Hesburgh had hope, and also presence. Critics labeled him a publicity-monger, dismissing his charitable concerns. Yet there were those, many students among them, who prized Hesburgh's friendship. He lived, they said, as he created—with intelligence and a comely, almost Thespian flair. Even now, Hesburgh gloried in the role of national avatar, convivial with newsmen, at home amid the ruling powers. His career was his fortune, perhaps the family he would never have.

"If you're trying to relive the early 1970s, you've done right, I hope, by coming here," he started, self-esteem merging with working pride. "No one can understand what the era meant, how the exuberance hurt and lifted us all, without focusing on the college. Everything that mattered had its inception here—the fight to end the war, the fight to create equality, the attempt to understand our place in the scheme of things, the battle over values and manners and life."

"Lifted us?"

"Oh, yes," he said while straddling a chair. "Don't forget, college's role historically has been to question, to challenge established authorities, to cry out for change when progress is due. Today, with our so-called anesthetized students, we have to excite them; back then, our task was to harness the vast excitement we had. And that's what we tried to do. We did it well, many colleges, anyway. But remember, if many people in college hadn't been out there marching, there would have been no one there to fill their shoes."

" 'All 'er nothing,' " I injected, stealing a song from *Oklahoma.*

"You bet," he snapped. "If there was a bond between college students of the era—and I think there was—it was because they realized that if they didn't fight Washington together, they *would* get nothing. And nothing could have pleased our friends in the federal government more."

Recount, I urged, the decade's inception. "What do you remember about 1970?"

"How," he responded, "do you answer a question like that? It wasn't just 1970, it was the year before, and the couple years after. So you make a mistake by focusing on one year." Emphatic in his ideology, Hesburgh could turn unyielding. "I know what you're getting at, though. That was the year the roof came off. It seemed to sum up all the fury—in war, morality, drugs, you name it. It made for a time impossible to be quiet about." Theodore Hesburgh, one sensed, was rather expressive too.

Born in Syracuse, New York, Hesburgh entered Notre

Dame in 1934, then transferred to Gregorian University in
Rome, earning his baccalaureate degree in 1940. Ordained
three years later, he became chaplain of Notre Dame's
Veterans Club in 1945, emerging as assistant professor and
head of the Religion Department in 1948. The following
summer Hesburgh was named executive vice president, was
appointed president in 1952, and has remained the head of
America's leading Catholic university. Though one of the most
widely celebrated universities in the world, Notre Dame was,
until the early 1970s, an institution largely middle class, wholly
male, and almost exclusively white. As president, Hesburgh
moved it from control by the church to a lay board of trustees;
elevated the quality of faculty and curriculum; struggled to
maintain the school's moral stature ("We stress values here;
American universities have become obsessed with objectivity"); and in 1972 instituted his most pervasive reform—making
the college coed. He also became among the nation's most
vocal advocates of human rights—for traditional Notre Dame,
a phenomenon almost akin to Spiro T. Agnew lionizing the
patriotism of the Left.

Hesburgh endorsed the use of affirmative action, mandated an increase in minority admissions, saw the percentage
of black students at Notre Dame leap from less than 1 percent
in 1952 to 6 percent fourteen years later, scored the Nixon
administration as callous to non-Caucasian desires. In November 1972, having been named by Nixon three years earlier to
chair the Commission on Civil Rights, Hesburgh—at the
president's insistence—was fired. Two days later he issued a
missive chiding Nixon for "betraying all the progress in race
relations this country has made in the last ten years."

"What was it," I asked, "that so appalled you about the
president? After all, you'd known him for two decades. You
were friends personally, and even once politically."

I repeated John Mitchell's contention that in the first three
years of the Nixon administration, the federal budget for civil
rights activities tripled; his claim—factually true—that although 40 percent of black students attended all-black schools
when Nixon became president, by 1972 the number was 12
percent; his reminder that, under Nixon, high school equiva-
lency programs and special language courses were imple-

mented for Spanish-speaking peoples; his boast that Nixon
created the first program, called the "Philadelphia Plan," which
specifically required companies receiving federal contracts to
allocate a fixed numerical percentage of funds to minority
businesses.

"In the area of black and white," Mitchell had told me, "the
press always paints us as the Big, Bad, Boogie Bear. But the
numbers, they tell a different tale."

"It wasn't the numbers," Hesburgh jabbed back, "it was
the *attitude*. Nixon's courting of George Wallace, his pandering
to the Wallace constituency; his decision in '69 to abandon
administrative action for court action in desegregation cases, a
step sure to cripple integration; his southern strategy; his
nomination of Haynsworth and Carswell to the Supreme
Court; his opposition to busing—all these created an impression that the people in power were, if not antagonistic toward
the plight of poor people, at least unsympathetic.

"I couldn't live with that attitude; that's why I spoke out
consistently, even though I knew that Nixon, because we were
friends, had expected I wouldn't push him. But I felt a need for
urgency—that we couldn't ignore what the 1960s had left
undone. Nixon didn't. And that's why I was canned."

Even now, he implored, community leaders must show
renewed concern for the voices of torment, of deprivation—
the voices which had despaired of being heard. For their part,
spokesmen for America's indigent must realize that neither
violence nor cynicism would help abate their longings. For its
part, he said, echoing "The Boogie Bear," government must
provide more tax credits and other incentives for business to
become involved in steering private enterprise toward minority employment; involved in bridging the gulf between promise and achievement in America's two-century-old search for
a just and abundant dream.

Hesburgh halted, reaching for a pipe. What, I asked,
passing him a lighter, had become of the violence of the early
1970s? Had America not learned that progress, to be permanent, must be peaceful?

"Yes," he said, slowly choosing his words, "and I think that
more and more black leaders are understanding that while the
wrongs of past centuries can't be cured overnight, they realize

that great legislative and judicial advancement has already
been achieved." Hesburgh stared at the sunlight. "In the 1960s
we went, in effect, from apartheid to a semblance of equality.
That was tremendous progress. And that's why I was so
opposed to what Nixon was trying to do. Today, unlike fifteen
years ago—where the emphasis was on judicial matters—now
it's economic. We have to get capitalism and minority residents
intertwined—so that our cities can be rebuilt and more jobs
created," and housing projects begun in those areas that require
them most.

"When I said," he continued, "that today, as opposed to a
decade ago, we don't have as much hope, that's not entirely
true. Race is an exception. We have officials today more
sympathetic to the plight of blacks, the handicapped, the poor.
In life, as in politics, it's the caring that counts."

Still, Hesburgh was a religious, not a political, fixture;
indeed, during 1969-73, with Bishop Fulton Sheen aging and
Cardinal Spellman dead, he rivaled Richard Cardinal Cushing
as titular head of America's 48 million Roman Catholics.

Studying his clerical collar, I reviewed my ecumenical ties.
Living in upstate New York, my father (a Protestant) had spent
his childhood in the Wyoming County hamlet of Pike, population 400. Exactly one of its families was Catholic. In 1960,
during the Nixon-Kennedy presidential campaign, a fight arose
in my back yard—the two combatants, a friend and I, both age
eight—over the Democratic candidate's Catholicism. Nixon
lost the election, but I won the fight. Nine years later,
graduating from high school, I attended my class's baccalaureate ceremonies at St. Columba's Church, Caledonia, New
York. "Doesn't this look like a gypsy carnival?" a Methodist
classmate of mine asked, my grandmother nodding sagely at
my side.

Finally, in a penultimate gesture, I began dating—"seriously," several relatives feared—an attractive friend from
North Tonawanda, a Buffalo suburb. Polish. A senior in
college. Above all, *Catholic*. My parents were nonplussed; who
was less likely to attract a Papist than I? When the romance
ended, I confessed that had they not protested—"Man, you
should have been still!"—matters would have ceased several
months earlier; to display my independence, not an uncommon
wish, I professed an affection I did not feel.

My ecumenical leanings were shallow and ephemeral, tenuously planted and incessantly abused, but as the 1970s unfolded, I came to understand—belatedly—the canon and mythology which made Roman Catholicism thrive.

The Catholic Church, I suggested to Hesburgh, offered a life of certitude—no doubts, no misgivings, no blurring of right and wrong. Amid the upheavals which accompanied 1970—the moral wilderness which abducted us all—its faith lent order to chaos and reaffirmed America's fundamental worth.

I remembered Nixon's wistful aside to aide Charles Colson, months before Watergate submerged him, "You know, Chuck, I could be a Roman Catholic. I honestly could. You know, it's beautiful to think about, the fact that there is something you can really grab ahold of, something real and meaningful, something really stable"; related how a friend once said of me, "He's culturally Protestant, morally Catholic, and intellectually Jewish"; and conjectured that while times change, principles should not, and that the Catholic hierarchy esteemed that truth.

"That's what you learned? Well, better late than never," Hesburgh said, laughing, as my story unfurled.

"Your story is an unusual one," he observed, more seriously. "A lot of people your age went in the opposite direction, leaving the Church—any church—for other options, other convictions, other ways of expressing their thirst or hunger. Not many, I regret, came to see what you did in the *way* that you did.

"What it all proves, I suspect, is first, the Kennedy election over Nixon in 1960 was a watershed event in ending religious prejudice. Even more, it shows the ferment of the early 1970s— Catholic and Protestant, orthodox and avant-garde, all crossed paths at some time in their search for the mystery of eternity; spiritual fulfillment. And that," he concluded, slamming the table in mock disgust, "is what made the age so memorable.

"It was a time of learning, of being exposed to other points of view, of colliding with opposing ideas—because only if you were in a vacuum in the early seventies could you escape the give and take. And what did it produce? In religion—as with you—and in civil rights, a tolerance we could only have dreamt of a decade before."

Hesburgh loved the Catholic Church—its pomp and

ritual, its rules and covenants, its mystery and sacred law. "Why shouldn't he love it?" a colleague asked. "It's made him the biggest Catholic big shot in the country today." And values, besieged but holy, he revered as well. "You know that stern, formal, moralistic facade of his?" questioned another. "Well, what you see is what you get. He's a doer, not an intellectual seeking some kind of abstract hope." When Hesburgh talked about decorum, the professor explained, "he means it." When he spoke of the heart-bond that linked black and white, a short, fleeting smile illumined his entire face.

Whatever else marked his life—"like all of us," said a psychology teacher at Notre Dame, "he has his sincerity and hypocrisy, and probably a great deal of each"—his faith in America and what it meant loomed untarnished, unmarred by the cynicism which warps our times.

Like many of his colleagues, Hesburgh was opposed to the war, disdainful of the Nixon administration ("at least," he said, "in human rights"), highly tolerant of black militancy, sympathetic toward embittered youth. He was dismayed by Nixon's secret bombing of Cambodia, appalled at America's floodtide of B-52 raids, and supportive of the McGovern-Hatfield Amendment to End the War (first introduced in the Senate on April 30, 1970), which demanded total withdrawal of U.S. forces and an end to all American operations in and over Laos, Cambodia, and Viet Nam.

In 1970, when delegations of antiwar students descended upon Washington, Hesburgh lent his approval. In 1972, when George McGovern thundered, "Our government would rather burn down school buses and school children in Asia than build schools for Americans at home," Hesburgh nodded assent. He visited patients mangled by shrapnel, echoed the travail of Americans trapped in a conflict they had not sought and could not understand, decried the animus which led Nixon to scold H.R. Haldeman, "Dammit, I want no more Ivy League bastards on my staff," rejected the mentality of William F. Buckley's immortal observation that he would rather be governed by the first hundred names in the Boston telephone directory than by the faculty of Harvard University.

His liberalism was authentic, his compassion unfeigned. He was not unreceptive to an essentially poetic view of the

1960s; not disturbed when Yale's Kingman Brewster led more than a thousand students and faculty to Washington to lobby against administration policies; not angered when the presidents of seventeen colleges and universities drafted a joint letter to Nixon protesting the "incalculable dangers of unprecedented alienation of America's youth" because of the Cambodian invasion.

Hesburgh was eloquent, forceful, persuasive. But cleaving from his antiwar brethren—many of whom felt that truth was what made one *feel* good and that reality was merely sensory, intuitive, instinctively gleaned—he did not believe that rule by mobs should supplant rule by democracy. "Violence," he said, "is a dead-end street." To the president of Notre Dame, American society was *not* repressive. Genocide was *not* inflicted on Viet Nam abroad and the Black Panthers at home. The United States was *not* brutal and imperialistic. Students did *not* exist to be exploited and pandered to. To end the war, one need *not* demand amnesty for deserters and reparations for Hanoi.

Hesburgh's bent was classic, grounded on rational, observable facts. "Yes," he said, "I took firm stands. But people need—and I think want—to have a line drawn for them, to know how far they can go. If anything goes, you'll get anything. On campuses today—as in the early seventies—we've got a bunch of faint fellows who don't want to make educational waves. The sixties took a terrific toll. We lost a whole generation of university presidents. Most of them didn't understand that when one guy impinges on another's rights, you're on the brink of anarchy."

On February 17, 1969, in a letter later published in the *New York Times*, Hesburgh warned that any students resorting to the use of force would be given fifteen minutes to disperse; failing that, they would be suspended. Five minutes later, if the disturbance persisted, they would be expelled. Severity meant clarity, and clarity calm.

If he did not, parroting Nixon, claim that whether South Viet Nam had a chance to decide its future was an issue of moral and human concern, neither did he argue that a minority had the right to impose its will on society at large.

If he did not, mirroring Agnew, claim that the preservation

of the American-supported Thieu government was essential to Southeast Asia, neither did he state—as did liberals like Father Robert Drinan, Bella Abzug, Ronald Dellums, and the Reverend Joseph Duffey—that national catharsis required admission of American guilt.

If he did not, endorsing national security advisor Henry Kissinger, claim that the February 1971 South Vietnamese invasion of Laos—a venture that saw ARVN forces panic, then retreat, then cling helplessly to the bottom of U.S. helicopters sent to retrieve them—in some way augured military success, neither did he nurture violence at home or justify illegality by those who felt "alienated," "turned off," "dropped out," or any of the other catchwords which demeaned and trivialized the age.

He was his own man, aloof and iconoclastic, admired by the Left and Right, trusted fully by neither side. He could deplore the barbarism of My Lai—site of a March 16, 1968, American massacre of more than 130 Vietnamese women, babies, and old men—and still rebuff those who equated irrationality with creativity and who infused students with visions of a messianic calling, intoxicating them with self-righteousness. "The arrogance of moral superiority," he said presently, relighting his match, "destroys those who hold it, those whom they hold it against, and any hopes for peace, internal or otherwise. Nothing showed that more lethally than the college years of yours."

Hesburgh's office door opened. His secretary reappeared. Accepting a long-distance call, he reached for the phone. As Hesburgh debated, I searched a calendar on his wall. Exactly ten years earlier, I told him when the dialogue ceased, New York University Professor Sidney Hook—declaring that "American colleges and universities today face the greatest crisis in their history"—damned "the problem and threat" confronting American schools. The danger rested, he said, not in academic disquiet, "but academic disruption and violence which flow from substituting for the academic goal of learning, the political goal of action."

Unbuckling my briefcase, I placed Hook's speech inside. "What," I began, "did..."

"That's fine," Hesburgh injected, "but what exactly did the good professor object to?"

Not to controversy, I said, retrieving the article, for "intellectual controversy," Hook claimed, "was the life of the mind. The public objection is to how controversy is carried out—to the use of bombs, arson, vandalism, physical assault, and other expressions of violent strife and turmoil." How could academic freedom flourish, he asked, when extremists disrupted with impunity—crashing seminars, mistreating guest lecturers, seeing their excesses answered with an absence of steel? "In the last analysis," Hook wrote, bemoaning colleges' reluctance to enforce disciplinary action, "it has been the faculties... who have lacked the moral courage to uphold the professional standards of their calling as teachers and seekers of the truth."

Hesburgh shrugged. Self-effacement gentled his face. "What he said is true," he agreed, "and it's something I said a decade ago. But many wouldn't listen then—and they're not going to listen now, even though many teachers, by altering their behavior since then and behaving as teachers should, have in effect conceded the point. Let's face it; crow isn't edible in public places."

Time out. The reverend must puff anew. "Anyway," Hesburgh continued, flashing his pipe, "all I'm doing is acknowledging that the forms of protest—intimidation, bullying, physical violence—got out of hand. There was never any question that what they were protesting *against*—the war in Viet Nam—was wrong. Catastrophic. Immoral. Of course," he said, wry mockery mixed with smoke, "perhaps someone of your political persuasion would have difficulty understanding that."

"Not necessarily," I replied. In college, I told him, I was one of 14.3 million Americans between the ages of eighteen and twenty-one; of those between twenty and twenty-four, 23 percent were enrolled in school.

Among us, many were—in Murray Kempton's phrase—shabby-genteel. My own identification lay with the middle, not upper, class. I was not the son of a doctor or dentist. My father was a teacher, my grandfather a farmer, laborer, railroad engineer. My mother was a working woman. My grandmother reminded me of no one as much as Marjorie Main ("It's a good thing Curtis can write," she once said of me, winking. "He never was any good at farm work"). Discarding white bucks and cashmere sweaters, I favored blue jeans and high-topped sneakers. When I entered country clubs, it was as a reporter or nonpaying guest; self-styled better people, as I called them, belonged to other families, not mine. My class origins were clear, prideful, almost rhapsodically square. I rooted for any dog that was under—Don Knotts and Phyllis Diller, Patricia Nixon during Watergate, the Boston Red Sox every day.

"Sound familiar?" I asked. "I'll bet it does." Was there no role left for Americans like these, I wondered—men who drank beer and cherished Chester A. Riley; women who scrubbed floors and laughed at Ethel Mertz; people who watched "The Andy Griffith Show" and loved their country, and whose eyes misted shamelessly as the flag marched by?

Hesburgh's old liberalism spoke to such people; FDR and LaGuardia provided guidance, symbolism, hope. Hubert Humphrey once labeled them the "ordinary Americans"; instinctively, I understood them, and while an undergraduate often sided with their heirs.

"How so?" said Hesburgh, more softly than usual, the exhausting conversationalist now searching and questioning.

"Just a couple ways," I replied, "that might show something, even indirectly, about the dimensions of the Viet Nam War." I supported gun control, Father Hesburgh learned presently; even now, having grown to maturity amid the woods and rifle ranges of upstate New York, I have never fired a bullet (nor do I intend to try). In college, I let my hair grow long; "reedy" was the term most frequently applied. I drove a used Renault (in 1972, more than 85 percent of this country's foreign-car owners voted for George McGovern); inhabited leftist-leaning bars; despised the folk-totem figures of Big Business, not for their venality—as many Democrats supposed—but because they were obsequious, too fawning to stand up for themselves.

My favorite movie was *To Kill a Mockingbird*, its message subdued and evocative and pacifist-inclined. My favorite sport was baseball, its solitary grace not obscured in a bedlam of bodies, or in a jarring crash near the backboard, or in a madcap scramble near the goal. Was the summer game slow and sedentary? Perhaps. But for decades the ardor of America's working class (and of liberal luminaries like James Farley and

Eugene McCarthy) allowed it to endure and prosper, the most artistic of their nation's sports and ultimately, the most beloved. Most of my friends were liberal, poles removed from my ideological bent. Emotionally, I empathized with "Make Love, Not War," but my mind tilted toward the right.

"Make any sense?" I inquired.

"So far, yes," Hesburgh adjudged, "but how exactly does it relate to Viet Nam?"

Did he remember the early 1970s, I asked? Antiwar critics often talked of freedom, liberty, candor—but they were unconcerned about the freedom of 17 million South Vietnamese; unworried that, if the United States fled Southeast Asia, Communist barbarism might (and did) unfold; unwilling to admit that their hatred of bloodshed arose no more from ideological principle than from one overriding interest—Self.

Almost invariably, counterculture leaders arose from upper-income, Establishment, well-endowed families. They were the offspring of Benjamin Spock's America—largely liberal, overwhelmingly affluent, convinced of their superiority, and disdainful of the past. Adored by the nation's tastemakers, their excesses excused by slack, plu-tolerant parents, they were indulged and patronized. They agitated against the war as a way to escape the draft, to protect their hide, as usual, to get their way.

Some, like McGovern and Ramsey Clark, opposed the war because of deeply felt, humanitarian concern. Others, their idealism passionate but superficial, embronzed as their motto "Me—First and Forever," their hypocrisy matched only by their venom. They cared chiefly about themselves. Why? Because they were selfish. Why were they selfish? Because too often they were spoiled. Did not the cause of peace, I now asked Hesburgh, deserve much more than that?

Hesburgh whistled quietly. "Don't be so subtle," he jested. "Tell me how you *really* feel."

"I don't believe in questioning motives," he said, more forcibly, flinging to the side his hand. "Just remember the zeal of the boys and girls you castigate." He believed in the people who upheld those beliefs and was proud to have been their spokesman in the sunburst of the seventies' dawn.

Had antiwar stalwarts been self-righteous? Yes, but surety

of conviction is an undergraduate's lot. Had they deserted their government? No, precisely the opposite was true. Had hypocrisy outflanked their idealism? Perhaps, but whose intent is exactly what it seems? Amid the age's agony, had protest meant abandonment, a cursing of the country's worth? No, he said. There lay beneath all they said a silence that could not be silenced, an unspoken fear that the nation they loved had turned to betrayal, or at the very least passed them by.

"I understand your feelings, and those who opposed you too," Hesburgh proclaimed, rising from his desk, "but at least people were concerned, agonized, agitated, involved. At least they were committed. And that, let's face it, is a lot better than we often have today." Style was all that mattered; moral substance had become the forgotten ground.

"What an age it was," he said, escorting me to the door. "Sometimes I wonder, 'Would we want to relive it?' And I realize the answer is no; it was the most difficult time of my life. I'd wake up in the morning with a knot in my stomach, just praying I wouldn't do something that day to destroy the place. It didn't take much. Remember, colleges were crumbling all over the country. Careers were ruined, presidents destroyed, because no one knew how to deal with the frenzy. We'd never seen anything like it before."

Greeting his secretary, Hesburgh leafed through a newspaper on her desk. He pointed to the morning's major headline, "Carter Blasts Reagan as Irresponsible."

"The stories change, but not the politics," he said. "Would we want to relive a decade ago?" Hesburgh repeated, his voice distant and demure. "Only if we could keep the caring and somehow erase the hurt." And then he was gone, seeking again the comfort of his office, left to accept his solitude and pray for peace.

8
Dutch

WE HAD BEEN HERE, I ALMOST BELIEVED, MANY TIMES BEFORE.
The man rising toward me, a smile spread across his wizened
face, was as familiar as the scene he dwarfed.

"Yes," he said, a chuckle erupting in his breast, "when
you've seen one hotel suite, you *have* seen them all." Undaunted by age, a probing, often sardonic press, and memorable deflations of the past, he was now within reach of the goal
that, even a few turns of the calendar ago, seemed both cruel
and mocking—the presidency of the United States.

Ronald Wilson Reagan was his full name, but "Dutch"
described him best. Born in 1911, he still delighted in casual
self-deprecation, still retained the polish and urgency that had
always marked his platform presence; his public appearances
were as adroit and unblemished as ever. He was still the child of
near-poverty who grew up in downstate Illinois—struggling,
striving, determined to earn the stature his parents had not so
that he could make his own way in the world.

"We're all the sum of our parts," he said while serving tea,
"and my parts were formed in the stores and streets and quiet
homes of the Middle West."

The son of a shoe salesman, his youth tinged by a series of

77

small timeless towns, Ronald Reagan cherished what Sinclair Lewis scorned—the Main Street of "my parents and of their parents before them." He knew himself to be an old-fashioned man. He spoke of an earlier era; his bearing reflected self-knowledge and self-acceptance. "The old ways *can* be best," he insisted. "If I had one message to tell America, it wouldn't consist of fancy economic theories or complicated details. It would consist of five words. Family. Work. Neighborhood. Freedom. Peace."

When I was a student Reagan was governor of California—preaching to the choir, seeking converts to the conservative cause, espousing self-reliance and military preparedness and simple (albeit oft-unfashionable) truths.

He was first elected in 1966, trouncing incumbent Edmund G. (Pat) Brown by nearly 1 million votes; four years later he won again. In Sacramento Reagan raised state spending, taxes, and aid to education; restricted the growth of state employment; unveiled a welfare program that slashed the number of recipients by two hundred and twenty thousand and the costs by $1 billion; and left Jerry Brown, his successor, with a far more buoyant economy than he himself inherited.

"There were those," he said, his smile now minus warmth, "who babbled that there were no simple answers to complex problems. I think what we showed in the late sixties and early seventies is that there *were* simple answers—just not *easy* ones."

The sun of the "early seventies" flooded my memory. The years, I noted, had become a part of myself; they were something to be proud of, something to be explored. Reagan nodded. "Well," he said, "it was a time unlike any I've ever seen," at turns chaotic and seductive and free.

Reagan came on slowly, his voice dispassionate and calm. The infant 1970s, he said, comprised a conflict over values, and the way those values would be determined, and by whom.

Ironically, I sensed, Reagan had been ill-prepared by temperament for a clash in which only passions could prevail. He was not a hater; he sought endlessly to understand other points of view. To evoke real anger, one must fearfully provoke him; even his jibes and put-downs were whimsically cast:

How do you describe the typical Washington economic adviser? "He has a Phi Beta Kappa key on his watch chain—and no watch on the other end."

What was unique, asked Reagan in 1967, about farm union leader Cesar Chavez? "He's the only man I know," he answered, "who gained weight during a hunger strike."

One year later, addressing a Republican rally, he spied several unkempt protesters armed with "Make Love, Not War" signs. As usual, Reagan was ready with his response. "They don't look," the governor quipped, "as if they're capable of doing either."

As governor, Reagan's rhetoric was often fiercer than his record. "If it takes a blood bath" to quell campus riots, he challenged California students, "let's get on with it." He was derisive toward those who fomented campus rebellion; fond of administrators (like Father Hesburgh and S.I. Hayakawa) who deplored the use "of force instead of rational persuasion"; prepared, indeed anxious, to condemn those who demanded that the State Board of Regents "financially subsidize intellectual curiosity." Beneath such verbal ardor lay an affable, earnestly engaging man. Norman Mailer described Reagan's manner as "a tripped on-my-shoelace, aw-shucks variety of confusion," and William F. Buckley called him "both too fatalistic and modest to be a crusader." Among even those who detested his convictions, who cringed when he cursed the wreckage born of big government, many were disarmed by his honesty and craft.

A look of hurt afflicted Reagan's eyes. "What I remember about that time," he said softly, "is how inflamed the era was. Some of the stuff I said, I suppose, was pretty mild in comparison, but even then it was sometimes overdone. There wasn't much room for compromise, for quarter, for any kind of reason to emerge."

"Neither side would allow it," I said.

"No," he granted. "There was more than enough sanctimony to go around. Looking back, probably all of us were too self-righteous, too sure of ourselves."

Reagan's reply faltered, then came gushing forth. "But I think that was especially true about many on the other side, radicals like Tom Hayden and Fonda and Bella Abzug"—

people, he mused, who would not "recognize the *real* America if it were wrapped in red, white, and blue bunting and draped in a Betsy Ross–made flag."

"The Age of Aquarius did not become you."

"Our visions were different, that's all," he shrugged. "The people I understood were the producers, people who get up every day and go to work, look after their children, support their churches and schools, believe in standards of right and wrong—and ask nothing more from their government than simply to be left alone."

In Reagan, surely, these Americans saw a champion as well as friend—voters worried about the need to reaffirm old values; worried about the future and security of their children; worried that few leaders listened to what they had to say. "If I have a rapport with them, it's because I'm one of them. I know what they believe in—family life and religious fiber, safe streets and social order—the ideals that made this country great."

I labeled the Reagan constituency America's "good, quiet people." Yes, he suggested, they were "too busy working" to picket or protest or publicly complain. Their vision was *his* vision—frozen in amber, perhaps, but resolute and unchanging, the final vestige of an America gone forever.

Even now, nostalgia tugged at Reagan's sleeve. He often thought about his childhood environs, he confessed. "Everyone has to have a place to go back to. Dixon," he said of his Illinois home, "is that place for me."

Reagan spoke of its sober masses, its placid, neatly scrubbed lawns, its credulity and homespun wont, its seeming warmth and goodness. "It was a marvelous life," he said, turning toward me. "I could never have hoped for anything more then or now."

"But is that *enough* today?" I wondered.

The candidate grimaced, then saw an arrival cut short his response. Nancy Reagan, thirteen years her husband's junior, entered the room, a lithe, slender-faced woman. Meeting guests, she bore herself elegantly, and there was a kindness to her manner that belied the verbal image spun by an associate and long-time friend—"She's the governor's closest ally and his top staff sergeant too."

"Is it true," I asked, nodding toward Mrs. Reagan, "that the two of you cry during moments of 'Little House on the Prairie?', " a program which like his other favored television fare, "The Waltons," bespoke the uncomplicated virtues of Reagan's secure and idyllic youth.

"Well," she said, "you know, Michael Landon"—the show's director, producer, and leading man—"is a great friend of ours."

"True," Reagan added quickly, "but you have to remember"—unfurling that short, knowing smile—"that Nancy, she cries even when the laundry is sent out."

She turned toward him, feigned astonishment in her eyes. I had heard, I said, that children and homeless dogs lured Nancy's greatest rapport. Both, one suspected, released her humor and affection; each lifted her from interminable public obligations—to smile when hurt and suffer silently while striving; to endure politics' pomp and egomania, the self-serving machinations of self-seeking men.

"Yes, and you should see her with *stray* dogs," Reagan observed. "If she had her way, we'd have kennels built all over Southern California to house them. Out I go, in they come. At least," he said, shaking his head, "we know who rates."

Delight invaded Reagan's face. He grinned—is there any other word to describe how?—*winsomely*. They exchanged soft looks of respect and love and shared understanding, almost to confirm that here—in this, a profession where hard, sodden figures vied as pretenders for Reagan's trust—she remained his one unflagging friend.

His wife departed. I looked at the man sitting to my left, serene and full-framed, eased onto a sofa. A graduate of 250-student Eureka College, a Disciples of Christ school ("I worked my way through college. The first year I washed dishes in my fraternity. The second year, because of a rule that only freshmen could wash dishes there, I switched to doing the same thing at a girls' dorm. I guess that's progress"), Reagan later became a sportscaster at radio station WHO in Des Moines; there the name "Dutch," derived from his father calling him a fat Dutchman at birth, initially took hold. In 1939 he went to Hollywood, obtaining a screen test at Warner Brothers and $200 a week; made fifty movies, among them the classic *King's*

Row and the immortal *Bedtime for Bonzo;* and became—in his own words—the Errol Flynn of the B's. "I made quite a few movies," he said, "where they didn't necessarily want them good—they wanted them Tuesday."

Elected in 1947 to the first of six terms as president of the Screen Actors Guild, Reagan—once a decided leftist—turned conservative as the 1950s progressed. He was named host of the weekly "General Electric Theatre"; toured the country as G.E.'s national spokesman; became a highly sought speaker at Republican dinners and rallies; and served in 1964 as cochairman of California Citizens for Barry Goldwater, bursting into national prominence with a masterful October 27 network television address—"If freedom is lost here," he said, his voice swelling with emotion, "there is no place to escape to"—which censured Lyndon Johnson and "ultra-liberal thought." When Goldwater was buried, carrying five states to Johnson's forty-five, Reagan became heir apparent, the new darling of the resurgent right.

Four years later, now governor, he surfaced briefly as a Republican candidate for president, losing ignominiously to Richard Nixon. In 1976, he again contended for the presidency, staging the most successful challenge against an incumbent since Theodore Roosevelt chose 1912 to clash with William Howard Taft.

Amid his changing fortunes, a single constant lingered; only in the small towns of America, far beyond the cities he toured, in the prairies and provinces—only here was his echo true. These people loved Dutch Reagan in a quiet way too deep for applause. They believed what he told them—that America was great because America was good and that greatness arose not from government giving more to people, "but through people giving more of themselves."

"But in the 1980s, is that enough?"

"I think so," said Reagan. "I've never thought you had to needlessly complicate issues just so some intellectual could think of you as a partner in soul." One remembered Nancy Reagan saying, "Ronnie doesn't make snap decisions, but he doesn't tend to overthink, either."

For years this penchant had caused critics to question Reagan's depth and knowledge, his ability to comprehend issues and interpret events. They wondered whether the world as he described it was really the way it was, painted in the black and white of conflicting hues; worried about his zeal for simplicities and slogans and one-line clichés; charged that his assault against budget deficits, the bloated bureaucracy, and social engineering—"the sins," he said, "that tie the Gordian Knot"—would ravage the fabric of accepted law.

Would all of these misgivings, I asked, rise again to strike his doctrine down?

"Not at all," he said, waving his hand as though to dismiss my qualms. "Let me put it in a wider perspective. You see, my philosophy is the same today as it's always been. I haven't changed. The *nation* has changed." While America was not ready for Goldwater in 1964, he theorized, it might well accept Reagan now. "But with someone of my persuasion, to be effective you have to be able to empathize with common people's values—to talk in emotional terms—and still have the good manners, the civility, if you will, so that those who disagree with you don't become convinced that you're a Neanderthal man. We have a lot of good men and women in public life—Republicans especially—who *are* civil, who are kind to their dogs and don't beat their children, but who don't understand what moves people. They're afraid to stand for something, to oppose busing, for example, or support a strong police. They don't want to be labeled square."

Reagan flashed his grin. "Call me romantic. Call me old-timey. Call me an old-fashioned square," he said. The old actor paused. "Let me tell you something. I've been called a whole lot worse."

"A decade ago," he continued, "when the 1970s began, you had public officials who *did* speak to ordinary people, who knew what blue-collar people believed, who understood that patriotism and the work ethic mattered, who had the guts to talk straight.

"The problem was," he noted, "that because they weren't pictured as civil, because they spoke in a way that their opponents could distort, they allowed themselves to be portrayed as troublemakers, rabble-rousers, men bent on division and harm."

"George Wallace?" I volunteered. "And Agnew too?"

The once and future Huck Finn tilted his head. "You have to understand that they *weren't* demagogues," he said. "I think both were patriotic, gutsy Americans who said what they thought. They didn't care if we were liked around the world; they just wanted us to be respected. And they were honest about standing up for an electorate tired of being bullied by the very officials they had elected to serve.

"*But*," and here Reagan smiled a hard smile, "by being so frontal and direct; by slugging away when a few light jabs would have done more; by not realizing that because people in journalism disliked them, they could not get away with what many liberals could—they infuriated many people who later helped do them in."

Self-made and pugnacious, Agnew and Wallace refused to cajole, to flatter, to cultivate. "Liberals thought of them as many things," said Reagan wryly, "but civilized was not one of them."

"Was Richard Nixon?"

"Richard Nixon," he repeated, almost wistfully. Even the savage season of Watergate had not stilled Reagan's affection for that remote and perplexing man.

"His greatest fault was in trying to protect others," Reagan said. "There was a sense of insecurity in him too, and of course he was wrong to deceive the American public. But he was brilliant. What he did in foreign policy during the early 1970s is something I don't think we'll ever see again. He had us on the right track; while traveling abroad, I got that direct from many heads of state. Almost to a man they respected him, trusted him to defend America's honor in a way that would still allow their countries to maintain face and dignity."

A frown blackened Reagan's face. "He and his wife were very fine, considerate people."

"Considerate?" I asked.

"Look, you have to remember what he was up against," he replied. "The press was against him. The universities. The Congress. None of that excuses, obviously, what happened in Watergate; that just snowballed and multiplied and ran out of control. But think of the people who opposed him—the extremists of the left. They were rancorous, strident, uncompromising."

I mentioned George McGovern; the frown instantly reappeared. "He was shrill. He impugned motives. He was sanctimonious," Reagan said. Three for three, I thought; the former sportscaster could still compute.

"Of course," he added, "George may have changed his positions since a decade ago. I know a few liberals who have."

The telephone rang. Reagan rose to answer. I thought about the linkage between emotion and civility; it seemed to me both perceptive and true. Several months earlier, working in the John Connally campaign, I had sought to describe the public's curious definition of importance; Reagan's fondness for "The Waltons," I wrote, probably gained him more support than did Connally's avowal of capital formation and productivity.

"Politics," I argued in an interstaff memo, "is only minimally a rational science, and no matter how persuasive our convictions, they will be effective only if we can first get people to make the *emotional* leap." The American voter, I said, "responds best to instinctual, not intellectual appeals; candidates who run intellectually oriented campaigns are hampered, disadvantaged, doomed."

Superbly qualified, rousing on the stump, praised by CBS Television as "perhaps the most experienced candidate to run for president in this century," Connally dwelt on *issues* and was abruptly ousted from the race. Reagan's approach differed widely. He knew that most Americans have only a peripheral interest in issues and an even vaguer understanding of them; that passion, not programs, tilts elections; that Norman Rockwell's America, not the Fortune 500 Club, is the electorate's decisive bloc; and that subjects that Americans readily comprehend—busing and pornography, quotas and permissiveness, prayer in school and order in the streets—most influence what H.L. Mencken called this country's "great unwashed"; the unsung, the slightly soiled, people less little than neglected and abused.

Because Reagan understood them, they felt, he could be trusted to act on their behalf. If his philosophy was ridiculed in Georgetown, Manhattan, and Harvard Yard, it was applauded in Albuquerque, Peoria, and the sweeping farmlands of Ohio. "Maybe they didn't know that a decade ago," Reagan said. "Maybe I didn't shout loud enough for them to hear me."

Strangely miscast in the early 1970s, lacking the rancor

which colored others' remarks, he was more at home in this softer, settled age. His place had changed because the times had changed. If Reagan was, as some suggested, a small-town innocent, he was also—in that nearly extinct term—a *gentleman*, and he bore an eerie charisma that blended privacy and warmth, and a gentle, almost courtly veneer.

The phone dialogue ended, Reagan returned to the couch. Who, I asked him, was the man who had most enriched his life? John Wayne, maybe? Even Buddy Ebsen, perhaps.

"You probably don't expect this," the church-going Presbyterian said, "but when you look back over the years, as I sometimes do, only one name emerges: the Man from Galilee."

A meeting pressed, Reagan explained; he must shortly leave. I extended my hand and moved toward the door. "Good luck, Governor," I said to the man who would be president one day.

He smiled, then departed, as had August the night before. "See you in November," he said.

9
Natural Woman

"WHAT WAS THE MOST IMPORTANT THING THAT'S HAPPENED since 1960?" Hubert Humphrey queried as the 1970s broke, a decade before Ronald Reagan clasped the presidency.

"Not Viet Nam; we've had conflicts before. And not even President Kennedy's murder; that was the most *unforgettable* event, but we've seen a lot of tragic killings. No, the most crucial thing that happened—the phenomenon that changed our lives—was the Negro revolution."

Crossing 64th Street in lower Manhattan, my destination the building at One Lincoln Plaza, I thought of the transpontine tumult which marked the revolution—its marches, its speeches, its bloodshed and poetry. The struggle for racial equality sought to protect those disfranchised by color and disinherited by birth. With its emphasis on liberty, it also made possible, in a strange and ancillary way, the most important phenomenon of the *1970s*—the pursuit by women of dignity, the demand by women for rights.

The war was over; Humphrey dead. Even George McGovern would sorrow, "You know, civil rights, no one seems to give a damn any more."

What remained, though, and what had changed almost every American home, was the discipleship started by the woman who now grasped her doorknob, opening an entrance to her apartment—ex-suburban housewife; disgruntled play-mate; ultimately, social pioneer.

Of her, my sister would say, as did thousands of like-minded women, "She has changed my life." She was the mother of America's feminist movement. Her name was Betty Friedan.

Late in 1968, in a curiously soaring climax to a death-inflicted year, men had first flown around the moon. Surveying the globe's lunar orbit, Archibald MacLeish ordained, "To see the earth as it truly is—small and blue and beautiful—in that eternal silence where it flourishes—is to see ourselves as 'riders on the earth' together—brothers on that bright loveliness in the eternal cold. Brothers who know now that they are truly brothers." Writing now, the poet would doubtless shun the term *brother;* it lay amid feminism's wreckage, victim to the crusade for equity in language as well as work.

"Good trip?" Friedan asked, her face much as the *New York Times* once described it, "a combination of Hermione Gingold and Bette Davis."

"Yeah. Not bad at all," I said, reliving every bruise of my three-hour train trek from Washington, D.C. "I love the railroads. They're so leisurely you can work up a hangover and sleep it off before the ride even ends."

Friedan and trains; a dissimilar pairing, I mused. Few treasures once matched the splendor of America's railroads—their imperial power and influence, the romance and folklore woven in their fabric. Even in their infancy, trains connoted calm; they were an enduring relic, fixed, unchanging, a vestige of seasons when life implied placidity and men were men and women found fulfillment in garden outings and Tupperware parties and bridge.

But what was that, I wondered, to Betty Friedan—changing, not impervious; urban, not pastoral; one who meant that accepted order must crumble so that the tentacles of rebellion could emerge. Her modes of travel would cling less to mist-shrouded cabooses than to the 747—"Why," she jested, "how did you ever guess?"—especially if the pilot was a woman and the stewards were men. Trains bowed no man's spirit, but their heritage differed from the feminist cause and what they wished to summon too.

"Yes," concurred Friedan, smiling broadly, "the last thing we wanted to do was memorialize the past.

"After all, let's face it," she said, "everything in the history of America—our textbooks, advertising, the teachings of sociologists and psychologists—had taught us that women should be subservient, that their place was in the home and their primary role in life to make their husband happy, that they could have a place in society not through what they were able to do but only through their families, as if they were incapable of psychic and emotional independence—which they weren't—and as if they were frightened of being anything but a shadow figure—which they were."

"And you rejected that," I said.

"Pronto. Unequivocally. And, I must say, with results surpassing my wildest, my most bizarre and uplifting dreams. These college students I go around lecturing to today, they take the equality, the freedom to decide, for granted, like a Messiah-provided gift. They can't know how hard it was," Friedan noted. "They can't know how far we've come."

Born in Peoria, Illinois, Betty Naomi Goldstein was Jewish, bright, and drawn to journalism. In high school, she founded a magazine, then went east to Smith College where she gained a literary prize for her editorials, became editor of the school newspaper, and helped to create the *Smith Literary Magazine*.

In 1942, graduating summa cum laude, Friedan accepted a research fellowship at the University of California at Berkeley, moved west, won another fellowship the following year (rejecting it because—as she once confessed—a boyfriend told her, "Nothing can come of this, between us. I'll never win a fellowship like yours"), and fled to New York City, living in Greenwich Village "with a flock of other girls from Vassar and Smith, finding an oceanful of conscious or unconscious or semiconscious reasons to work on the mundane kinds of boring, menial jobs that led to the same address. Nowhere."

On June 21, 1947, she married advertising executive Carl Friedan, then a professor of summer stock. From Greenwich Village they moved to Parkway Village, a family community in the borough of Queens and, in 1957, to a Victorian home in suburban Rockland County, its eleven rooms, three baths, and landscaped acre towering above the Hudson River. There, as her husband embraced his work, Betty Friedan endured the conventions and expectations of the dogged employee's muted wife—"schizophrenic years," she later wrote, "of trying to be the woman I wasn't, of too many unnecessary arguments, too many days spent with, but not really seeing, my lovely, exciting children, too much cocktail party chit-chat with the same people because they were the only people there."

She was affluent.

"So why wasn't I delighted? I kept asking myself? I mean, for Lord's sake, I was in the suburbs, we had money, all the conveniences, free time. I was living the American housewife's dream."

Respectable.

"I did all the right things, and oh, did I keep busy," she said, her voice edged with sarcasm. "The endless minutiae, the never-halting details of husband, children, home. Not that they're bad by themselves—they were bad because I felt trapped into accepting them."

Wasted. Bored.

"'Is this all there is to existence?' I kept asking myself. I'd given up my search for achievement. Here I had education and skills and talent—I'd worked as a clinical psychologist—and my identity was still wrapped up in others. I knew what women were told they should be—and I knew, separate from that, what they really were, and even more, what they could become."

Fifteen years after graduation, refining a questionnaire for Smith College classmates, Friedan first realized the degree to which this dilemma—"the problem," she said, "which has no name"—was shared by other women. Among many of the respondents, and thus, Friedan believed, perhaps millions of women, the nameless travail lingered, leaving them, even before middle age, with a "mysterious ailment"—a conviction that their lives, which might have mattered, lacked the self-respect of choice.

What followed in 1963, Friedan's epoch-marking book, *The Feminine Mystique,* excoriated a dogma as old as America—the doctrine that women could find meaning only through child-bearing, the philosophy that women's proper role revolved around homemaker, mother, wife.

"Each suburban wife struggled with it [the problem]

alone," her best-selling treatise read. "As she made the bed, shopped for groceries... chauffeured Cub Scouts and Brownies, lay beside her husband at night—she was afraid to ask even of herself the silent question—'Is this all?'....

"Other women were satisfied with their lives, she thought. What kind of woman was she if she did not feel this mysterious fulfillment waxing the kitchen floor? She was so ashamed to admit her dissatisfaction that she never knew how many women shared it."

Alternately praised and vilified, her book translated into thirteen languages, Betty Friedan became—at age forty-two— abruptly, a household word.

"Some people were running around like lunatics, charging that I said, 'Women of the world unite—the only thing you have to lose is your men,'" she said, living again the uproar. "It wasn't true. What I said was, 'You have nothing to lose but your vacuum cleaners.'"

"And the reaction?" I asked.

"Everything you can think of," she replied. "I was called everything from a lesbian to Joan of Arc, from the nation's savior to a Communist spy. I was picketed, applauded, got obscene calls, had vulgarities thrown at me. Once in Detroit, being interviewed on a radio station, the switchboard was pelted by calls saying I should be shut up, gagged, thrown off the air.

"New York was being hit by a newspaper strike at the time the book came out. So the reaction to it, nationwide, was mostly word of mouth. I'd have people call me in the middle of the night—saying they'd been saved. One woman called from Pittsburgh; she'd been out all night looking for the book in different stores, her kids were in the station wagon with their pajamas on, and all the stores were sold out. She was desperate. 'Where can I get a book?' she pleaded.

"Then there were the haters, probably a majority then, for sure a minority now, but the same terrorized people who are falling for Phyllis Schlafly's hypocrisies. They couldn't face what I was saying, that realities were changing, the fact that there was a world out there waiting for them; they *wanted* to be trapped. They were too insecure, too frightened, to change their lives. At cocktail parties, they'd try to tear the hair out of women who defended me—and God, they hadn't even read the book. Afraid. Afraid to face the truth."

A look toward the window. "I'd have people come up to me and say, 'My mother wants to burn you at the stake.' And ten years later I'd have the same person come up and grab me. 'My mother believes everything you're saying.'" Friedan chuckled, lightly. "Lord Almighty, it's been rough and ready, but it hasn't been dull."

Buoyed by her response, Friedan spanned the country, addressing women's clubs, entreating college students, insisting that her sex—which now constituted 53 percent of the populace—was "the world's only discriminated-against majority."

In 1966, believing that the need for a women's movement had "reached the point," she wrote, "of subterranean explosive urgency," Friedan founded the National Organization for Women. NOW sought equality in employment, abortion on demand, the creation of child-care centers for working mothers, the revision of laws to permit deductions for housekeeping and child-care expenses. Among its splintered interests, the economy counted most. "The name of the game is confrontation and action," she declared in late 1969, "and equal employment is the top issue; the one that lodges in the gut."

She was, said admirers, the heir to Susan B. Anthony and Elizabeth Cady Stanton, her zealotry reminiscent of Alice Paul, author of the first equal rights amendment in 1923 and leader of the National Women's Party. "I have always thought that once you put your hand to the plow," Alice Paul had bandied, "you don't remove it until you get to the end of the row."

Hands were joined on August 26, 1970, the fiftieth anniversary of women's suffrage. Aided, belatedly, by the U.S. House of Representatives (which two weeks earlier adopted an amendment to the Constitution prohibiting bias on the basis of sex) and spurred by an outpouring in New York, where twenty-five thousand marchers paraded, arms locked, up Fifth Avenue, Americans in forty cities—many bearing placards reading, "I Am Not a Barbie Doll," "Don't Call Me Doll, Chick, Girl, or Broad"—struck for equality and (blessed) liberation, the largest expanse of women's sentiment since Warren Harding occupied the White House and Babe Ruth wove magic with his bat.

"That day," she related, eleven years later, "was an instant revolution against sexual oppression. It completed the great change in consciousness that began in '63.

"You see, I sensed that the country's identification with the women's movement was much broader than with Women's Lib—remember, the bra-burners, the radicals who were taking over in the headlines—and the message of our movement was being distorted. We were in danger of being known as kooks.

"So I called for a one-day protest. What for?" she asked. "To hit home our two goals. The personhood of women. Equality of opportunity. And in twenty-four hours we became a political movement—with a message, with troops to march, with clout to force politicians to listen, and eventually, to hear. We dove into the mainstream—and we've never left."

The afterglow of 1970, regarded fondly, vibrated around the room. "You have to recall what the 1950s and early 1960s were like for women. We weren't looking to find resources in ourselves. Too many said, 'All I want is a man to take care of me the rest of my life.' It was safe, and it was empty. Our whole reach of focus could have exploded in one great wave of boredom.

"But now," she exclaimed, gesturing broadly, striking with her palm a piece of Victorian furniture, "now it's changed. Look at me. I'm unbored. I can get mad as hell. I get exasperated. But, damn it, I'm *absorbed*. I love what I'm doing. And I know that we've changed the nation, brought women into the concrete realities of life, and in great ways, changed ourselves."

How had they changed, though, and what was the cost? Since 1955, women in the paid work force had more than doubled; of the entire labor mass, 42 percent were women (43 million in 1980). Child-care facilities had multiplied, career options been enlarged. Personal liberty and the soapbox merged—ERA proponents ratified, housewives boycotted, homosexuals protested, convictions hardened.

I reminded Friedan of an early-seventies cover of *Ms* Magazine, a man, beleagueredly, asking a woman, "Do you know the women's movement has no sense of humor?"

"No," the women said, glumly, "but hum a few bars, and I'll fake it."

From Friedan to Bella Abzug to Martha Mitchell ("I don't

believe in that no-comment business," she blurted in 1970. "I always have a comment") to Gloria Steinem, women demanded an openness of power and grandness of control—of one's body, one's career, one's ability to choose.

"Marriage, home, motherhood, it was all so neatly arranged," said Friedan, divorced in 1969. "We knew what our function was—to be a sponge. We were to be concerned with a man, not ourselves—his job, his advancement, his growth. Everything was mapped out for us. What we tried to do was change the route signs, to find some different roads to take."

Among feminists' anxieties, none loomed larger than the fear of that ineffable quality—the human heart and spirit—being heedlessly, irreparably harmed. More and more, they sensed, women seemed alone and powerless; they sought to have a say in things, to have a voice—and to have that voice *heard*. "Until we had a core of self-respect, we wouldn't earn respect from others," said Friedan. "Until we learned to love ourselves, we'd be incapable of extending true love—as opposed to affection in exchange for security—to anyone."

"Does that account," I asked, "for the shrillness of your voice in the early 1970s?"

"Partially," she replied, almost in a semimocking vein. "*Shrillness?* If we'd been men, we'd have been called aggressive. We were called brazen; the same quality in a man, you'd term him forthright. Hypocrisy. And even if we *were* shrill, I mean, did we have any other choice? Look at what we were up against." I thought of Helen Reddy, in 1972, singing, "Yes, I've paid the price, but look how much I've gained."

"We had to break through barriers that kept women from working, earning, moving in the mainstream," Friedan continued. "We had to convince women they could find an identity separate from men and marriage, that they deserved equal opportunity, that they had this right—the human obligation—to detail their grievances against men at home and work.

"Those weren't accepted concepts—they were revolutionary. And does this mean we had to be loud, unyielding, shrill in order to be heard? What in the devil do you think it meant? You bet it did."

By 1980, 43 percent of American wives with children under the age of six were working, some because of economic necessity, some because they yearned—in that fashionable phrase— to "find themselves." Women submerged the marketplace—in law schools, service academies, government contracts, and major corporations; in all-boy choirs and all-male social clubs; in positions where formerly "Only Men Need Apply." A decade after the phenomenon of August 26, 1970, only 17 percent of American households included a father as the sole wage earner, the mother as the fulltime homemaker, and one or more children. "And less than 7 percent," Friedan accented, "live in the kind of arrangement Norman Rockwell would cherish—mommy as the housewife, daddy as the breadwinner, two children plus a cat and a dog."

Twenty-eight percent of American households were composed of a father and mother as dual wage earners, with one or more children living at home; 32.4 percent were comprised of married couples with no children (or none living at home), and 22 percent consisted of one person living alone, fully a third of them women over sixty-five. "The traditional family needs all the help it can get," columnist Carl Rowan wrote in 1979. "The time-honored family portrait of dad at work, mom home cooking apple pie, the kids playing with gramps, is barely recognizable. Nowadays, chances are mom's at work, too; dad may have been laid off; the kids are tempted by drugs; and grandpa has been shunted off to a nursing home."

"Not bad for a decade's work," I said.

"Well," she offered, "especially when you consider that we were up against centuries of stereotypes."

The bell sounded at One Lincoln Plaza. Rising, the Feminist Mother moved slowly toward the door. During the early 1970s, I thought as she excused herself, America's Royal Family was "an arrangement" Rockwell *had* cherished—housewife Patricia, daddy Dick, children Julie and Tricia, husbands David Eisenhower and Edward Cox, and a poodle and an Irish Setter. "Often we were called square," Nixon would write in his *Memoirs*, "and as far as we were concerned, that was just fine." What blessings, I asked when she returned, did the women's movement, born in the second year of the Nixon presidency, receive from his administration?

"You've got to be kidding," she said, disdain splitting her face. "Sure, Nixon supported the ERA [signing the amendment, approved by both houses of Congress, in 1972], but don't forget, it was an election year. Even forgetting his dangers to American freedoms—and how marvelously our Constitution worked to protect us—he never understood our cause, our people, what we were trying to achieve. Where he came from, the kind of family he had, the Neanderthals who were his biggest supporters, they represented everything we had to overcome."

"And his wife?" I said.

"Mrs. Nixon?" Friedan said. "Oh, she was a gem. I suppose she was a nice enough person. Very refined. But as far as doing anything, or being her own person, or giving encouragement to those of us who fought the forces of reaction, forget it. It was as if she didn't exist."

"Not like her successor," I stated. To many feminists, viewing in Patricia Nixon the counterculture's bane, Betty Bloomer Ford was starkly different, almost heroine-worshipped—a synthesis of Eleanor Roosevelt, Florence Nightingale, and Carrie Nation.

"No, not at all," she replied. "She didn't live her life through her husband and children. She wasn't perfect, she had faults, but she was complex, not afraid to bust out on her own."

Pausing, Friedan stroked her chair. "I think the important thing about Betty Ford is that more so than almost anyone else—more than Carter, for example, who bungled his chances to help us, or Reagan, whose sensitivities are two hundred years old—she *legitimized* what we were trying to do, gave credibility to our efforts, even among traditionalists who saw us as crackpots bent on ruining the American home.

"She was a gutsy, gutsy dame. Superb. She stuck her neck out for ERA; she was honest about her problems; she wasn't a hypocrite—direct about her daughter and affairs and so forth—and she had something you can't rent or borrow. Backbone."

Like the war for racial equality, which—post Martin Luther King—often had spokesmen less worthy than its cause, the feminist revolution set in conflict one's beliefs.

No one need tell me, I suggested (with ample sanctimony) to Friedan, how *truly* liberated women behave. My mother was a marvelous teacher and a working wife. Physically, she reminded friends of Eve Arden. Emotionally, she made us more alive, more caring, more cognizant of life and love. With my youngest brother still in elementary school, she returned to college for her post-graduate degree—becoming a public school librarian (with five children to raise, two paychecks outflanked one), showing her family that even with home environs that were loving and supportive, only with career fulfillment could she sense herself complete. Both of my sisters graduated from college, one of them earning a master's diploma. "It's a good thing," I told them, "at least *some* of us are educated."

I understood, I hoped, the importance of creativity, of being free—vocationally—to expand and employ one's gifts; realized how various reports, among them the Manhattan Longitudinal Study and National Center for Health Statistics, verified that in the 1970s—as the feminist message blossomed—the psychological well-being of women improved; felt that marriage (or any relationship) could thrive only when women owned what Friedan demanded—the power of self-expression, the pride of self-respect.

If I relied (excerpting from *The Feminine Mystique*) on "waxing the kitchen floor for mysterious fulfillment," I too would go mad or to a distillery, whichever came first.

Feminism's goals, then, were laudable, but their influence—though NOW leaders denied it—was far more variable. Many of its deified figures, i.e., Abzug and Steinem, were caustic, spiteful, irretrievably rude. Striving to exhibit their independence, determined to prove they could compete with men, they discarded—almost gleefully, it seemed—the vestments that made *humanity*, not just femininity, worthwhile: grace and selflessness, tolerance and concern.

They were implacable toward groups that opposed them, disdainful of those who—cleaving from their views—found pride in housework; unburdened by the fact that their mission often reverted from a crusade for fairness into a vulgarization of self. "Charity is compassion," network sportscaster Buddy Blattner once advised me, "and that's the hardest thing in life to find. Nobody gives a damn about anybody anymore. What is life, anyway, without that, without those kind of feelings? Without them, you become hard and vengeful."

Friedan's gaze was riveting. The women's movement, I argued, celebrated decency, generosity, freedom. But what was decent about solely "looking out for number 1?" What was generous about caring chiefly for oneself? What was liberated about a cause that, rushing to display its prowess, left parents embittered, spouses deserted, children injured, marriages wrecked?

These questions were already troubling Friedan and led in 1981 to the release of another book, *The Second Stage*, which examined the rewards and dilemmas of changing roles. For many of her colleagues, though, absorbed in the search for "I," they were questions to be ridiculed, not examined, and dismissed as irrelevant. They were not irrelevant to millions of American homes. They were not irrelevant to history.

"I understand what you're saying," Friedan countered, her hands thrashing freely, "but I think your exaggerations are extreme. When men cared about themselves—and expected their wives to fawn all over them—do you call that selfish? No. So what's different for us? It's not a question of selfishness in our movement. It's a question of survival, and what's more, it's the only way we can relate to each other as people, honestly, candidly, without all the pathologies inbred in us from youth emerging to kill every feeling we have."

"In men and women?" I asked.

"For women, allowing our feelings to be genuine. For men, freeing them from the expectations that they had to be a jock, a macho man, no sensitivity, afraid to love or cry. But none of that can happen until women's identity allows all of us—women *and* men—to adjust to the new balance. And that's where men have balked."

"Maybe," I said. "I'm not sure." Was it possible that like the quest to end racial discrimination—a goal perverted, eventually, into reverse discrimination—the women's movement had been transfigured? Could women not laud ideals more elevated than feminine identity, or hope that even as people's self-images varied, their values would remain unchanged?

Rising since 1963, the divorce rate had doubled in the 1970s; more than 1 million unmarried couples lived together by 1978. As commitments became more casual, their meaning evanesced. We had become a nation of provisional loyalties.

Exchangeable relationships. Disposable husbands. Expendable wives. If the new morality—mirrored in the phrase "instant gratification"—ensured greater candor and independence, it could also make ready to hurt. The promise of feminism was manifest, but its disillusion—the cruelty it could inflict on others—that was genuine too.

"So what would you do?" Friedan challenged. "Erase all the advances of the women's movement? Put us back in the kitchen, barefoot and pregnant? Retreat to the days before ERA, before abortion came out of the backroom and equality out of the closet? Because that's what a lot of people want—the right-wing domesticated barbarians in the country.

"They talk about fairness—but what they really want is fairness on their terms. They talk about a partnership—but they want one partner, them, more equal than the other. It's easy to talk a good game, but those of us who've trudged in the trenches know talk doesn't do much except keep the downtrodden down. Is that what you want?"

No, I answered; before we could talk, I suggested, remembering Plato, let us first define our terms. What, precisely, did women's liberation mean? "I still don't know, entirely," I said. The most admired woman of the 1970s, said the Gallup Poll, was the "gem" Friedan had derided an hour earlier—Thelma Patricia Ryan Nixon—and to many, I proposed, she was among the most liberated.

"Ridiculous," snapped Friedan.

"Not wholly, perhaps," I smiled.

Since the women's movement cherished choice, I suggested, and since one career option—by that definition—was not superior to another, and since (further) Friedan acknowledged that feminists often insulted (needlessly) nonworking wives, Pat Nixon—like any woman—could be judged only by example, by the manner of her life.

What, after all, did feminists insist upon? That women be strong and authentic, if needed, solitary, capable of fending for themselves.

During her husband's presidency, Pat Nixon was more her own woman than many of the reporters who resorted to "Pluperfect," "Perfect Pat," "Plastic Pat," and other disparagements. She did exactly what she wanted—represent America as graciously as any woman who ever lived. Her dignity, Henry Kissinger wrote, "never wavered. She made no claims on anyone; her fortitude had been awesome and not a little inspiring because one sensed that it had been wrested from an essential gentleness." She asked for little, yielded much, uplifted others, and steeled herself. She differed from feminists, I proposed, only in her interests; her qualities—courtesy and courage and self-deprecatory humor—would enrich any offspring, daughter *or* son.

"What you're saying," Friedan injected, "is that in the early seventies people on both sides of the feminist issue—reactionaries and us—sometimes ignored the human equation, the parts making up an individual, because the sexual roles we were fighting against dominated public discussion. Biased stereotypes made understanding impossible."

"Yes," I said.

"Both sides were shadowboxing, you know? What were the cave dwellers defending? Woman as pawn, defenseless, a crutch. What were we denouncing? The same image. But the image was a fraud. It never existed. There was never any merit behind it—and when America got wise to the fact, the feminine mystique was gone."

"And both sides were blinded," I nodded.

"What?" she said.

"Well, powers on the right denied your right to freedom, to liberation," I remembered. "And people on the left—believing that you couldn't be liberated if they didn't agree with you—denied that a Pat Nixon, say, was free. Not because she wasn't liberated, but because once liberated, she chose a different means of expression."

"All of which goes to prove?" Friedan said, teaching.

"Yes?"

"That all the trauma, the conflict, the explosions of the women's movement aren't going to leave us for ten years, or twenty, or the rest of our lives."

"And all of that," I repeated, "goes to prove..."

"You're a good straight man," she said, laughing. "What it proves is that what we started is one of the milestones in the history of this country."

"How so?" I wondered.

"Few events," she exclaimed, proudly, "make people change the way they think, how they feel, what they believe about themselves, relatives, roles. We did. And because we did, millions of people woke up—and started to understand what all of life could mean. Not all reached my conclusions. But at least they're aware, involved. Even if one does think Pat Nixon is among America's most liberated women."

Outflanked, I winked my reply. "Comes with the territory, I guess."

Unlike John Newton Mitchell or Ramsey Clark, unlike some of my classmates thirty years her junior, Betty Friedan's profile was unfinished—because her movement was unfinished too.

Leaving this attractive woman, with her olive, sunlit skin, I thought of those affected by her calling—my mother, sisters, college friends, loves. It had begun, for me, amid the groves and midlands of Allegheny College. It would end, for many, when their yearning for identity, still rising, yielded to the grave.

If my embrace was not total, as it was not, it was because dignity, I felt, could not be bequeathed by a movement. Dignity must be earned, not acquired; it was personal, the sum of how we conducted ourselves.

If others, disagreeing, became Friedan apostles, it was because they believed the imagery of singer Cat Stevens— "You're only dancing on this earth for a short while"—and because while here, they hoped to matter, if only the insanity of the moment would give them the chance.

Entering Grand Central Station, eight hours by train from western New York, I passed a newsstand in the western foyer of the Main Concourse. Drawing closer, I saw a political journal with two Illinoisans on its cover. "Anderson no Lincoln," the title read.

One hundred and twenty years earlier, leaving Springfield to assume the presidency, Lincoln had addressed his home people at the Great Western Railway Station. "All the strange checkered past," he told them, "seems now to crowd upon my mind."

I purchased my ticket and boarded a train. From New York City, where the present was overarching, the Salt City

Express swerved toward the north and west, where the past overwhelmed.

Book Two

We spun so fast we couldn't tell
The gold ring from the carousel.
How could we know the ride would turn out bad?
Everything we wanted was everything we had. °

°"The Hungry Years"

10
Sweet Summer

IF DIXON, ILLINOIS, WAS RONALD REAGAN'S VALHALLA, Geneseo, New York, was mine. With its wandering cobblestones and cathedral-vaulted homes, its small shops and maples and Indian names, it was—as Theodore Roosevelt once wrote of his summer White House, Sagamore Hill—"the offspring of the years as surely as is a reef of coral."

As a student at Geneseo State University, I shared with classmates in common limbo—having said good-bye to childhood, I had not learned what it meant to be a man. Buffeted by cynicism and always, it seemed, exuberance, we yearned, above all, for sense of self. Definitions evolved less in the classroom (where forums on war, criminality, and terrorism were tilted by the bias of individual professors, and where we not infrequently rejected substance for show) than in dining halls and dormitories and the rathskeller and college union, where what one did determined who one was.

Formerly a state teachers college, now among the most selective colleges in New York's State University System, Geneseo in 1971–73 still housed the heirs of Middle America—middle income, middle class, demonstrably middlebrow. Larger (enrollment, 4,200) than Allegheny College, it was somehow more intimate.

"We've got some self-consciously fashionable people here," a friend of mine, one year older, conceded in the first week of my junior year, "and we've got some poor people, but mostly what we've got are a lot of kids just looking for some way monetarily to get the hell through school." Ten years later, proposing that homogeneity meant solidarity, an admissions counselor at Brockport State, Geneseo's sister college, said, "Whether it's because of the school's remote location [thirty-five miles southwest of Rochester], or its standing near knolls and hills, or whatever the reason, word of mouth kept telling us that Geneseo was divided in what its students thought, but united in temperament, (informal) and alike in what (lack of pretense) its students prized." And in my twenty-one months as a student there, reflective of the nation too.

At Geneseo, while many undergraduates lauded beer, brawls, and Greek society—not for nothing were they called the "*Silent* Majority"—others gathered petitions, drafted editorials, denounced institutions, canvassed homes. They were influenced by teachers, said Andrew Greeley of the University of Chicago, "who, if they compare the United States frequently enough to Nazi Germany, begin to believe that there are Nazi stormtroopers in the streets, that Richard Nixon actually is an Adolf Hitler who intends to cancel the 1972 election, that John Mitchell really is a Heinrich Himmler who is setting up concentration camps, that the United States has really embarked on a policy of genocide against the black and brown people in its midst, and that Daniel Berrigan, in a mad exercise of romantic narcissism, has become Deitrich Bonhoffer reincarnate."

In Meadville, activists had adopted a single doctrine—opposition to Viet Nam, to conventional morality, to existing vestiges of authority and rule. But by late 1971, with the war receding and soldiers coming home (United States troops in Southeast Asia declined to one hundred and thirty-nine thousand by year's end), with arms limitation negotiations near consummation and Nixon's trek to China already announced, and with Nixon emerging among the most respected (which is not to say beloved) presidents of post-World War II America, targets of the counterculture—no longer silent—began crying out for some measure of respect.

Their pleas reeked not of bigotry but rather injured

pride—a resentment against the harm *they* had done to this country—and reverberated most loudly in those places where the royalty of intellectual fashion seldom neared. Portland, Oregon, and Portland, Maine. Nebraska and Ohio. And the small burgs and cities, the retirees and attendants, the town halls and shopping malls of upstate New York.

"My years in college were the finest of my life," I remembered Nick Miletti, owner of baseball's Cleveland Indians, saying in 1972. "What was unusual—that wasn't—was that I realized so at the time." Miletti's counsel was unerring.

Amid the decade's brilliance, I found at Geneseo a contentment that had not previously impelled me, and that has not embraced me since. In an age that solemnized disquiet, I found at college hope—partly because, as some suggested, one could thrive on turbulence; partly because as one became outspoken, one might also become unafraid. Could deeds alone dim night's spirit and make of the early 1970s—this fascinating mix—an ordered and coherent time? Wanting to believe so, I believed.

Reticent at Allegheny, I grew vocal in New York. Restless, I bought my first car—small, treasured, and flagrantly inexpensive. Solitary, I fell in love; our times were glorious, as fine as any we could hope for, and when bad times confronted us they were as bad as any we had known. Thespian, I found peace in public-address announcing, in charity variety shows, and in public readings of prose from Carl Sandburg's *The Prairie Years* to Walt Disney's *Bongo* to *The Bridge of San Luis Rey* to *Going to the Fourth*, a novella combining Grant Wood serenity and familial affection.

Reveling in what a professor called "the role that most avante-garde students think they have a monopoly on—the voice in the wilderness," one could drink gin at breakfast and coffee at night, praise James Fenimore Cooper while others celebrated John Updike, and in environs where—to many— liberalism meant enlightenment, write political columns that prompted two death threats, obscene phone calls, and a visit to my dormitory room, unsolicited, by several soul sisters protesting my equation of black campus violence with "behavior that has been shabby and gutter-level, bordering on the obscene." Exaggeration, we know now, was not a leftist monopoly.

Nowhere was extravagance richer than in the fury en-

circling Nixon. Instinctively, I felt affinity. I knew of his roots
("I remember our mother used to get up at five o'clock every
morning at our little country store to bake pies so that I and my
five brothers could get the education my father didn't have")
and of his courage ("No matter what else you say, he was a
leader," Jimmy Carter said of his predecessor, once-removed,
in the first of the 1976 televised debates). He was, as commer-
cials for Ronald Reagan boasted in the 1980 presidential
campaign, "so clearly one of us." His critics hailed from what
John Anderson, seeking support in that same ill-starred election, would enlist as the "Volvo and brie-cheese crowd."

   Endorsing him, I defined myself. Defending his administration, I defended my past and aligned myself with what my
parents and grandparents—bullied, like millions of other
people, by those who professed to be the self-anointed judge
and jury of all that transpired in American life—had never
known before. A Voice.

   "Middle America had been without a great leader for
generations," Theodore White later wrote, "and in Richard
Nixon it had elevated a man of talent and ability, a president so
powerful as to change the world, so powerful that Richard
Nixon alone had been able to destroy Richard Nixon." He
forced students (for better *and* worse) to examine the conse-
quences of government policy, and by his complexities as
president, shadowed the campus proletariat to a degree that
Eisenhower and Kennedy never equaled and that Carter would
not approach. If, in our search for identity, we saw ourselves as
Hamlet, Richard Nixon was Hamlet's ghost.

   Ironically, among the decade's personae, it was a boxer—
former heavyweight champion Floyd Patterson—who best
embodied this search: for "serenity of mind, of a peace within
myself," he said, wistfully, in October 1972, "an identity and
purpose that will last, that won't make one feel ashamed of
being different."

   Burlesquely miscast among boxing's calloused men, Patterson that fall was dismissed by the nation's ring public, KO'd
in a fight with Muhammad Ali—the debacle thwarting an
agonized comeback and effectively ending his career. For ten
years Patterson had sought to regain the title Sonny Liston
stripped from him in 1962. Bruised, battered, scorned by his

rivals and derided by the press—back from the boxing dead he came, winging his way into the million memories of America. The road was tumultuous and ultimately doomed to fail; reporters called him a paper tiger, a heavyweight in name alone. Yet even in defeat Patterson dared as greatly as he bowed, and in his comeback—his groping for a modicum of self-respect—he left America to marvel at the arching human spirit, oft-abused yet free.

Elaborately gentle, a noncombative figure in an intensely violent sport, Patterson's tenor echoed with qualities alien to the early 1970s—the dignity, the humility, the innocence, all these more apparent than before.

"People said I didn't have the killer instinct," he acknowledged. "Well, it's something I never wanted. They said maybe I was too meek. Well, maybe they were right, but I couldn't be other than myself." Once a stranger, even among supposed friends, Patterson found himself as he *was* himself, and learned that even, curiously, in a time which enshrined ill-temper—as he found millions with him, with him because they loved him, and sensed himself complete—a man of kindness could survive.

In his quest for "purpose," Floyd Patterson was Everyman. At Geneseo, three weeks before Patterson was pummeled by Ali, I went to see a movie, *Five Easy Pieces,* fictional cinema, that bespoke more than it intended. Near the picture's end, its leading character, played by Jack Nicholson—accompanied by three flunkies, all unemployed and touring the country—strutted into a roadside diner and, mocking their waitress, ordered food not on the menu. With the waitress unable to comply, Nicholson maligned her, swept the table clean of dishes, silverware, saucers, and cups and —presumably now a bigger man—swaggered out of the bistro, leaving the utensils in pieces and the waitress in tears.

I was surrounded by eighty people in Geneseo's Riviera Theatre, and almost alone, it seemed, was repelled by Nicholson's behavior. Most were delighted; cheering, they rose to their feet. Watching Patterson twenty days later, I thought of Nicholson and Ali. They cherished crassness, boorishness. To adversity, they responded with self-pity; they came on as almost aggressively mean. To misfortune, Patterson countered with self-discipline. Seldom would he peel away defenses. Seldom were emotions unveiled. He etched a strong, consoling profile when what he really wanted was to reach out and be consoled.

Between Nicholson and Patterson, my classmates and me, responses varied widely, but all sought resolution of a ferment which voided pause. "You cannot be given a life by someone else," one college textbook advised us. "Of all the people you will know in a lifetime, you are the only one you will never leave or lose. To the question of your life, you are the only answer. To the problem of your life, you are the only solution." Was self the only truth we could rely upon? In the town of Geneseo, where, as the past was measured against the present, men and women hoped for normalcy, and at Geneseo State, where students hoped for something more, change's sword attacked our throatlatch. Some were elevated. Some succumbed.

A decade later, retracing Geneseo's fallswept streets, I found both fates resurrected and remembered how a single moment—to me, October 20, 1972—perhaps joined them best. Writing in the *Lamron*, the college's weekly newspaper, I had dwelt on the presidential election, then eighteen days away, and in pages usually devoted to the unmaking of Richard Nixon, berated his opponent, George McGovern, for "a campaign lacking decency, lacking principle, and in November, sadly lacking votes.

"The McGovern mystique," the column read, "has been shattered by a series of McGovern mistakes—errors that have punctured his false facade, blunders that have transformed May's 'Honest George' into October's 'Lonesome George.'

"He has time and again abandoned programs, principles, and yes, even his own vice president—and on November 7, the American people will abandon him."

The October 20 editorial, later called by a *Lamron* colleague "the most nauseous of this election campaign, more full of half-truths and distortions than Richard Nixon himself could think of in ten years," reached Geneseo dormitories shortly after noon.

In that same hour, four hundred miles removed, Nixon appeared at Independence Hall, there to sign a revenue-sharing act. With McGovern's candidacy collapsing and Nixon near the greatest victory in the history of the presidency, he recalled how on the last day of the Constitutional Convention in 1787, Benjamin Franklin had looked at the president's chair and observed that he wondered during Philadelphia's "long, hot summer" whether the sun painted on the chair was rising or setting. "But now at length," Franklin concluded, "I have the happiness to know that it is a rising and not a setting sun."

Like Franklin, Nixon said, "we can be confident, as we approach our two hundredth anniversary, that the sun is rising for America." Seemingly invulnerable, exhilarated by the presidency—as many of us were by college—Nixon stood, as Edmund Burke once declaimed, at "the summit. He may live long, he may do much. But... he can never exceed what he does this day."

What he could not know, as we did not, either, was that in the flowering of future months—for him, and us, and America—the sun would almost disappear.

11
The Dignity of Man

WHEN I ENTERED GENESEO, SIX STATES AND SEVEN HUN-
dred miles from the Georgia State Capitol, whose doors I now
converged upon, Martin Luther King had been dead for 1,243
days.

His murder made of civil rights an interregnum, deprived
apostles of the man who most swayed America's white
majority stock, and left this country—King's oratory gone—
with no black who understood equally, and could, as such,
convey the grandiloquence of rhetoric, the primacy of words.

Five years earlier, reflecting the adoration of two hundred
thousand Americans at the Lincoln Memorial, King had
celebrated the one hundredth anniversary of Negro emancipa-
tion. "I still have a dream," trumpeted the future recipient of a
Nobel Prize, "that one day this nation will rise up and live out
the true meaning of its creed: 'We hold these truths to be self-
evident, that all men are created equal.'"

With King's death, what became "self-evident"—as black
leaders rushed to occupy his void—was that none were "equal"
in ability.

Ralph Abernathy, King's successor as president of the
Southern Christian Leadership Conference, proved posturing
and ineffective; by 1980, removed to the periphery, he was
reduced to endorsing Ronald Reagan for the presidency, a

112

Top left: John Mitchell, attorney general from 1962 to 1972, shown delivering an after-dinner speech. To many American's, he was "Martha's husband." (*Wide World photo.*)
Top right: Ramsey Clark, "a voice of liberty and piety," writes the most vocal critics. (*Wide World photo.*) Above: Billy Graham, preaching at an early-1970s crusade (left), had evolved by 1982 as an ardent foe of "this foolish, destructive nuclear race." (*Photo at left from Wide World, at right courtesy of Mr. Graham.*)

Allegheny College's Jeanne Braham (in 1971, on left, and today): "The most remarkable teacher I ever met," recalls the author. Above: Allegheny College students held a candle-light procession to protest Kent State. (*All photos courtesy of Allegheny College.*)

Allegheny College's Bentley Hall (top) and the Ford Chapel. (*Allegheny College.*)

President of the University of Notre Dame, chairman of the President's Commission on Civil Rights, Father Theodore Hesburgh (top left) broke with Administration foreign and domestic policy. (*Photo by Gary Mills.*) Ronald Reagan campaigning for Nixon (top right) and preparing to horseback. (*Top from Wide World; below by Michael Evans, The White House.*) Betty Friedan (bottom left), Mother of the Feminist Movement. (*Courtesy of Ms. Friedan.*)

Julian Bond (top), with an unlikely colleague, Lester Maddox. "Sure, quotas divide," said Bond. "They polarize. But it's a necessary polarization." (*Wide World photo.*) After the May 1972 shooting that paralyzed him, George Wallace was visited in the hospital by Hubert Humphrey, a rival for the Democratic nomination. (*Wide World photo; recent photo of Wallace at right is courtesy of Mr. Wallace.*)

"If Dixon, Illinois, was Ronald Reagan's Valhalla," the author writes, "Geneseo, New York, was mine." Clockwise from top left: the picturesque Genesee Valley; Old Main, on campus; a mist-shrouded view of campus; and the town's Main street.

Spiro Agnew (top left), appearing on Dinah Shore's television program, where he played the piano and prepared linquine. (*Wide World photo.*) John Chancellor (top right), looking much the same as he had during the 1970s, when he became recognized as one of America's leading journalists. (*Photo courtesy of NBC News.*) Jerry Rubin (below), circa 1968: "I just believe," he said in 1981, "I can be more effective now, considering the way the country has changed, wearing a suit and tie." (*Wide World photo.*)

The age's preeminent figure, clockwise from top left: presiding over a press conference; celebrating his landslide over McGovern; reporting to the nation upon his return from China. "He was the lodestar," the author writes of Richard Nixon, "around whom our years in college turned."

stroke King's widow Coretta termed "the machinations of a man desperate for publicity at any cost." Jesse Jackson, by turns persuasive and egomaniacal, did not emerge as a major black spokesman until the late 1970s, when his call for academic self-discipline—"lacking motivation and effort, the best opportunity in the world will pass you by"—angered those opting for dependency over racial and personal pride.

Rather, in the early seventies, as Roy Wilkins and Whitney Young grew older, as Floyd McKissick grew more intemperate, and as Andrew Young perfected what ultimately became his national hallmark—sanctimony—the man deemed most likely to seize King's mantle was mild and thin and eloquent, Georgia's Julian Bond.

The descendant of a freed slave, Bond first met prominence in the late 1960s, as the agenda for civil rights was shifting—from voluntary desegregation to compulsory integration; from an emphasis on quality education to the whirlpool of busing; from statutes barring discrimination in public facilities, voting, education, and employment to administrative laws that imposed reverse discrimination; from "the elimination of racial barriers," cried skeptics, among them Justice William Douglas, "to their creating in order to satisfy our *theory* as to how society ought to be organized."

"Different decade, different land," said Bond, a state senator in the Georgia Legislature, looking much as he had in 1968, the year *Life* magazine called him "a comer, perhaps the prototype of a whole new breed on the political scene—the young, articulate, well-educated, and determined Negro politician who must be included in the political equation from now on."

Forthright and handsome, his nature earnest, my host flung to his side an arm. Outside, Atlanta sparkled, and as dawn became mid-morning, the city's warmth belied its February date.

Black concerns had changed, Bond started, because their needs had changed. While biases persisted and inequity remained, the freedom *from* that King solicited—from want, shame, and bigotry—had evolved, as the 1970s began, into demands for a new, more eclectic freedom *to*—to own, create, and manage.

"Today, in the civil rights movement," he said, reclining in a chair, "you have a lot of miniscule, separate local groups that don't know their right arm from the left. One isn't involved with the other. One's interested in bilingual education, another in school guard crossings. It's fragmented, torn apart. But in the sixties, cresting about the time you're writing about, our movement was single-minded, single-directed. We acted with a united voice. We acted as one."

By 1970, he recounted, America had already heeded—"for the most part, that is"—the counsel of Lyndon Baines Johnson, delivered in his first presidential address to Congress. "We have talked long enough in this country about equal rights. We have talked for one hundred years or more. It is time now to write the next chapter and to write it in the book of law."

Johnson spoke on November 27, 1963. In late June, invoking cloture to end a southern filibuster, the Senate adopted a civil rights bill—extending suffrage, integrating public accommodations, authorizing federal bureaus to with-hold funds from federally-assisted projects imbued with racial discrimination.

Nine months later, Alabama state police—wheeling clubs, bullwhips, and tear gas—halted a black voting rights march from Selma to Montgomery. The dissonance pierced one's cognizance, and when King led a March 25 pilgrimage to the base of the state capitol, concluding the trek to Montgomery, twenty-five thousand Americans encircled him. "We are on the move," he told supporters, "and no wave of racism can stop us."

On August 6, the president signed the Voting Rights Act of 1965, ordering its full compliance and, insisting upon black involvement in future state and local elections, announced the Justice Department would file suit against the four states that required payment of a poll tax as a prerequisite to voting. By the election of 1968, when, ironically, George Wallace swept the region, four hundred and sixty-thousand new blacks were enrolled as voters in states of the Deep South; in Alabama, the percentage of blacks registered to vote—only 14 percent in 1960—had spurted to fifty-three.

"That's what I mean about a singularity of purpose," Bond affirmed. "The different segments of our movement banded together in the early sixties for dignity, then for voting rights, and in the years, say, between '66 and '69, for budding political power. Not that we accomplished what we wanted to—the record shows we didn't—but at least we knew together what we wanted to do.

"Remember the riots of '67?" he asked. After their cessation, the National Commission on Civil Disorders—warning that more than a quarter of all black teenagers seeking jobs could not find them and that 75 percent of all black grade-school pupils in metropolitan areas attended predominantly black schools—said starkly: "Our nation is moving toward two societies, one black, one white—separate and unequal." The report said also, Bond continued, that under the Great Society's swell of legislation, extending from the Economic Opportunity Act of 1964 to the passage, four years later, of an Open Housing Act, barriers to freedom were orderly and lawfully abridged.

When Johnson left the presidency, only one-third of Northern blacks still lived in urban ghettos, one-third of all black family incomes exceeded $7,000, and in Fayette, Mississippi, the state where six years earlier a field secretary for the National Association for the Advancement of Colored People, Medgar Evers, was murdered, blacks—now an electoral presence—elected as mayor his brother, Charles. "Most people don't realize what we accomplished in about five short years," Father Hesburgh of Notre Dame had earlier reminded me. "We went from the equivalent of almost total apartheid in this land to a situation where we could actually talk about equality, and even see it on the horizon. It was unprecedented. And in retrospect, absolutely essential if this country—*literally*—was to survive."

Laughing softly, Bond appraised the recollection. "Sounds dramatic, doesn't it?" he said. Flanked by notes and papers, we sat alone in his basement office. "Well, it was—the marches, the protests, the sit-ins, the songs. But the romance died when King was shot, and when Bobby Kennedy died two months later, so many said, 'What's the use? They've taken all we have.'

"If they had lived, if King had been one of the country's consciences and Kennedy its president—as I think they would—we would have built on the freedoms the 1960s gave us, not spent every waking moment trying to preserve them from extremists, and ushered in social reconstruction that might have

made the next decade a lot different than it was. We had all the
blocks in place—the legislation, the leverage over the demagogues of the right." A turn of the head, glancing downward.
"We had everything but power. Had we had a president ready
to implement the laws on the books, the seventies could had
been the brightest decade ever. But Nixon came to office at
exactly the wrong time. When we had the buttons to push, we
had no one to push them.

"I remember," Bond continued, "I'd go around to campuses in the late sixties and early seventies and the students—
they hadn't adapted to the alterations we had to face. When I
put ideas on the table, they'd turn them down.

"If I said, 'Get involved in a political campaign,' they'd say,
'That's plebian.'

"If I asked them, 'Try to better the community around
your school,' they'd say, 'That smacks of paternalism.'

"They didn't want to help five people. They wanted to
help a hundred thousand people. And because they couldn't
help the hundred thousand, they wouldn't help the five. They
didn't understand that all the struggle for equality was going to
be harder—and a lot less glamorous—than in the 1960s. They
couldn't be bothered. They didn't realize that for all of us, the
days of wine and roses were gone. What worked on the streets
of Selma wouldn't work in the Nixon White House. We had to
nickel and dime our way for every goal we wanted."

Born in Nashville, the son of a Negro college president,
Bond had witnessed (as many of the students had not) the tidal
discontent afflicting Black America—the 1954 Supreme Court
Decision, *Brown v. Board of Education of Topeka*, which
ruled that segregation in public schools was unconstitutional;
the fifty-four-week boycott, begun in 1955 and led by King,
which forced Montgomery to integrate its city buses; the fourth
Wednesday of September 1957, when bayonet-armed National
Guardsmen protected the first Negro students to attend a
southern desegregated school; the wave of militancy begun on
February 1, 1960, when four freshmen from a black college in
North Carolina sat down at a segregated lunch counter in
Greensboro, and when a waitress refused to accept their order,
refused to leave.

As Negroes conducted sit-ins (by mid-1962, more than
fifty thousand people had demonstrated in one hundred cities)

and wade-ins (attacking the exclusivity of segregated beaches and pools) and boycotts and protest marches; as the federal government dispatched armed officials in September 1962 to guarantee Negro James Meredith's admission to the University of Mississippi, and in May of 1963 to quell riot-scarred Birmingham, and the next month to allow two blacks to enter the University of Alabama; and as—further—segregationists unleashed police dogs and fire hoses on demonstrators, beat civil rights workers and, bombing a black church, killed four small girls at Sunday School—the cleavage was defined by King, who spoke of escalating duality: "The worst of American life...the best of American instincts."

Enrolled at Morehouse College, where he took a philosophy course under King and graduated in 1961, Bond learned of peaceful resistance, Gandhi's creed turned American, and saw his teacher assailed by Southern segregationists—who cloaked their racism in states rights—and by extremists on the left, who echoed Malcolm X's gospel, "I don't see any American Dream. I see an American nightmare," and who equated patience with repression, nonviolence with defeat.

He became a reporter, eventually managing editor, for the *Atlanta Inquirer*, a Negro weekly newspaper, and created a communications office on the Student Non-Violent Coordinating Committee (SNCC). In 1965, when reapportionment formed a largely black district in southwest Atlanta, Bond—at twenty-five—ran for the state legislature, won, and was barred from the House of Representatives. It objected, said members, to Bond's endorsement of a SNCC document accusing the United States of "an aggressive [Viet Nam] policy in violation of international law." Finally, elected twice more, he was sworn in as a member of the Georgia House on January 9, 1967, one month after the Supreme Court ruled his exclusion unconstitutional.

"Was all the turmoil because you were against the war," I said, "or because you were black?"

"Is this an either/or exam?" he retorted.

"Well," I said, laughing, "you get my drift."

"Who knows?" he said. "I suspect one would have been sufficient to many of the members. But the combination, well, that was too much to beat."

Nineteen months later, charging that Negroes were excluded from Georgia's Democratic organization, Bond led an insurgent delegation to the party's national convention. There, among Democrats inured to blood and violence, and fearful that Nixon would defeat Humphrey in November (he did, by 499,704 votes), Bond seconded the nomination of Eugene McCarthy for president, preached on behalf of human rights, and found himself, then twenty-eight, nominated for the vice presidency. "I have not yet reached the age necessary [thirty-five] to be a candidate," he told the convention, but as proceedings adjourned in Chicago on August 29, many delegates wondered if, unlike Spiro Agnew—who three weeks earlier said to newsmen, "My name is not a household word"— Julian Bond had been already blessed.

"Me a household word? Like Agnew?" he scoffed. "I've been linked with many people, but never with him.

"No, the reason I was nominated was that people on the McCarthy staff—Dick Goodwin came and asked me—wanted to nominate someone other than Ed Muskie, Humphrey's choice. They wanted me to make some statements, wanted to go on record against the police violence in the streets. So I figured, 'Why not? I'll do it.'"

With Nixon elected, and Bond now known, focus shifted to priorities and whether, as the latter once canted, "This nation, for these people, is likely to fail as long as Saigon holds priority over Selma and men on the moon over men on earth."

"What did Nixon get in the '68 election?" Bond asked. "Thirteen, 14 percent of the black vote? No more. He didn't owe blacks anything, didn't know us, didn't understand what could be lost if we didn't use the gains of the 1960s to build upon. And to be blunt, we didn't expect anything from him. And to be even blunter, he didn't disappoint. Stridency, fear, the government became a hostile force. The man who told us to lower our voices couldn't stop shouting at us." Pause. "And just think. If Humphrey had got one more black vote per district across the country, he'd have won."

Between them, the American president and college president's son clashed over doctrine and philosophy—the scope and intent of government; whether federal officials were benign or condescending (or both); the wisdom (or lack thereof) of dispersing and relocating authority; whether "Washington Knows Best" was reality or fraud.

Nixon believed, as he said in a 1972 radio address, "You can be sure of this: On matters affecting basic human values— on the way Americans live their lives and bring up their children—I am going to respect and reflect the opinion of the people themselves." Bond's rejoinder was less discreet. "The same people who believe that nonsense," he said, "are the same jokers who thought Bull Connor was a patriot and Spiro Agnew an honest man."

No concept better defined this schism than Nixon's hope, disclosed as part of what he grandiosely called the New American Revolution, to efface the old system of categorical grants that had—in speechwriter Raymond K. Price's words— "federal bureaucrats second-guessing every sort of local decision from the height of buildings to the location of sewer lines."

These grants rose in number from 160 to more than 1,000 in the ten years after 1962, and were composed, said an official for the Department of Health, Education, and Welfare, of "federal money taken from the states with no strings attached and then given back to the states by Washington with a whole ball of yarn attached."

Critics warned that they eroded local responsibility, inserting federal judgment for local pride. In education, urban renewal, and manpower development, they said, local officials were engulfed by red tape and paperwork, most of it emanating from Washington. "The federal government is very good at collecting revenues," recited Daniel Patrick Moynihan, special assistant to the president, "but very bad at dispensing services."

Could decentralized government, I asked Bond, not reduce this disparity? Nixon had consciously favored "block grants," where states and localities—receiving federal funds for *general*, not specific, purposes—defined their own priorities; it made him a political Santa Claus and enabled revenue sharing to blossom. Its success limited the function of the federal government while restoring local incentive (and not incidentally, reinforcing a sense of community that Johnson's Great Society, often unconsciously, had helped dismantle).

"Despite the fact that both decentralizing and centralizing proposals were part of the Nixon program, the important direction of change was decentralization," Richard Nathan of the Brookings Institution said. "Coming at the end of a thirty-year period in which the predominant trend of domestic policy had been to increase the responsibility of the federal government, Nixon's own program marked an important shift. At its root, the New Federalism program involved basic social values; it was designed to . . . increase the capacity of individuals to influence events."

"That's an interesting scenario, a marvelous theory," Bond admitted. "The only problem is, it's ludicrous." He smiled a half-smile. "Say you give a million dollars unattached to a community like Tupello, Mississippi. And say, as is true in hundreds of communities, the black population is in need of funds. Not to mention deserving.

"In a lot of these places, you have local officials who don't give a shit about the black population. If there's no one to look after how the money is spent, you have money that comes from *all* the people going to advance the benefit of those who control the local power. Too often their pigment is white. They're not going to spend money to build playgrounds for the poor. They're going to spend it on tennis courts for the rich."

If revenue sharing symbolized Nixon's legislative proclivity, his Supreme Court nominees crystallized the judicial. Throughout the 1968 campaign, Nixon had stormed against that branch's activism, tarring federal courts as intrusive, demanding that judges clarify, not amend, the Constitution. As president, he said, he would uphold the principle of judicial restraint, and in his appointments—most notably to the Supreme Court—seek "strict constructionists" whose decisions would not slight the perogatives of Congress and who were not inclined to usurp policy areas reserved for localities and states.

To replace retiring Chief Justice Earl Warren, Nixon selected Warren Burger, a justice of the United States Court of Appeals in Washington. To succeed Associate Justice Abe Fortas, the president chose Clement Haynsworth of South Carolina, and when Haynsworth was rejected by the Senate, Georgia's G. Harrold Carswell. Both were conservative. Both believed that judges should interpret existing laws, not indulge in social mandates for change. Both were endorsed by southern senators of both parties (as was Harry Blackmun of Minnesota, later confirmed to fill Fortas's vacancy)—and both were ousted by a coalition symbolized by George Meany and the NAACP.

"They were a joke, those nominations," said Bond. "Burger and Blackmun, I called them the Minnesota Twins. And Haynsworth. Remember his confirmation fight? It showed that he was guilty of conflict of interest, sitting in on cases in which he had a financial interest in the outcome."

"What about Carswell?" I said.

"Roman Hruska," Bond replied.

"What?"

"He was the Republican senator [Nebraska] who said that although Carswell was mediocre, mediocrity deserved representation on the Supreme Court. That's not a marvelously appealing way to have to support a guy for the highest court in the land."

To organized labor, mediocrity was a minor flaw; opposition confronted Carswell (like Haynsworth before him) because lower court rulings repelled union leaders. For Bond, as for the civil rights community, the course posed even less self-doubt. Neither judge, they knew, would parallel black views on busing, or integration, or affirmative action; and falsely tabbed as racist, Haynsworth and Carswell were denied Fortas's seat.

"When you strip away all the hypocrisy," glowered Nixon bitterly on April 8, 1970, after the Senate's rebuff of Carswell, 51-45, "the real reason for their rejection was their legal philosophy, a philosophy that I share, of strict construction of the Constitution, and also the accident of their birth, the fact that they were born in the South."

Grimacing broadly, Bond swept aside Nixon's anger. "The president had no business being bitter," he said. "We're the ones who should have felt that way."

"Why? You won," I reminded him.

"The very thought that the leader of this country would nominate someone of their persuasion, their philosophy—four nominations in a row, if you count, in fact, Burger and Blackmun—shows that he simply was not concerned about the rights of people like us. He had no feelings about us; felt no responsibility toward us. Worse, he didn't even count us into the equation. We weren't just discounted; we were ignored. That's the worse kind of discrimination."

Since the early 1970s, a time in which Bond became—

progressively—columnist, network commentator, and prospective candidate for president, among the issues proliferating in rancor was affirmative action, or, as those who scorned it said, *reverse* discrimination.

It sought to impose ratios and quotas in employment, education, and political endeavor (irrespective of merit)— dividing Americans into many conflicting elements; granting preferential status to minority interests; making innocent Americans pay a debt owed by society as a whole. Reverse discrimination, said its opponents, only replaced an old form of injustice with a new form of injustice; the victims had changed but not the practice.

"Yes, I know that's an argument a lot of conservatives use," said Bond. "I know they claim America's greatness owes its origins to the talented, the enterprising, and those who make of the work ethic a continuing creed."

"Doesn't a lot of it?" I asked.

"To some extent, but a lot of people in this country—black people especially—have never had the education to show their talents, or the opportunity to be enterprising, or the confidence that even if they worked, it would make any difference in a society where whites prevail."

"But are quotas the answer?"

"When nothing else works, yes," Bond insisted. "Sure, quotas divide. They polarize. But it's a necessary polarization. We're not asking for a lifetime of dependency, and we weren't either a decade ago. All we're asking is for a helping hand—that those who have been denied access historically be granted access now—and that's natural for any group. Black. Brown. Or lemon-turquoise."

Black. Brown. Or lemon-turquoise. What could one prefer about preferential treatment? How long could America remain a nation of angry and embattled parts? I recalled John F. Kennedy's admonition of August 29, 1963: "I don't think we can undo the past," Kennedy said. "I don't think quotas are a good idea. I think we'd get into a good deal of trouble." It was unjust, he observed, to insist that undue advantage be given members of one group because of past discrimination against *other* members of that group. A good society could—and should— provide equality of opportunity for all its citizens. But it could not provide—nor should it ever strive to mandate—equality of results.

"That was almost twenty years ago, that statement," Bond protested. "A lot of things have changed since then. We didn't possess the urgency that the late sixties brought about. We didn't realize the importance of pluralism. Black people were less forceful, more servile, more patient and because that was a fact, so was the lack of demand for quotas and things to rectify all that happened to us over three hundred years."

Ironically (and to many liberals, improbably), Nixon—who in his 1972 acceptance speech, would proclaim, "Americans don't want to be part of a quota, they want to be part of America"—was a founder of reverse discrimination.

In 1969, aware of bias against blacks in hiring and promotion, the president announced formation of the Philadelphia Plan, its intent (despised by organized labor) to require contractors awarded federally-funded construction projects to increase minority employment. The program established "goals," not quotas—the distinction later blurred—and demanded "affirmative action" to meet pre-determined percentages; i.e., among construction employees, the increase in Philadelphia of minority members from 4 percent in 1969 to 26 percent four years later.

In this, as in the expansion of minority business (in Nixon's first four years as president, its amount received through federal contracts rose from $8 million to $242 million, and receipts of black-owned enterprises, $4.5 billion in 1968, soared to $7.2 billion in 1972), the rhetoric of Bond and the president clashed savagely, but as Nixon excoriated quotas, and Bond deplored the president, what sprang from administration policy did not displease the other.

"It had potential, the Philadelphia Plan," said Bond, loosening his tie, "but the administration wouldn't pressure either employers or the unions hard enough to really make it work." Gentle laughter. "When did you ever hear of *this* administration refusing to play hardball before?"

Even quotas paled beside the firestorm of busing. "How long are we going to allow federal bureaucrats in the Justice Department to torment the little children of America?" Jesse Helms asked his Senate colleagues in November 1980. "The vast majority of Americans, black and white, are fed up to here seeing their children hauled past neighborhood schools, sometimes as far away as fifteen miles."

Compulsory busing turned explosive in the late 1960s— condemned by conservatives like Helms of North Carolina; decried, said the Gallup Poll, by more than 80 percent of all Americans; defended by Bond, Abernathy, and other black spokesmen; and seemingly cherished by state and federal courts, who made of busing decrees a sort of judicial tyranny. It polarized the nation as did the Ku Klux Klan and, because of its emotionalism, made compromise difficult, reason passe. To advocates, busing was the last, best hope of real integration; court mandates meant enlightenment, and those who disputed them were racist or Neanderthal. To opponents, busing was a colossal failure, a reprehensible tool by which children were torn away from their own communities, carted from district to district and city to town, so that the goal of racial balance in public schools—regardless of human and cultural cost—could be summarily attained.

Bond was fourteen when the Supreme Court, in its 1954 decision, ruled that separate but equal schools were illegal (and unequal): America's dual school system, it said, must disappear "with all deliberate speed." Yet by 1969, when Nixon became president, fewer than 6 percent of all black children in southern states were in schools termed by the courts "unitary systems." Thus, when on October 29 the Supreme Court ruled unanimously that school districts must end segregation "at *once*" and operate integrated systems "*now* and hereafter," many judges favored busing as the means to most quickly (and they believed, completely) erase the patina of racial imbalance.

"You supported the court's decision," I said.

"Of course," Bond recalled. "You only need look at the statistics in 1969 to see the pathetic progress that had been made since the 1954 decision for 'all deliberate speed.' We'd had a lot of deliberation. We hadn't had much speed."

"But integrate now . . . at once?"

"I know the South bemoaned its predicament," he said. "'We can't do it all at once,' they said. 'It's going to take some time.' And remember, Nixon's Justice Department backed them up. Arguing before the Court—the Court rejected this view entirely—the Justice Department said delays were permissible in requiring integration in some districts and that providing a quality education should take precedence over enforcing social justice. But America had *had* time—and all it had done was delay."

"So the court said, 'Integrate now, litigate later,'" I remembered.

"Well, the idea that quality education and social justice should be at odds is something only John Mitchell would have thought up. And finally, in '69, the Court had had it. 'No more excuses. Get on with the job.' "

In 1971, the number of black southern students in "unitary systems" surpassed 90 percent. "How did we do it?" Nixon asked later. "We weren't self-righteous. We tried to help. We tried to show respect for the communities involved. Most importantly, we treated the problem of segregation as a national, not regional, problem and got local and state leaders— both black and white—involved. We told them, 'Integration is going to happen; the courts have spoken. It's up to you, though, whether it's peaceful or violent, and whether once integration is accomplished, rancor remains.'"

Whether, in fact, Nixon's pride was justifiable, or whether— as Bond said—"he got pushed by the courts toward an end he had consciously tried to gut"—*de jure* segregation (resulting from law or the deliberate actions of school officials) did crumble, and dual systems dissolved.

Where progress faltered, and busing begat hate, was *de facto* segregation—racial imbalance not deliberate and therefore, the administration claimed, not in violation of the Constitution. "*De facto* segregation," Nixon wrote in a 1970 statement, "results from residential housing patterns . . . . School authorities are not constitutionally required to take any positive steps to correct the imbalance."

Bond, like most civil rights proponents, admitted to no distinction between *de jure* and *de facto;* racial balance, he implied, was a constitutional principle. Many courts, agreeing, issued busing orders that voided the concept of the neighborhood school.

"Sure, we needed to transport kids to other schools. Otherwise, integration would have been a joke," Bond said.

"You could pour money into upgrading urban schools, improve the curriculum and faculty, and still you wouldn't have the advantages of exposing black students to white schools, and white to black. That's what made busing necessary. Those blacks who disagreed, too often they were political prostitutes, the accomplices, willingly, of the fascist forces in America who saw in a retreat from busing a retreat from the commitment to achieve equality in race."

Ultimately, in 1974 the Supreme Court clarified its October 29 ruling. Busing was not required to rectify *de facto* segregation, and as Burger stated, "no singular tradition in public education is more deeply rooted than local control." To Bond, such minutiae mattered little; busing discomfited, but segregation reviled.

"It's only bad, busing is, in the sense that it's disruptive," he amended. "No parent likes to see his Johnny carted around on a bus twenty miles a day. But only 4 percent of all kids bused today are for the purpose of promoting integration—and nearly 40 percent of all kids are bused—so you can see that race isn't a major factor.

"But that doesn't matter to most people, of course," Bond noted, "because they get emotional. And it all ties in with the fact that they think busing is bad if it's for integration. And integration, you may not believe this"—and as he spoke, his face believed—"is a goal millions of Americans still oppose."

"Still, aren't you considering everyone but the kids?" I said. "Busing is enormously unpopular. Even a majority of black people dislike it."

"We're not supposed to be polltakers," he countered. "Now or in the Age of Tricky Dick. We have to be concerned with what's decent. And if only through busing can we get quality education—take black students out of lousy schools and put them in places that are superior, where they can learn— then, as far as we're concerned, and studies have shown that it's almost invariably a success, it's the right thing to do."

For whom, though, and to what avail? Reaching for his overcoat, Bond thrust forth a response. "Pain brings progress," he said, rising from his chair. "Busing isn't easy. But neither were the marches. Neither were the sit-ins. Neither were the deaths we paid from Selma to South Boston, and the bigots we've encountered along the way—Louise Day Hicks, Frank Rizzo, and George Corley Wallace."

He must leave Atlanta this evening, Bond confessed; a speech, one of more than ninety annually—"those are just the ones I'm paid for, and the ones outside this city"—waited several hundred miles away.

He enjoyed these functions, King's adherent insisted, "not the speechmaking, necessarily," but the chance to mix with college students. "They're more personally oriented now," he offered. "The 'Me Generation' has homesteaded the New Frontier. Not that they're not as interested in knowing what the problems are as your age was. They are. They're just not interested in doing anything about them."

Bond grinned slightly. "You don't believe me?" he said.

"Yeah, but what does that portend for the 1980s?"

"River City," he conceded. "The country's more conservative now—you can read it in the tea leaves—and the Congress, and the courts. We're in for a rough decade, I'm afraid, and the worst of it is that Reagan is a nice, adept, clever man—more clever than Eisenhower, nicer than Nixon. He can say absurdities—for sure, he's had enough practice—and people still smile."

"Come 1990, will you?" I said.

"Oh, we'll survive. We've come a long way, further than our parents would have thought possible. And how?" Bond challenged, not awaiting a reply. "Not by being mealy-mouthed, ready to accept whatever crumbs established politicians wanted to toss us. We've had to jostle every inch of the way—for the decision of '54, for an end to Jim Crow a decade later, for busing and affirmative action today.

"After all," he said, wryly, escorting me from his office, "all we're talking about is the dignity of man."

12
The Prophet
from Montgomery

NOW, AS TWENTY, FIFTY, A HUNDRED YEARS AGO, THE
South took refuge in its separate culture, the folkways incessant
turmoil bore—in mores and literature, idiom and commerce, in the prideful singularity its isolation spawned. Entering Alabama, I passed fields and lumber and mangled sheds,
and nearing the state capital, noticed that in an outlying freight
yard, a lone boxcar was marooned. "Illinois Central," it read:
"Main Line of Middle America." Montgomery had changed
little since George Corley Wallace began.

Here, in the spiritual home of the Old Confederacy, where
warmth and passion merged, George Wallace helped change a
nation. Was he, as his enemies proclaimed, a demagogue,
seizing power through racism? Or, as defined literally by
Webster's Dictionary, a prophet—"A person who predicts
future events in any way"? Or would history decide? Already,
perhaps, America had.

Too bluff, too scarred by tragedy, too tinged by past
segregation, Wallace never ascended to the presidency. Yet by
1980, when Ronald Reagan reached the same office, burying
the New Deal in an electoral tide, his campaign slogan of eight
springs earlier—"Send Them a Message"—had been absorbed
by every politician in the country.

"Where once it was the party of the people," Wallace wrote of the Democratic Party in 1972, "along the way it lost contact with the working man and the businessman. It has been transformed into a party controlled by intellectual snobs. The American people are fed up with the interference of government. They want to be left alone." The Prophet from Montgomery, yes.

"Come on in," he said, greeting me in his office, one block from the state capitol; the address, One Court Square. He was older now, past sixty, the eyes brown and wistful, the bulk rounder than before.

Behind him, on a white wall, loomed the Seal of Alabama; elsewhere hung photos and magazine covers, letters from noteworthies, cartoons combed from forgotten files. Wallace's desk swelled with items of correspondence; one corner held a book, *Let Us Now Praise Famous Men.* Through a picture window, its skyline muted, downtown Montgomery wilted in the rain.

"Doin' pretty well," the three-term former governor announced. Wallace, his upper torso thick from exercise—"I do a lot of work each day with the bar, lifting weights, you know, keeping in shape"—sat in a wheelchair, his frame beside the desk. He could not walk or use his legs or feet.

"I've been here since 1979, when I left as governor. Been director of the college's Rehabilitation Resources Center [University of Alabama] since then. I spend part of my time in Birmingham and part of my energies here. And not only has it given me hope," he said, dramatically, gesturing to his arms and chest, "but a lot of other people who've been through the same kind of what they thought was hell."

During the early 1970s, bemoaning the troubled currents in America, Wallace had been prescient, feisty; he was outspoken; he never bored. Now somehow less adamant, his manner was more discreet, and there seemed in what he said, even in appraising his misfortune, an absence of bitterness, of the pity and hostility, which might have marred his *Weltanschauung.*

"George has never been less in the public eye," a former legislative assistant told me, "and probably never closer to the people here." These people were his friends, more so than the plastic allies of the past; he enjoyed them because he trusted them, because he shed his bravura, the image that the nation knew, and found Alabama reveling in what lay beneath—the small-town native whose nativeness sufficed.

By ancestry and upbringing, the man to my right was southern-cradled, and like the state he governed, both proud and insecure. Alabama's patriotism was militant; service was respected, the flag held high. Alabama was conservative; not oblivious to change, but averse to reformation. Alabama was anxious too, afraid of the leftist demon-tides which might emerge to wrench. "Do we have a persecution complex here?" he mouthed, repeating my question. "No, not as much as maybe a few decades ago. But some, I guess, and it's not hard to see why."

Wallace paused, pointing to *Let Us Now Praise Famous Men.* "You see that book?" he demanded sternly, his hands thrusting upward. "That's why I ran for the presidency. You know who 'famous men' are? They're the people I grew up with—the sharecroppers, the tenant farmers, the people who live in shacks. They were semi-illiterate. I was luckier; my folks had some education, they'd gone to school—but we were way behind the rest of the country. We didn't have the skills.

"But that's not the way we were pictured. You-all in the North—they looked down at our accents, our customs. They didn't say we didn't have education. They said we were animals. They called us subhuman," he said, his animation rising. "They didn't insult our schoolin', they insulted our dignity. And it made us band together, become close-knit. It made us determined never to sell out; to say what we thought. And as we banded together, it made us strong."

Amenities passed and nostalgia flourished. Once robust, Wallace today was less than strong. His voice was throaty, rasping; he tired easily; he drank water freely from a pitcher. He wore a pin-striped suit, which he delighted in, and a hearing aid, which he did not. "George is lucky to be alive," the assistant said. "With what's happened to him physically, emotionally, above all, psychologically, most men would have become a vegetable. But George? You know what magazine story he liked best? In the middle 1970s. *The Saturday Evening Post.* 'Thou Shalt Not Kill George Wallace.'"

He had endured much, friends said, since, campaigning for president in 1968, he uttered ad nauseam his most obstinantly memorable line: "If any demonstrator ever lies down in front of my car when I'm president, it'll be the last car he ever lies down in front of." The death, slowly, of his cancer-stricken first wife, Lurleen. The divorce, ugly and sensational, from his second wife, Cornelia. The frustration evoked by a Democratic Party hierarchy which, even as Wallace's precepts were assimilated by Americans, refused to acknowledge his influence. The madness of May 15, 1972, when a would-be assassin's bullet left Wallace paralyzed from the waist down and, in a media age where liabilities were magnified, removed him as a would-be president.

"I don't think much about those days," said the former Sunday school superintendent, almost, I felt later, to convince himself.

"I have a lot to busy myself with now. My job here. Serving as a counselor to the governor. Reading. Talking with officials who come and see me. You know, most of 'em are from this state, politicians who pay a visit before they decide to run for this or that office. And I tell 'em, 'Say it like you feel. And don't second-guess the voters. They'll outsmart you every time.'

"I do anything to help 'em, help Alabama. After all, I never really lived anyplace else."

Wallace met adolescence in the county seat of Alabama's Barbour County, intersected by the Central of Georgia Railway Line. Immersed in studies, prize fighting (he was Golden Gloves bantamweight champion of Alabama), and debate, he graduated from the University of Alabama, his class 1942, his major, law. He enlisted in the Air Force, was a flight mechanic on bombing raids over Japan, and suffered a 10 percent "nervous disability" allowance, prompting an honorable discharge from the war.

Home in Alabama, politics consumed him. Wallace entered the state legislature in 1946. Six years later he won election as a circuit judge, gambling in 1958 on the governorship, where he was beaten for the first—and only—time by a candidate more conservative than he. "John Patterson out-niggahed me," he explained, according to biographer Marshall Frady. "And boys, I'm not going to be out-niggahed again." Vying for governor in 1962, Wallace this time won. "I draw the line in the dust and toss the gauntlet before the feet of tyranny," his Inaugural Address proclaimed, "and I say, 'Segregation now . . . segregation tomorrow . . . segregation forever.' "

Was Wallace a racist? "They called me one," he said, throwing out both hands in harsh emotion. "Just like they called us 'The Bombsey Twins' in 1968 [Wallace, a third-party candidate for president, and his running mate, General Curtis LeMay] when all we said was that we wanted to prevent war, and the only way you could do that was be so strong no one could threaten peace."

"Were you?" I asked.

"What?" he said, not hearing.

"A racist?"

"Never. You just look at the record," he said, his jaw jutting forward. "All I objected to—and all the politicians do now, ever' one—was the asinine combinations, the busing and the quotas, breaking the back of every family in America."

"But your record says otherwise," I said.

"You learn," he retorted. "You grow."

He did not, Wallace knew, hate blacks; if apartheid crippled them, one remembered Lewis Carroll's Walrus, devouring the oysters, saying, "I weep for you. I deeply sympathize." As governor, had Wallace not increased funding for mental health and nursing homes, hospital care and education? Had his administration not created more than a dozen new junior colleges, benefiting Alabamians, black and white? Yet if that was true, so was Wallace's past espousal of segregation, his belief that America's two major races should associate but not join, and the vulgarity of June 1963, when the newly elected governor—honoring a campaign pledge—stood "in the schoolhouse door" of the University of Alabama to bar the admission of two blacks (briefly, it evolved) and the resumption of integration in his state's education system.

In defeat, he became a household word, and even when two conservatives—Nixon in 1968, Reagan twelve years later— captured the White House, expanding their normal realm of Republican support, it was George Wallace who first exposed liberal vulnerability among America's blue-collar bloc; Wallace who first expressed worker discontent with social engineers; Wallace who first scorched the timidity of America's military resolve; Wallace who first etched the peril of an overweening bureaucracy, and who, as early as the mid-1960s, spoke of "tax revolt...spiritual bankruptcy...conspiracy against the everyday American."

Writing in 1968, columnist Joseph Kraft divined the Wallace tableau as "Middle America"; a year later Nixon first spoke of the "Silent Majority," its needs and sensitivities shunned. Wallace had known for years what Kraft and Nixon echoed. Long before the late 1970s, when even liberals cloaked themselves in conservative dogma—George McGovern solemnizing military defense, Frank Church pledging law and order, Jerry Brown being moved to pontificate, "The liberalism of the sixties is dead"—he assailed the growth of government and its "briefcase-totin' bureaucrats," the "pluperfect hypocrites" inhabiting Washington, D.C.

"We don't need guidelines to advise us, and we don't need half a billion dollars of your hard-earned tax money being spent on bureaucrats in Washington to check every school system, every hospital, every seniority list of a labor union," he stormed in 1967.

Public education? "Busing is the most atrocious, callous, asinine thing you can do to little children. Washington is the hypocrite capital of the world."

Public housing? "Any time the federal government lays down the law for people, fixing the terms and conditions in which they can sell their own homes, folks won't stand for it."

Law and order? "The people are fed up with the sissy attitude of officials with less backbone than Bozo the Clown."

The Supreme Court? "It's a lousy, bum-ridden, no-account outfit."

And what of "intellectual morons," "ivory-tower counselors," and "uninterested politicians"? They would famish under George Wallace. As president, his America would change.

To Wallace, the foreign policy of the United States relied upon facade and window dressing, and symbolized our weakness, not strength, the confusion of our president, not the courage of our people. American policies, he said, invited even neutral powers to swagger; we ensured that enemy nations would treat us as a punching bag—and all we would do is shrug.

What America needed, said the gospel according to George, was a president who knew that if any nation bullied him, others would follow suit; who knew that if we betrayed our allies, no allies would exist to betray; who knew that if America did not stand up to its adversaries, soon its adversaries would be standing over us. "What we've got to do," said Wallace about the morass in Viet Nam, "is win. We've got to pour it on."

At home, Wallace's doctrine was urgent, unblurred. His appeal was gut-wrenching, not intellectual. If his bent prompted fear and loathing (as it did in millions of Americans), millions of others found in him a spokesman, and as he discoursed on social values, not one's knowledge of capital formation, Wallace found an electorate with grievances, wanting to be spoken *to*, but finding both parties mute.

Wallace bewailed the plight of the middle class and denounced the eclipse of morality; chastening permissiveness, he praised the nobility of toil. Stumping through primaries, delivering his Grade-B speech, Wallace's romance, the music that adorned his lyrics, stemmed from the fantasy he stirred. If he made us less than we were—less gentle, less united, less sensitive to want and hunger—he also touched what much of his nation still cherished—military prowess and populist poetry, the longing for old-time authority and old-style ways.

The America of his childhood, vowed the candidate (born in Clio, Alabama, population 850), was the *real* America. Its locals formed the country's backbone. Politically, they comprised the country's largest flock. Yet within the nation's largest papers, on its television screens, in the programs which shaped its emerging ethics, they were a psychic island—unable to rule or reason, to explain the spiritual collapse endangering all they stood for and all they had built.

Middle America respected Wallace for exactly those tenets many newsmen found repulsive—his principles, his philosophy, his blunt and combative wont.

If he could not, as did Nixon, engrave his vision of how the middle class might lead America, he could (and did) articulate its fears, its resentments, its hostilities.

If his background, denying equality, exuded states rights, his message became, in the early 1970s, a cry of equal rights for all Americans, not preferential treatment for some.

If his doctrine was bereft of kindness, it was not devoid of compassion—for Americans overtaxed and overregulated, burdened by indulgence, fearful of rising tyranny by the federal courts, and unable to outlast the inexorable certainty of the 1960s. Government's intrusion into their lives.

"You just look back at what I was saying fifteen years ago," I heard him saying now.

"What do you remember?" I asked.

"A professor at the university here compared our platform in '68 with the platforms of the Republicans and Democrats in '80. You know what he found? Practically identical."

"Where, especially in defense?"

"Not just there," he said, and refilling his glass, he reached back to my years in college, for the George Corley Wallace of his prime.

"What was I talking about?" he started. "About how the government hired a horde of regulators who operated by Parkinson's Law. You hire one bureaucrat and then hire two more to give the first somethin' to do. Then you hire four more to take care of the two guys, then eight for the four.

"I talked about how inflation was a wasteful, invisible parasite."

"But only for the middle masses," I protested. "That's all you ever talked about."

He hesitated. "For *everybody*. But it's the middle masses who give order and stability. That's why I wanted a revamping of the income tax system that was destroying them. They held the country together, and I thought of 'em like Oliver Goldsmith—'course they weren't peasants—but he said, 'Once the peasantry is destroyed, it will never be resupplied.' We were destroying initiative."

"How?"

"The super ultra-rich had their tax exemptions," he said, "and the do-gooders had their social programs to give more money to the problems they imagined. I always thought there was a pact between 'em. The do-gooders got their programs, the super-rich their exemptions."

Jousting, I tapped his desk. "And the rest?"

"The middle class," he said, "got stiffed. I talked about welfare programs, how they destroy incentive, and how every job depends on whether the U.S. is strong enough to defend itself in the Middle East, and how I'd negotiate with the Soviet Union, but I'd recognize that they hadn't kept a single agreement since Potsdam and Yalta.

"I talked about order," Wallace reminisced, "and how if we didn't get a handle on it, you wouldn't be able to ride, let alone walk in the streets, and how if we didn't—and the courts have destroyed the effectiveness of policemen—we'd have anarchy.

"And I talked about how the Communists believed through Lenin and Marx that they could lie or cheat or do anything if it was useful, and how the average American knew Castro was a Communist while the *New York Times* was inviting him to tea." On he went, jabbing, gesturing, vocalizing, for near a half an hour, his eyes completely closed, like an evangelist at revival meetings, seeking comfort in the past.

Wallace halted. Did I remember 1968? he asked. Four years earlier, invading the northern primaries, he had lured 30 percent of the Democratic vote in Indiana, 34 percent in Wisconsin, 43 percent in Maryland—sweeping all white precincts of the textile city of Gary; doing well in the Serb and Italian precincts of Milwaukee; molding a bond with working men and women, ignored, abandoned, their drudgery and hopes termed unworthy or immoral. "And by '68," he chortled, "remember what happened then?"

What happened was that Wallace became a phenomenon. The candidate of the American Independent Party, an impromptu, disheveled group, Wallace lured 9.9 million ballots and 14 percent of the total vote, emerging as a national totem in the general election, the most successful third-party candidate since Robert LaFollette in 1924.

"Fourteen percent," he recalled, proudly, "and I had 22 percent of the vote in a September Gallup Poll—against Nixon and Humphrey, against the two major parties. And even though I slipped off some—you know, 'A vote for Wallace is a wasted vote. He can't win. Vote for Humphrey,' and the Nixon people were saying the same thing for them—I knew I had somethin' going for '72. Even ol' Walter Cronkite must have seen that."

"But your percentage of the vote fell badly the last month of the campaign," I said. "How could you have had any confidence about four years later?"

"I outdrew 'em both, for one thing," he offered, his vibrato sounding remarkably like Ethel Merman's. "Humphrey used to tell me later, 'You know, in '68 we monitored your speeches,' and I asked him why. He said, 'Cause you always got better crowds than I did. So I asked my aides what the reason was,'" Wallace recounted, "and they'd say, 'Hubert, you know how to make butter melt, but Wallace, he says it even hotter.'"

Wallace grinned at my laughter. "Why'd I outdraw 'em? Move ahead to 1976. I was running in the Massachusetts primary and the *Boston Globe*, they hated me. They blacked out my campaign—didn't even report I was alive. So I went to meet their editorial board—you know, the highfalutin' writers and the editorialists—and I got outside their offices, and here there are hundreds of linotype operators, printers, pressmen, all from the *Globe*, and they're outside *cheering* for me. Same paper, different mind.

"And I told 'em, 'The editorial board of your paper wants to interview me. They want to see what makes me tick. They don't know what makes me tick—but *you* know what makes me tick,'" he said, his face gleaming. "'They're not going to vote for me—'cause they don't think like I do. But you're going to vote for me, 'cause you *do* think like I do,' and the roof practically fell off, they were roaring so hard."

"Yes, but your appeal had slipped by '76," I reminded him. "What about 1972?"

A curious tenderness invaded Wallace's eyes. "Nineteen seventy-two," he said, slowly, quietly. "That was my time. The ideas in the minds of average people, they were just like the ones I had. I'd have been on the ticket. I could'a beaten Nixon. I'd have beaten anybody. I would'a been president, you see."

Among Democrats in the last twenty years, only 1976's Jimmy Carter rivaled Wallace's surge through the early 1972 primaries, his campaign at once base and exhilarating, his shadow ever longer than before. In Florida, he buried all opponents, winning the northern panhandle (redneck country) and liberal Dade County, of which Miami was heart. In Wisconsin, with no state organization, only George McGovern beat him, and in Michigan, marshaled against Hubert Humphrey, he demolished the guardian of organized labor, taking 52 percent of the vote.

By mid-May, armed with an issue—busing—that enraged Americans and with his constituency—unlike 1968—composed of white collars as well as blue, Wallace had lured more popular votes than any Democrat. With only McGovern (already regarded as immoderate) and Humphrey (already tainted with defeat) looming as major rivals, it was not inconceivable (though still improbable) that the party of Franklin Roosevelt, Dean Acheson, and Adlai Stevenson might nominate George Corley Wallace for president of the United States.

"They called me a radical racist," he repeated, "'cause I was talking about problems nobody else would touch. All other politicians, they were just weaslin' around." Wallace opted for the water pitcher. "Still are, you know. All the problems I talked about are still with us—'cause we ain't had a strong president to whip that old bureaucracy around and point it in shape.

"I'd have been that strong president, I'll tell you," he said, jauntily, sipping from a glass. "And if I'd have been even vice president on the ticket in '72, I would'a made sure the *president* was strong. I would'a been in on policy. We would have got a start on problems ignored now for a decade—turned the country around."

Wallace paused. Looking, I saw his face whiten. His eyes again were closed.

"Humphrey and I had a date set for May 25," he began.

"Our aides had been talking for over a month, and the gist was this—I was going to be on the ticket. Hubert and I had agreed. We knew that between us, we could take care of McGovern, deprive him of a majority. And whoever had the most delegates at the convention, Humphrey or me, he was going to be the nominee for president; the other would throw his support to him. Then the reverse would happen—whoever had the second-highest delegate count among us would be vice president.

"We'd already met once before," he said, "Humphrey and

I, and now the details were being worked out, and on the 25th we were going to see that the compact was sealed."

"No doubt in your mind the deal would come about," I said.

"None," he stated. "Hubert was an honest man."

Fantasy crumbled on May 15. That afternoon, campaigning at a shopping plaza in Laurel, Maryland, Wallace was shot by a madman named Arthur Bremer. The bullet paralyzed its victim, and as George Wallace lay immobile, all bravado—and hope for the presidency—dissolved.

"We were on our way," he boasted. "We could have gone to the convention [at Miami in July] with the largest number of committed delegates. I might have won the nomination. Who knows? I would have been a presence, affected the hearings, the platform. They wouldn't have gone way over the edge with me the way they did eventually—going McGovern's way, out-fiddlin' Castro."

"Even given that," I granted, "what about the fall elections? How could you have beaten Nixon?"

Gazing out the window, Wallace seemed not to hear. "That dear sweet man," he said, halting between words.

"Humphrey?"

"He called me on New Year's Eve of 1978," Wallace noted, "just about a week before he died. Mondale told me later that he had a WATS line. He had a list of people he was calling up to wish them a good year, and I was on the list. Happy New Year? What he was really doing was saying good-bye.

"You know, we were in total conflict on the issues, but he didn't have an ounce of pessimism in his body. So Hubert said—and this was when his body was riddled by cancer—he said, 'George, you're going to have a good year, and I'm going to have a good year,' and I just about broke down on the phone." Wallace stared at me and added, "And I bet he *had* a good year, you know, where he went, up there, probably still gabbing up a storm."

I noticed his eyes film with tears. "Oh, I guess I'm just old-timey," he said, recovering.

Yes, I mused, Wallace *was* self-consciously unfashionable. To social engineers, he offered ridicule. To custodians of liberalism, he lambasted the influence upon them of special interests. "Pointy-headed bureaucrats" he dismissed as leeches, and he mocked those who indulged "the slumbering, the willfully poor, and all those who hurt our society today."

He appealed to Americans for whom the word *conserva-tive* was leprous—union members, ethnic laborers, middle-income Catholics, orthodox Jews. In a nation where—implausibly—to defend the working middle brought the risk of being dubbed a racist, Wallace showed (for the first time) how social confluences could move a nation and, flanked by leaders who prized timidity, showed disdain for compromise.

He was loud, profane, divisive. His tenure in Alabama disqualified him for the presidency. But he was spirited. Courageous. And on issues from reverse discrimination to burgeoning taxation, invariably, almost eerily, attuned to the electorate.

"I remember what they used to say about me," Wallace said. "I was a Neanderthal. I'd just stepped in from the Ice Age. But," he continued, shaking his head, "they never understood. Those elites—they wouldn't know the truth if it up and jumped on the dinner table. They didn't know what I meant by talking about the 'average man.' All they ever knew was the issues they saw on the CBS and in *TIME*—the environment and the need for integration and how we were spending too much for defense and all that drivel."

"Integration?" I replied. "What kind of drivel is that?"

"Well, you never read about the *real* issues—how taxes were killing people, how we were becoming weak, how people were getting sick and tired of paying for people who could have worked and didn't."

"But you weren't the only one to speak for them," I suggested. "What about the president? And Spiro T.?"

"Nah," he said, gruffly. "They just grabbed my sails and flew. Where were they when I was going to the Harvard campus in the sixties and getting my car rocked by students, having bags of urine thrown at me, drowned out by pickets trying to stop me from speaking? They didn't say nothin'—not until the time came when they saw the American people had had their fill. Then they started to protest. Funny, the timing."

"What about your *own* party?" I said.

"Deaf. Dumb. Blind. They disowned me for a decade and

when they finally woke up to the fact that I understood the American people and they didn't, they had apoplexy. Just about broke out in St. Vitus's Dance."

Grasping his wheelchair, Wallace halted in mid-thought. "Remember how it was? We had 'em on the run. The *New York Times*. The CBS. The NBC. All the judges who'd ruined the country. They couldn't park their bicycles straight. They were double-dealing, two-timing phonies. And they all hated me, 'cause I called 'em what they deserved.

"The spring of 1972, I was second in Oregon—never stepped in the state, almost. I ran well in Nebraska and Arizona and womped 'em in Florida—not just some parts, but everywhere. And Maryland, we killed them. And Michigan," he said, relishing each syllable, "they called me a cave man there once.

"They wouldn't even let me speak at a Jefferson-Jackson Day dinner there that year—invited every other Democrat but me in '72. So we cooked up a counterdinner, and I spoke and thirty-five thousand people showed up. Traffic was blocked, backed up for miles. I couldn't even get a 'howdy-do' from the state officials and then comes the primary, and I carried every county in the state," and as he glowed, I marveled—at the stories and anecdotes, the homilies and commandments, and at how he remembered (to the percentage, even decimal, point) his vote in the Democratic primaries of 1972, much like old baseball fans, born to reminisce, find sweetest memories in distant games.

Even now, Wallace lived in the early 1970s; he loved them, as in a time warp, an experience diffuse and yet central to his being; they made him feel alive.

"Was it my age? You bet it was. And they couldn't do a thing in '72 to stop me. Not one damn thing," he scowled, his sallow eyes reliving Laurel. "Only one thing stopped me, and you know, I never saw it coming." Listening, I felt close to this strange, encumbered man, lost amid his musings, closer than to Clark or Mitchell or Hesburgh or Reagan, and looking at my note pad, I felt tears to rival his. Who, among his contemporaries, had suffered more than Wallace? The time had left him crippled, physically; my classmates and I, what kind of cripples were we?

Forsaking silence, Wallace grabbed my arm. He was

troubled, he said, not by his disability—"I used to be bitter," he said, almost shyly. "I couldn't understand why God had deserted me. I still can't understand it, honestly, but I'm not blaming anyone. There's a reason, and He'll tell me some day"—but by what, in retrospect, one bullet had cost.

Wallace's voice became gentle, his bearing austere. Even more than urban blacks, who used the 1960s—he conceded—as a forum for outrage, the South's rural brethren bore the barnacles of want and neglect. Most politicians had deserted them; even Wallace could not now diminish their concerns. Few would deny that they were impoverished or that they seemed alone. Yet poverty had warped neither their decency nor stoicism, and there was a poignancy to their struggle which underscored the dignity they brought to life and love.

"When I'd talk about the middle class around the country, I'd really be talking about the folks at home," Wallace said, almost inaudibly, as if talking to himself. "They don't complain, don't ask for nothing. Subhuman? Hell. Just quiet, decent people. You might not believe it—but I loved 'em. And I could have helped 'em, could'a helped . . . this country, it's changed so much."

The wheelchair pivoted. The former governor smiled. I remembered his oft-spoken adage from the 1968 campaign. "When you're down," he said of America, "you get up again." Defeat, to George Wallace, was but a momentary hardship. Paralysis, for all its ultimacy, seemed little more than that.

13
The War Both Sides Lost

"AND SO MY POINT IS," THE STAR OF *THE NIXON INTER-
views with David Frost,* reveling in combat, said in May of
1977, "let's just not have all this sanctimonious business about
the poor repressed press.

"I went through it all the years I've been in public life and I
have...they never have been repressed as far as I am
concerned. I don't want them repressed, but believe me when
they take me on, or when they take any public figure on,
Democrat or Republican, liberal or conservative, I think the
public figure ought to come back and crack 'em right in the
puss."

While I was in college, the president "cracked" the media,
and the media scarred the president, and each diminished the
other, and both demeaned themselves. In 1969-73, no conflict
was more intemperate than the Press v. Richard Nixon. None
was more implacable. None harmed the nation more.

If Nixon was tormented, as he said in the third year of his
presidency, "by one of the most hostile and unfair presses that
any president has ever had," he had not—as he claimed seconds
later—"developed a philosophical attitude about it."

For more than two decades (their discord born when a
young congressman—pursuing the scalp of Alger Hiss—first

magnetized America), Milhous and the Eastern media had impugned each other's motives, derided one another's integrity, insisted that their vision of America more exactly neared the norm. To most columnists and commentators, Nixon was churlish, unprincipled, square. As senator, vice president, and finally president, their victim/accuser seethed with parallel contempt. The media, he thought, were ruthless, arrogant, their perspective biased and effete; they were unreflective of the nation's will. Each side denied the other's scruples. Both were convinced of their views as truth.

The new president's Inaugural Address, delivered on January 20, 1969, under mellow, gray-tinged skies, vowed "to celebrate the simple things, the basic things—such as goodness, decency, love, kindness. . . . To lower our voices," said Nixon, "would be a simple thing," but by late autumn—the clash of press and president exploding—bombast was even simpler, and only silence was still.

The armistice ended in early November when Nixon, unveiling the concept of Vietnamization in his televised "Silent Majority" speech, was followed—Spiro Agnew, addressing a Midwest Regional Republican Committee meeting in Des Moines, Iowa, charged ten days later—by "a small band of network commentators and self-appointed analysts, the majority of whom expressed, in one way or another, hostility to what he had to say."

With his superior's benediction, Agnew lacerated network television for its "narrow and distorted picture of America. . . . A small and unelected elite," he said, residing wholly in the "geographical and intellectual confines of Washington, D.C. or New York City," engaged in "instant analysis and querulous criticism," focused on an "endless pursuit of controversy," refused to "turn their critical powers on themselves." Americans, he urged, must "let the networks know that they want their news straight and objective." They "must defend themselves. . . . The Citizen—not the government—must be the reformer."

Reporters were affronted by the frontal attack, and when, on November 30, Agnew traveled to Montgomery, Alabama, and declared, "I do not seek to intimidate the press, the networks, or anyone else from speaking out. But the time for blind acceptance of their opinions is past. And the time for naive belief in their neutrality is gone," the chamber of commerce applauded, but the news media—already enraged by the vice president's broadside in Des Moines—treated the speech as an assault on the First Amendment.

Richard Nixon, Walter Cronkite would say in 1973, had contended "in every possible way that the press has no privileges in this society," and "created two Americas—one that believes in freedom of speech and one that doesn't." His rancor was echoed by Julian Goodman, president of NBC, who said of Agnew, "Evidently he would prefer a different kind of television reporting—one that would be subservient to whatever political group was in authority at the time"; by CBS President Frank Stanton, accusing the vice president of striving "to intimidate a news medium"; by George McGovern, his indignation piqued, who called Agnew's speech "perhaps the most frightening single statement ever to come from a high government official in my public career"; and by John Chancellor of the National Broadcasting Company, who christened Nixon's Avis "a small man who speaks in big generalities, an apostle of some of the worst instincts any administration could espouse."

Reporter, author, influence, Chancellor was among his network's more civil wordsmen, an accomplished writer who viewed the world skeptically, even cynically, but without the vitriol emitted by his peers. Less combative than Agnew (who found solace in the role of "lightning rod"), less defensive than Nixon (who was, after all, the object of greater abuse), his wont was matter-of-fact, paternal. He relied on the breadth of network television (its evening newscasts reaching more than 50 million viewers) to reaffirm his creed. Presiding on NBC, a genial, reassuring presence, Chancellor graced each evening of the "Nightly News," and his manner disarmed Nixon's frequently cited judgment of the news media—"the press," he barked, "is the enemy"—an elitist clique bidding America tearful welcome to calamity.

John Chancellor was not the most commanding broadcaster of the early 1970s; Cronkite's shadow towered Olympussized. He was not the most flamboyant; CBS's Dan Rather, a frequent Nixon duelist, earned that appellation. Nor was

Chancellor, perhaps, even America's most trusted announcer;. like George Romney, of whom admirers once asserted, "He looks like a president" (sadly, for Romney, the resemblance ended there), Howard K. Smith of ABC seemed typecast by providence for the role of "Commentator, Network. Salary—astronomical. Exposure—unrivalled. Qualities required—dignity, austerity, elegance."

Yet, like Ronald Reagan a decade later, whose "very niceness," an aide to Jimmy Carter mourned, "makes our stabs at painting him as a right-wing nut look ridiculous," Chancellor's placidity became a curious virtue. Because he appeared objective, he was credible. Because of his credibility, he was, feared Nixon, a figure who could couch leftist ideology in conservative garb, and so impress—as more garish liberals could not—even those calling themselves "Nixon Republicans," Americans who thought Chancellor to be reasonable. Because he was a gentleman, he was a formidable man.

"Nice guys finish first?" I asked him, tentatively, in the Rockefeller Plaza quarters of NBC News.

"You, me, or Agnew?" jibed Chancellor.

"Take your pick," I said.

"Well," he began, "I don't know you that well, and I know of Agnew, perhaps too well." Pausing, the NBC anchorman relished his stab at whimsy. "So I suppose that only leaves me."

"And?"

"Oh, I guess I'm sort of understated, low-key. But what the devil?" he shrugged. "I couldn't be other than what I was. People see through fakers. And anyway, I always felt there was enough bluster in Washington in the time you're talking about without me adding to the fuel."

Now fifty-five and graying, Chancellor joined NBC in 1950, at a time when communications meant radio, the word *media* was alien, and Adlai Stevenson, ironically, could complain about a "one-party [Republican] press.... The overwhelming majority of the press is just against Democrats," intoned the future nominee of the party of Jefferson, Wilson, and Franklin Roosevelt. "And it is against Democrats, as far as I can see, not after a sober and considered review of the alternatives, but automatically, as dogs are against cats."

Born in Chicago and educated at the University of Illinois,

his philosophy centrist New Deal, Chancellor covered politics and the judiciary, civil rights and the Suez. His campaign baptism, Ike's second trouncing of Stevenson, showed Chancellor to be a wry, unruffled journalist ("Teddy White, who had hundreds of honors, and I, who had almost none, covered it together, and between us we became friends. Did he take me under his wing? It would embarrass him to say so, but wing it was. And Eisenhower and Stevenson, they disagreed politically, they were quite different men, almost polars in many ways, but they were genuine. Relaxed. And they had a nobility that almost seems to me we haven't reached again"). Four years later, having advanced to chief correspondent, he reported the election that capsulized Nixon's hatred of the national media and changed, perhaps irreversibly, how the media regarded themselves. "If we live another fifty years," said Chancellor, "we're still not going to see its likes.

"I look back upon that campaign with great nostalgia now," he related. "It changed American politics, it changed the country, and because Kennedy was killed before another presidential election could happen, it had a different historical texture than anything that's happened since."

The campaign of 1960, won with distinction and lost with honor, propelled America past a dividing line that, once crossed, many would not double back upon—from a culture founded upon tradition to a society that thrived on youth; from an administration led by Main Street and businessmen to a government laced with academicians, unionists, and civil rights activists; from a presidency for "Protestants only" to an office Catholics were not denied; from politicians who equated achievement with legislative policy to leaders who felt that among all the attributes of Camelot, none mattered more than style.

It also became, as even disciples of John F. Kennedy later granted, among the most flagrant episodes of press favoritism in post-World War II America—an election Willard Edwards of the *Chicago Tribune* named "one of the most, if not the most, shameful chapters of the American press in history"; one in which numerous reporters, discarding neutrality, opted openly for Kennedy against Nixon, and in which author Theodore H. White—who saw the Democratic candidate as a "hero"—wrote of how "in the last weeks of the campaign, those forty or fifty national correspondents who had followed Kennedy since the beginning of his electoral exertions into the November days had become more than a press corps—they had become his friends and, some of them, his most devoted admirers. When the bus or the plane rolled or flew through the night, they sang songs of their own composition about Mr. Nixon and the Republicans in chorus with the Kennedy staff and felt like they too were marching like soldiers of the Lord to the New Frontier."

Minutes elapsed. As Chancellor caressed his phone, engaged in long-distance conversation, I thought of Bryce Harlow, Eisenhower's chief speechwriter—respected by the hierarchy of both parties—and later congressional affairs assistant to Nixon. "I remember Bill Lawrence of the *New York Times* coming up to me at one of Dick's 1960 rallies and growling, 'How many people do you think the police commissioner said are here today, Bryce?' " Harlow had told me. "So I said to Bill, 'Well, the guy said ten thousand.' And Lawrence replied, 'Yeah, and I believe him, but tomorrow in the *Times*, my story's going to say five.' And it did. And it was typical, the bias, the prejudice.

"You know Pat Nixon? You know how strong she is? Well, she showed cracks only three times in the thirty years I've known her—once in 1974, when Dick Nixon resigned; once in 1960, the night he conceded to Kennedy; and once the month before—October—as the campaign peaked, when all of us were in Ontario, California.

"A bunch of us were sitting in a hotel. Dick was in the shower. And Pat burst into tears. She knew about Kennedy's morality, his philanderings around Washington, as most people in the capital did. And she couldn't believe that somebody like that could be elected president. So she said to me—Pat had great ethical standards, and she was crying—'What's going to happen to this country if someone with those morals gets into the White House? Why don't the people know? Why doesn't the press write about it?'

"And I said to her, 'Pat, forget it. It's not in the cards. You know the press is going to cover it up. It'll never get out. They'll do anything to help Kennedy get elected.' And," said Harlow, "they did."

The phone and Chancellor parted. What, I asked him, did *he* remember about the 1960 campaign? The grace of Kennedy, he answered, and the self-pity, the melancholy, the bittersweet bent of Nixon.

"They were more outgoing, more expansive, more fun," Chancellor observed of the Democrats. "Kennedy enjoyed the press; he could have been a writer. I remember his sense of style, his elegance. Remember how he used them against Nixon in the Great Debates? He understood language and the people who used it as a living. He'd written, remember, for the *Boston Globe* and the *Herald Tribune*. He'd won a Pulitzer Prize. And he was an exceptionally easy interview; he knew what you wanted—and were going—to ask." Chancellor laughed softly. "I always had the impression that he went through the motions of playing a politician in talks with us, laughing on the insides all the while at how ludicrous it was."

"Ironic detachment," I said.

"Yes," he said. "Far different than Nixon."

"He mistrusted you," I recollected.

"The press?" he said, "Oh, yes."

"And the press him?"

"Partly," he said. "And as a result, it affected some reporters, and . . . "

"You became advocates?"

"No," said Chancellor. "Oh, some did, I suppose. Human nature affects any job, and I have to say, yes, there's no question that when you go from one candidate who understands your profession to another who treats you almost as a leper, it's going to influence how you feel."

Lighting a pipe, his blue tie unfastened, Chancellor swept high his palm. "So," he affirmed, "if there was a disparity between how the candidates were talked about, and if some got caught up in what you call *advocacy journalism*, I can only say that one camp knew, I think, what the press stood for, and with the other, Nixon, there was always an undercurrent of nervous tension in each of his campaigns I covered, some of which were very professionally run. He couldn't relax, couldn't relate to us, and I think it caused so many of the problems that later cursed him."

Staggered by 1960, convinced that the press, not electorate, had chosen Kennedy, Nixon struck back two years later, greeting newsmen the morning after his gubernatorial defeat in California ("But as I leave you," he taunted, "just think how much you're going to be missing. You won't have Nixon to kick around anymore") with what became his most oft-repeated line.

During the mid-sixties, as the former vice president (a lawyer) re-entered private practice and the Johnson presidency succeeded Kennedy's; as the "good causes" (claimed fashionable doctrine) of Viet Nam, equality, and nuclear disarmament stirred those who found in journalism a creative resonance; and as graduate schools (and broadcast executives) valued reporters who saw as their function to persuade, not inform, the affection for advocacy rose.

By 1969, with Nixon in the White House, press revulsion toward its tenant—and the antipathy, often held, by liberal newsmen toward established institutions—merged to form a spirit that made irreconcilable war.

"It would have been tough, in any event," Chancellor said, "between the president and the press."

"Unlike, say, with Kennedy," I suggested.

"What?" he asked.

"Well, look at his press conferences, their transcripts, their tone. They were less combative than what we've seen since then, less hostile; the press identified with his ends."

"Maybe so," he conceded, "but don't forget that reporters coming out of college in the late sixties were of a higher caliber than decades ago—more educated, more erudite, more independent. And they were skeptical; they weren't about to believe everything said to them by officials who now had us embroiled in a war. So when you come to the period you're talking about, they weren't willing to kowtow. They were tough, more objective. They had no intention of depending on some press release from politicians for their newscast or morning story. They weren't about to get in bed."

"With Nixon?"

"Or anyone else," he said.

Chancellor grimaced. "Especially Nixon, I suppose," said the host of "Nightly News." "I covered him in the presidency and in 1960 and in '68, when he ran and won. And I remember one incident that showed why a lot of newsmen disliked him. It happened in California in 1962. Tom Wicker [of the *New York Times*] and Roscoe Drummond [*Christian Science Monitor*] and I went out from Washington one time that fall to report on his race for governor. There were only three of us, and we went to a Nixon rally with notepads in hand.

"So Nixon starts talking in his speech about how all the Washington press contingent is covering him. 'They're all out here,' he says. *All?* Three guys. We knew that. But to the average guy listening to him, there could have been three hundred. Nixon knew it wasn't true, but at every stop that day he kept repeating the same line. So at one point where he starts talking again about how he's attracting the Washington press, Roscoe, Tom, and I raised our hands." A fleeting smile. "A small protest. Maybe even a small point. But it goes to show how Nixon wouldn't miss any opportunity to *use* you, to manipulate."

Silence. "But even so," he continued, "Nixon might have gotten through."

"As president," I said.

"Yes," he said. "Look back at the clips. He got a pretty attractive press his first year as president. All the talk about the 'New Nixon.' Some reporters believed it. And look at how he performed in press conferences. Never a flub. So he was off to a good start, more than decent, in fact, when it all started to polarize in the fall of '69."

"Agnew, stage right."

"It was a declaration of battle," Chancellor said. "You couldn't interpret what he said in any other way. Sheer belligerency. I was in Helsinki at the time Agnew unloaded. Eric Sevareid came in with an advance copy of the speech, and he was absolutely outraged. He gave us the text, and we read it and *we* were outraged. What had been a difference of opinion—yes, some newsmen were ideologically opposed to Nixon—became a struggle for survival. Both sides lost perspective. And journalists came to feel that the people in power would do anything—*literally*—to bend our credibility and, in the end, to break us."

"But was there some truth," I asked, "in what Agnew had to say?"

"I doubt it," he said.

"Even a scintilla? How many staffers here supported Goldwater in 1964, or Nixon against Humphrey in '68, or voted, say, against George McGovern four years later?"

Looking behind me, Chancellor laughed. "At NBC, you mean? I'm not a polling booth," he said.

"True," I conceded, "But for all of Agnew's bombast, wasn't a central point your insularity? I mean, you and your colleagues *do* live in New York and Washington. You read the same newspapers, read *TIME* and *Newsweek*. They watch you on the news. You go to the same parties, see the same people, exchange what some might say are pretty much the same views. At least that was Agnew's theory."

"We're not incestuous, interchangeable clones," protested John Chancellor. "And what do you want me to do, move my family to Dubuque?"

"No," I replied, "but how does Buffalo sound?"

Chancellor battled a widening grin. "You've seen one iceberg," he said, "you've seen them all."

Brushing against his desk, the network anchorman rose. Where the administration erred—"grievously," he commented— was in the tenor of its criticism. "I'd like to say Nixon sent Agnew out to hit and slash," he noted, "but as far as the press was concerned, what it really was was more like search out and destroy.

"Look," he said, "I went over Agnew's charges. They were patently foolish. He said we work in Washington and New York City, as though it were a crime. Well, Washington is the nation's capital, for Christmas sake, and this [New York] has always been the communications hub. He charged we were the products of Ivy League snobbery. Scotty Reston and I went to the University of Illinois. Cronkite grew up in the Middle West. His claims didn't wash.

"What I really feel happened was that Nixon had had an arrow with the press's name on its shaft in his quiver for a long time. He just hadn't put it in his bow and let fly. He was looking, you know, for the proper moment. So in the autumn of 1969, *TIME* and *Newsweek* both ran cover stories the same week on how Nixon was in trouble, his White House in turmoil. And I think he saw this, and knew he was under siege, and thought to himself, 'If I can blame the press for these problems—and moratoriums and the rest—maybe I can help myself and bury them.' They were shook up, I believe, and so they struck out."

"Against you," I recalled.

"Yes, the press. And the times raised the stakes on all sides. The war exacerbated all the other divisions—over integration and morality, drugs, respect for established institutions—and it brought a sense of urgency, I hate to use the word *desperation*, to an administration that was never very secure and to a president who never really knew who he was."

"It put them under a magnifying glass, the differences," I said.

"Exactly. But criticism—even unfair criticism—comes with the territory. It's part of a president's lot. Look at Reagan. A lot of newsmen aren't in sympathy with his views. But he doesn't come on like he wants to shred his opponents."

Feigned amazement. "Usually we even feel he *likes* us. And that moderation helps him. No newsman wants to maim Ronald Reagan. Because like Eisenhower and Ford, Kennedy, even Johnson, he knows who he is, and the public pose is close to his private, and the press respects that, because then hypocrisies and differences don't exist in their postures.

"You know," Chancellor noted, "I've covered presidents since Eisenhower, when he employed a press secretary, Jim Hagerty, who understood the makings of the press and who was able to bring the information machinery of government into the White House for the first time. I remember, for instance, how Johnson would work tirelessly trying to get the press to do his bidding, like he tried to do with everyone else, and how domestically, he got a good press, and in Viet Nam, savage. Or with Ford, I remember him as being the easiest to interview on TV; there was a good-guy aura about him that was extremely attractive, and he was just what the country needed. Ford has as few enemies as anyone could possibly have in the press. He adopted a personae that suited him; he was comfortable with his thoughts. Then came Jimmy Carter, who got a bad press, and that was a singular disappointment, I think, because Carter wanted good relations, was immensely well-informed, but could never seem to grasp the big picture. You know, if you asked Carter what time it was, he'd tell you all about the clock—its inner makings and so on—but he'd forget to check the time. Even here, though, his weaknesses were analytical, not petty.

"But Nixon!" he gestured. "In an administration that thrived on secrecy, his disdain for the press was the worst-kept secret. And maybe even less disdain than simple discomfort, which in turn made the press uncomfortable. There was such a vivid contrast with Kennedy, you know. Kennedy had such an easy self-assurance, a sense of knowing his own charms, and even more, knowing that there was no gulf in culture between him and most reporters."

Chancellor paused. "Nixon, on the other hand, was very good programatically," he said. "He knew a lot about government. He knew an enormous amount about foreign affairs. But proximity in press relations was something he couldn't handle. My feeling was that he didn't want you to know who he was; the closer you got to him personally, the more he was nervous and uncomfortable. And he tended to blame the press. Add to the personal dislike some reporters had for him before he became president, his conduct as president—his distrust of their vocation—made it a professional grudge match too."

After November 1969, with all hope of rapprochement gone, Nixon's major animus focused not upon the Democratic National Committee, nor organized labor, nor (even in 1972) George Stanley McGovern—but upon the news media of America. He differed from their members in message, style, and purpose, in the manners they sought to celebrate, and in the ethos they esteemed.

"The president represents a group which is not fashionable or popular with the media," Daniel Patrick Moynihan, leaving the White House to return to Harvard, said in November 1970. "The 'Silent Majority' is silent because it has nothing to say. It has no popular intellectuals speaking for it. It represents no major cultural breakthrough, so everything it says is ridiculed or put down." To which author Allen Drury, writing eight months later, responded: "Day after day, hour after hour, month in, year out, hatred of Richard Nixon snarls from the news columns, sneers from the editorial pages, smirks and sniggers from screen and airwave. They wallow in their hatred, and it is a sad and shabby sight to see."

Pridefully, almost ostentatiously, the Nixon administration

defied the mores of America's avant-garde. More than the debate over United States conduct in Viet Nam, or whether rule by mob should supplant rule by law, or the schism between environmental sanctity and economic power, it was a clash of values—etched by the word-cluster *family, home, permissiveness, and patriotism*—that marked the age's cutting edge, and left both sides inflamed. Because they viewed the world differently, they would not concede the other's sight.

I related two Nixon homilies, both uttered in the early 1970s—"Nobody is a friend of ours, let's face it," to counsel John Dean, and "No more Harvard bastards in the White House. Find me somebody from Oklahoma State," to H.R. Haldeman, his alma mater the University of California at Los Angeles.

"What do you think," Chancellor was asked, "these kinds of statements meant?"

"Remember the context," he said. "The Nixon men were, I suppose, from an old culture—remember how many of them wore an American lapel pin, and they were always verbalizing the canons of diligence and the flag. And in some way, they saw the press and the bureaucracy, which they regarded as total allies, to be the couriers of fancy parties and as the apostles of Georgetown. And so in they came from California—the Haldemans and Ehrlichmans—and they thought we despised them as déclassé. They thought of us too, I think, as somehow the cause of, or at least in sympathy with, all the turmoil in the late sixties and early seventies. They kept seeing students who wore their hair long. And who experimented with drugs, perhaps, and accepted the advent of pornography and rebeled against religion and maybe even laughed at the flag. To the people around the president, this was a disease, and to them, *we* became the bad guys, as if we were the *carriers* of that disease."

"How so?" I wondered.

"The reason Agnew gave his speech, in part, and the reason it was accepted by many Americans," Chancellor said, "was that the White House had poll data showing a certain percentage of people in this country didn't like us."

"Why?"

"Because," he exclaimed, "we *had* become the bearers of

bad news. Network newscasts really came of age in 1963, when
they went from fifteen minutes to a half-hour in length, and by
1969, only six years later, we'd been through the Kennedy
assassination, Viet Nam, the freedom riders and unrest in the
South, riots all around the country, the dramatic change in
morals. Every night Americans were being assaulted by a
stream of unpleasantness.

"Older people, ones who grew up on newspapers and
magazines, were used to being their own editors, you see; in
print, you can read stories which please you—my Dad, for
example, would read sports and business pieces in the *Chicago
Tribune* but then skip articles on gossip and rape. My point is
this—in television you can't do that. You could watch a thirty-
minute newscast, but to do so you had to watch the whole
thing. And so some Americans—the guys Agnew really appealed to—were furious at us for blasting them with the bad
news they weren't accustomed to as well as the good news—
and there kept being less of it every year—they *were* used to
seeing. And Nixon milked that resentment, trying to make it
seem as if we were corrupting the country."

"To some people, you were," I said.

"No," he said, more sharply, "what we were doing was
reflecting the changes taking place. What *would* have been
corrupt is if we'd stuck our heads in the sand, pretended—as
Nixon would have liked us to—that the world of 1972 was the
same as when he'd been elected as vice president twenty years
earlier. It wasn't. And we couldn't. We didn't cause a social
upheaval. We reported it. But the administration could never
understand the difference."

Lighting a cigarette, I looked at Chancellor, decent, well-
mannered, and wondered how television's bearing rivaled his.
In 1969–73, what Newton Minow called "the wasteland" had
not been altogether blameless. When I first left for Allegheny,
his medium teemed with programs like "The Jackie Gleason
Show," "Gunsmoke," and "Gomer Pyle, U.S.M.C."; pre-1955
viewers, waking from a decade-long sleep, would find most
plots and stereotypes unaltered.

In college, you watch little television; other priorities
occupy time. Leaving Geneseo in 1973, a graduate free to
sample the networks' repast, I was startled by the enormity of

change. Accustomed to a frazzled Lucy, to fathers like Robert Young and mothers who wore pearls and hosiery while mopping the kitchen floor, and to families who ate together and attended church and resembled "The Real McCoys," I met homosexuality, vasectomy, abortion. If, as its agents hinted, television mirrored America, I could not understand the latter. Expecting Guy Lombardo, I was assaulted by David Bowie.

When I was in college, network programs like "The Beverly Hillbillies" and "Green Acres" (and almost a dozen more) were canceled, each pulled off the air, not because they were inadequately watched (their ratings were superb), but because they appealed to the *wrong* people—rural, white, middle-income Americans. The split was dissonant. Conservative and liberal, country and city, traditional and mod. Even nightly newscasts upheld the dichotomy. Free enterprise was scalded; the welfare state embronzed. Police were contemptible; their "victims" benign.

"About that picture you draw," Chancellor said.

"You mean you don't buy the image of network TV as a leftist domain?" I asked.

"Nope," he said. "As far as prime time is concerned, people get what they want—and what they watch. If shows are inferior, the public apparently likes them that way. I'm more familiar with the news segments, of course, and if you'll look at those years, I think you'll find that what you're talking about is a lot of right-wing propaganda by people who don't care to know the facts."

What was "propaganda," many inquired, though, in 1969–73 about the public's animosity toward compulsory busing—and television's avoidance of that fact? Why was Barry Goldwater an "ultra-conservative" and George McGovern not an "ultra-liberal"? Why, in 1970 and today, did network newscasts talk only of "right-wing Republicans" and "right-ward extremists," as if "left-wing Democrats" and "left-ward extremists" had vanished from the planet Earth (or at least the halls of Congress)? Why, under Nixon, were violent protesters "activists" and bomb-throwers "militants," but union leaders "hard-hats," and "redneck" the cherished trademark for Southern whites?

What was faulty about the analysis of *Newsweek's*

Kenneth Crawford, "In appealing for the support of a 'Silent Majority' and repudiating 'effete snobs' of the Northeastern intellectual-academic-journalistic complex, [Spiro Agnew] pressed an emotional release button of surprising potential. . . . It develops that millions of middle-class people, blue-collar to upper-suburban, feel that they have been patronized too long by a self-celebrated cultural elite. They may have got this notion from journalists who keep calling them know-nothings"? What was penetrative about David Brinkley's shibboleth, "News is what *I* say it is. It's something worth knowing by *my* standards"?

Chancellor nodded, slightly. "Anyone can be criticized," he began. "And there's no easier target—probably no one is more in the public's glare—than television. Ours is a subjective medium. So when viewers watch us, if they want to imagine editorializing in what we say, it's easy enough to do so. That, I suspect, is what you're talking about."

"Partly, yes," I said.

"If there was some imbalance in network reporting of that time," he reported, "and I don't think there was, and understand, all three networks are independent and are only responsible for what each one does, but if there *was* any imbalance, I can only say the administration helped bring it on itself. When you set out to destroy the credibility of the American press, you can't expect to have the press applaud."

"Or respond," I said, "'How sweet it is.'" Gleason, please forgive.

Rebuked by the president, network journalists disemboweled their foil. In 1970, the administration revealed an environmental protection policy, far-reaching and comprehensive, serious proposals deserving serious debate. The media derided it. The New American Revolution, announced in January of 1971, sought to reorganize the federal government and implement a family-assistance welfare program and institute revenue sharing and diffuse Washington's bureaucratic elite. Its purpose? To make government more workable, not an altogether unworthy goal, but the press preferred other goals, and the New American Revolution was ignored.

The media taunted Nixon as insensitive; scored as improper the Supreme Court nominations of, first, Clement

Haynsworth and then G. Harrold Carswell; labeled Vietnamization a failure.

When Nixon prejudged the guilt of accused murderer Charles Manson, calling him "a murderer" in 1970, newsmen chortled; the president "bespoke himself," press secretary Ronald Zeigler said.

When, two weeks before a summit conference in Moscow, Nixon acted in May of 1972 to thwart a Communist offensive, mining North Vietnamese ports and bombing rail, road, and military targets, reporters merged in shrillness. To Tom Jarriel of ABC, the blockages meant "a slap in the face" to the Soviet Union; to Sevareid of CBS, "a very drastic action . . . a serious challenge to the USSR"; to NBC's Moscow correspondent, an end "to prospects of a summit"; and to John Chancellor, "the summit is in jeopardy and a new phase of the war has begun." But the summit was not ended; a new (if fledgling) phase of nonproliferation began; and in Moscow, American and Soviet officials signed an agreement to limit the expansion of nuclear arms.

When, finally, in late December, Nixon renewed the bombing of North Viet Nam, a decision that made the Vietnamese negotiate, and—in effect—made possible "peace [temporarily] with honor," reaction turned apocalyptic. Americans, said the *Washington Post*, must "cringe in shame and wonder at their president's very sanity." At the *New York Times*, columnist James Reston wrote of the president's "war by tantrum" and Anthony Lewis likened Nixon to "a maddened tyrant." Media prejudice was not a Nixonian mirage. During my forty-four months as a college student, many newsmen were obstinant, vindictive, self-righteous, unfair. Their bias dishonored their veracity. Their hypocrisy discredited their craft.

Sadly, their "enemy" behaved no less ignobly. In the late 1970s, with Watergate coloring all, journalists would proclaim the Agnew Des Moines critique and what it implied the undoing of the Nixon administration—its demise, they argued, proved the vice president wrong. But Agnew's message had been forthright, direct; it exuded the quality (candor) to which writers devote collective paeans; it was endorsed by a 1969 Lou Harris Poll, whose results stated "by a ratio of nearly three to one, TV viewers believe that the camera can lie, a view that runs strongest among professional people, the college-educated, and the young" (and by dozens of other indices, including several Gallup surveys and, intriguingly, the *New York Times*, which reported a pro-Agnew letter ratio of twenty-four to one).

Having challenged the press's credibility, and knowing he was closer than most journalists to the country's pulse, Nixon might now have halted, and thus quieted, the paroxysms of media rage that eviscerated the last two years of his presidency. Instead, from 1969 to 1971, concerned that leaked material would imperil national security, Attorney General Mitchell approved—without legal sanction—wiretaps on five newsmen, departing from previous administrations, when to tap a journalist was "suicidal," said J. Edgar Hoover, and only the Communist *Daily Worker* was exempt. Under Nixon, the White House Office of Telecommunications attacked television's "ideological plugola" and urged local officials to demand from the networks objectivity, a device Zeigler defended as "long-overdue" and journalists called intimidation.

While aide Charles Colson traveled to New York, meeting with network officials and saying, "If you don't treat us better, we're going to have trouble," columnist Joseph Kraft's home was broken into, entered by John Caulfield—an appointee of John Ehrlichman—who sought proof of linkage between Kraft and foreign-policy leaks. While Haldeman requested (and received) Hoover's acquiescence for FBI harassment of Daniel Schorr, another reporter, *Newsday*'s Robert Greene, was targeted for an Internal Revenue Service probe. While several local stations were encumbered by administration officials, who warned that unless coverage became more favorable, their federal licenses might expire, Nixon brooded over how history would paint him and wondered—interminably—how Americans who preferred press to president could be somehow disabused.

One cannot read the White House transcripts, even during Nixon's golden year of 1972, without realizing that the president of the United States was obsessed by the press. "They will never irritate me, never affect me, never push me to any move I don't think is wise," Nixon said in March 1971, but as Drury wrote that August, "neither he nor his family nor his staff can ever forget they are there."

Adopting his own counsel, Richard Nixon would have done better to forget. Abhorred by liberal newspapers, most national magazines, and the three television networks, he still won, in the 1972 election, a landslide of phenomenal scope; the power of the media was enormous, but less than the president's to mold and transform events.

Nixon professed to "ignore" reporters. "We have to do the right thing and then be strong about it, and decent enough to take the criticism and not be bitter about it. You have to learn to laugh it off," he told his cabinet in the first year of his administration, but the president did not "laugh it off," nor greet "the criticism" with equanimity, as even a beleaguered president should.

Rather, he resembled Gulliver beset by Lilliputians. To bias that was hateful, he countered with hate and authorized directives that sought—more so than Agnew's Iowa sermonette—to curb the *freedom* (not bias) of the press, helping to generate the fear (the us-v.-them ideology) that later, during Watergate, burdened Nixon with what columnist Nicholas von Hoffman called "a worse press than Stalin had at the height of the Cold War."

"It's pretty much accepted," I said to Chancellor, who was leaving to attend a luncheon, "that in the conflict with Nixon, the media eventually won."

"I wouldn't use the term *won*," he cautioned. "I just like to think that common sense prevailed."

"Maybe," I conceded, "but you know what people forget? How close Nixon came to winning, how near he came to achieving what he set out to do—erase public confidence in you as journalists and as men."

Would Chancellor, I wondered, care to revisit February 1973? The war in Viet Nam had ended; its cease-fire, signed on January 27, was for Nixon a signal victory over his most zealous critics, the press not least among them. With prisoners of war leaving Southeast Asia and the stock market at its all-time high, and Nixon's public approval (as measured in the Gallup Poll) even more extravagant than his November rout of McGovern, the president loomed—said *Newsweek*, published by The

Washington Post Company—as "a stern, sure, and uncompromising man who disdained to conciliate his critics." He seemed invincible. In retrospect, the medium of David Brinkley, Eric Sevareid, and John Chancellor was salvaged by John Dean, Sam Ervin, and Judge John Sirica.

"I'm not sure I agree with your premise," Chancellor answered. "Not entirely, anyway. Actually, I think the administration attacks on us had already passed their peak several years before. I remember back to 1970; even my kids were saying to me, 'Why is the president saying these awful things about you?' But a year or two later, we weren't so much on the defensive. A lot of people realized how ludicrous their charges were."

"Even so," I said, "come early 1973, the president was on a roll."

"Yes," he said, "Nixon had some genuine accomplishments. And that's what made Watergate, and the *need* for Watergate—that screwball, senseless, imbecilic thing—all the more insipid."

"Didn't Watergate change everything?" I asked.

"Well, it didn't help Richard Nixon," he answered, smiling, "and it didn't hurt us."

"Nixon was at the pinnacle. Then scandal, disgrace, and soon," by late spring, by the time I left college, "for the press, resurrection."

"It was incredible," Chancellor recalled. "Almost like a Greek tragedy, and for the country, a cosmic disaster."

"Without Watergate, what would there have been to stop him?" I said. "All the worst must have seemed behind the president. And what a horizon he must have seen."

"The chance to remake America in his own image," my host noted.

"The chance to bring the press to heel."

John Chancellor smiled. "Not a very pleasant prospect," he added.

"Not a very pleasant chapter," I replied.

14
Interpassage II

"YOU COMING TO SEE ME?" HE LAUGHED, THE VOICE strong and familiar. "Last time I saw you was three years ago."

"Yep," I remembered. "You were sitting in the Vital Spot at Geneseo," fondling a glass. He had recognized my voice and, hailing a barmaid, ordered my favorite college drink—a Scarlett O'Hara, heavy on the Southern Comfort, light on the grenadine.

"Well, we'll have a lot to talk about," he answered. "Just one word of warning. Don't expect any physician's cures."

We called him Doctor Erotica. He was short, balding, rotund, and unforgettable. A resident, like me, of Jones Hall at Geneseo, he drank Boone's Farm strawberry wine, inhaling from the bottle; walked down our floor clad in swaddling clothes, dancing as he strode; and in the College Rathskeller, perched atop the juke box where Harry Chapin sang, dreamt of Little Richard and Buddy Holly and other signatures of his youth, when the Cold War turned frigid and drive-ins multiplied and rock 'n roll was young.

Because his bent was coarse, some recall him as unruly. Because he smoked incessantly, his room lay cast in pallor. Because he was older than my classmates, we draped him with respect. His Christian name was almost incidental. He preferred, more simply, "Doc."

163

Doctor Erotica was not the most noble part of the class of 1973. He was not its most elevated member, nor the most contemporary either: hearing the name "John Chancellor," he might have huffed, "Who's he play for? *Chancellor?* The Red Sox? No, maybe the Twins." But he *was* perhaps the most memorable and, as I sought out the meaning of the early 1970s, the most probable to say, "This was what helped mold our world, so that when we gaze back now we can state, 'there was its guts and heart, if only we had seen them.' "

He was a philosopher, friends said, but in truth, Doc resembled more a friend-seeker, zealous in his eagerness to be liked. We arrived at Geneseo on August 29, 1971, I a transfer from Allegheny College, he from Nassau Community College on Long Island, twenty minutes from his home. Already twenty-three, with his military servitude (three years, U.S. Army) complete, he yielded neither to age nor discipline.

"I'd look at other vets about as old as him," said classmate Doug Brown, "and they'd be pulling 3.5s out of 4.0, starring in grade point average and knowing after college what they wanted to do. Then I'd look at the Doc," indelible, often bellicose, and spectacularly unfulfilled.

"He'd bungle along with his C average. He didn't care. All he wanted was to be the center of focus. I think the term is *self-actualize.* He'd never done a lot before; he looked for college to fill a void in his life. And it did. Even those who were ticked-off by him were fascinated by him." To Doctor Erotica, life meant attention, and both blossomed, inexplicably, in the bars and dormitories of Livingston County, New York.

He became a campus landmark, this stooped, erstwhile rebel, a manchild who installed a scoreboard in the hallway (one point for kissing, five for something more), wore white socks and army boots, and each Sunday after darkness, drew floormates around him for a "fireside chat." Here, a Berle amid the minions, he told of conquests (real and imagined) like Lois and Fat Donna and Boops, the last a local girl who, aping the Doctor, paraded from his room to the foyer clad only in panties and bra.

My classmates were his courtiers. He was their clown, yet a clown not wholly without dignity, and with a tragicomic lure. He saw himself as our *paterfamilias*, less innocent than his colleagues; he reveled in the image of uncompromising manic. He was a timepiece, deceptively miscast, one who vocalized his fantasies, and by speaking, made them so. "I belong to the fifties," he would blurt without prompting, Chuck Berry blaring from his stereo. But he was not old, nor nearing finality, and in 1971–73, as college became—for him, like us—the Jerusalem of our existence, he showed an insight, often sad and intuitive, that seemed to bridge, not disengage, the years.

"How you doing?" he said, stout and full-faced. Home was in Massapeaqua Park, New York. Doctor Erotica was thirty-three years old.

"Can't complain," I responded.

"Good drive out?" he asked.

"Not bad." From New York City, 355 miles southeast of Geneseo, Doc's residence was twenty-five miles away.

"Lived here long?" I inquired.

"'Bout three years. Stayed around Geneseo awhile, working at Sonyea, the place for slow, problem kids. And I lived near the college. Remember?" he said, beaming. "That's where I ran into you a couple years ago. Winter? The Vital Spot? What was it, '78, '9?"

"Somewhere in there," I agreed.

"Well, I'd sort of bummed around all the years since graduating—did some jobs, got involved with a girl. And then—hell, it's not the same when you're not a student—I came on back to the Island." Without his court, the Doctor was not the Doctor still.

For Doc and I, as Geneseo students, our only full calendar year was 1972. The last four months of the preceding year (our first on the State University Campus) revolved around it, almost becoming its appendage, as did the first five months of 1973 (our last).

For the nation, it was not a golden time exactly, but neither was the future unmanageable. Just as Eisenhower's 1950s, once degraded by historians and political scientists, were rehabilitated by the trauma of its successors, so would the early 1970s—marred by linkage with another Republican president—emerge, in reflection, as a time of substance, one in which the Nixon administration "could easily claim legitimate victories of its own," confessed the *Boston Globe* in the final year of the decade, and where we expected to avoid Archibald MacLeish's 1955 prophecy, "We have entered the Age of Despondency, with the Age of Desperation just around the corner."

If one forgot the war (few could), the whole and periphery of 1972 were special in the life of the country, warranting (as most years do not) the epithet *historic*. "You just think so because you were in college then," a classmate once countered. "They're no more special than, say, twenty years before." No, I replied, the times sired hyperbole. "Just look at the calendar from the time we got to Geneseo till the day we left."

On August 15, 1971, Richard Nixon froze wages and prices, devalued United States currency ("the most significant monetary agreement," he exulted, "in the history of the world"), and severed the dollar's link to gold—measures that acted as shock therapy and which made the economy swell.

Amid the verisimilitude of "boom," 1972 evoked gloating and self-satisfaction. Inflation plummeted to 3.2 percent; unemployment dipped to 5.1 percent; the gross national product soared to $1.555 trillion; among 418 companies, *The Wall Street Journal* reported, profits leaped by 23.7 percent in the fourth quarter of the financial year. Of American families, more than one-half had annual incomes exceeding $10,000. One in four earned $15,000 or more. "Conditions," said *Newsweek*, "may be getting too good," and in January 1973 *The New York Times* proclaimed, "The United States is in the midst of a new economic boom that may prove to be unrivaled in scope, power, and influence by any previous expansion in history." Only black America seemed removed from favor. The president, said Clifford Alexander, Jr., former chairman of the Equal Employment Opportunity Commission, "actively opposes our goals." The nation, said Harold Sims of the National Urban League, "still lies in the grip of a selfish, not silent, majority." But in Bangor and Baton Rouge, the living was easy, and across America, the comfortable were joined.

Abroad, despite Viet Nam, Nixon engaged in diplomatic summitry, and helped end the postwar bipolar world. In February 1972, five years after writing in *Foreign Affairs*, "Taking the long view, we simply cannot afford to have China forever outside the family of nations, there to nurture its fantasies, cherish its hates and threaten its neighbors," and nine months after telling *TIME*, "If there is anything I want to do before I die, it is to go to China. If I don't, I want my children to," he did what his predecessors could not—visit the People's Republic of China.

As more than two decades of estrangement ended, and millions watched via satellite-transmitted television, and college students—even at Geneseo—interrupted regular viewing to applaud the president's party, Chinese and American officials toured the Great Wall, traveled to Hangchow and Shanghai, were enraptured by the Forbidden City, toasted one another in Peking.

Vowing "peaceful coexistence" (and the removal of all United States troops from Nationalist China), Nixon and Premier Chou En-lai halted a twenty-year embargo on trade, travel, and cultural relations. The week of February 21–28, electric in its symbolism, marked "the week that changed the world," said the president, extravagantly, and, not incidentally, blessed his presidential campaign. If we were not yet a "global village," in Marshall McLuhan's phraseology, at least, many journals rhapsodized, the times were on the side of peace.

Three months later, on a late-May odyssey to Moscow, détente was born in the dankness of the Kremlin. Nixon became the first postwar American president to visit the Soviet Union and, between bear hugs and vodka, joined Communist Party leader Leonid Brezhnev in signing the first agreement of the nuclear age to limit strategic nuclear arms. On June 1— after traveling from Moscow to state visits in Iran and Poland—he returned to Washington, there to tell a joint session of Congress, "The foundation has been laid for a new relationship between the two most powerful nations in the world." Nixon's arrival at the Capitol, the Marine helicopter settling on the plaza of the East Front, "was like Caesar coming to Rome," Harry Reasoner reflected in 1979, "except that all his conquests had been peaceful." Euphoric, briefly. Historic, yes.

From September 1971 through May 1973, as we doubted whether in its evolution the age would ever grasp a middle ground, America beheld violence at Attica Penitentiary (twenty miles from Geneseo, forty-eight men died in the nation's most violent prison insurrection) and at the Munich Summer Olympics (Palestinian terrorists, seizing Israeli wrestling team members as hostages, caused seventeen deaths). In Egypt, President Anwar Sadat hinted at a peace accord with Israel. In October 1972, Henry Kissinger professed—prematurely—that "peace [in Viet Nam] is at hand." In the Far East, Jane Fonda sponsored antiwar tours, thundering, "We must oppose with everything we have those blue-eyed murderers—Nixon, Laird, and all the rest of those ethnocentric American white male chauvinists." In what Archie Bunker called "the good old U.S. of A.," out went midi-length skirts, back came mini-skirts, Lewis Powell and William Rehnquist joined the Supreme Court (its ninety-ninth and one hundredth inhabitants), the Senate approved the Equal Rights Amendment, cocaine and the Jesus Movement vied, and in New York City the memoirs of Howard Hughes, written by Clifford Irving and thought to be genuine, were documented as a fraud.

Under Jimmy Carter, the electorate would assert, America exuded diminution. Not in 1971–73. As John Connally once expressed to me, Texas-style, "Everything about it was big." The roots of America's singularly epochal scandal were planted. Thomas Eagleton became the first vice-presidential candidate to withdraw voluntarily. Spiro Agnew campaigned (and was judged by most Americans, polls said) as a man without self-puffery and sham. George McGovern lost the republic's most one-sided presidential election. The Christmas bombing of North Viet Nam, announced on December 18, 1972, and ended twelve days later, prompted invective. Six weeks later, after Guy Lombardo welcomed the New Year with songs that included "Cabaret," "Silver Dollar," "Too Much Mustard," and "Boo Hoo," returning POWs met emotions nearer love.

None of this disturbed Doctor Erotica or much impressed him either. "Sure, I knew the events that were in the headlines," he said, uncorking a beer, "but what the hell was that to me? It wasn't my doing. Yours either. You couldn't affect them. And look at that lineup. I always knew Nixon was a crook, even when he was jetting off to Peking and Moscow. And what he's gotten away with since his pardon—the pension, the benefits, all the money from his books—that's the crime. Agnew? A dud. McGovern was a weakling. Right on a lot of issues. But he could never get his thoughts across. And Wallace was an ass."

"So what's the solution? Drop out?"

"Hell, no," he insisted. "You just realize what a bunch of fakers you're dealing with. I saw that in the Army. Saw it in a lot of teachers. Saw it in some of the prima donnas we got stuck with as students here. So you get to see that you'd better concern yourself with something you can do more than a little bit about."

"Like what, Doc?" I wondered.

"Like yourself," he replied.

"What do you mean?"

"Well, man, I could always have impact on what I did, you know. And that wasn't true of anything else. So I said to myself, 'Make up for lost time. Do what you've never done before.' And so I did, and lived it up and drank and had a blast, and maybe even taught you guys a thing or three"—the Doctor washed a smile with Budweiser—"and I never heard no complaints." Not in "fireside chats," for sure.

While Doctor Erotica "lived it up," others died. Noel Coward. J. Edgar Hoover. David Ben-Gurion. Walter Winchell. Roberto Clemente and Maurice Chevalier. Mahalia Jackson and Howard Johnson. The Duke of Windsor and Adam Clayton Powell. Lyndon Baines Johnson, of whom Nixon wrote, "He died of a broken heart." Harry S Truman, once told by Churchill, "You, more than any other man, have saved Western civilization." And Jackie Robinson, of whom Heywood Hale Broun said, "He lived a life richer in honor than happiness," and who bore the weight of a pioneer.

Doc knew of Robinson, for he understood baseball, and we both found its appeal enduring. As young men, we had cheered for the New York Yankees—he on the Island, I in upstate New York—and its announcer, Melvin Allen Israel, whose exuberant praise of Yankee feats stirred small burgs and cities and who brought joy to provinces located hundreds of miles from the ballyard in the Bronx.

Across America, baseball cults divided into two schools— those who proclaimed that Mel Allen was nearly as exciting as being at the park, and those who prayed that an attack of laryngitis would silence him forever. Partisans hung on every word. Critics claimed he talked too much, a complaint which masked their true intent. The woods were full of Yankee-haters, and Allen drew the haters' wrath. For a quarter of a century, he broadcast with expansive detail. Few questioned his talent or denied the impact he made. Listening, we revered the voice, deep and vibrant, the voice which lured and never tired. Allen began in 1939, an Alabamian in New York. In 1964 he was fired, a dismissal that savaged the Yankees (and made me a Red Sox fan).

Doctor Erotica often spoke of Allen and the Yankees, and of baseball in the 1950s, when Mays and Mantle dwarfed each summer and Williams and Musial lent a luster to their game. He liked two stories about the Voice of the Yankees—one a parody of a Schlitz beer commercial ("the beer that made Milwaukee famous") now ending "the beer that made Mel Famey walk us," the second Allen's recital of two teenagers trading kisses in the Yankee Stadium bleachers. "That's interesting," Allen supposedly observed. "He's kissing her on the strikes, and she's kissing him on the balls," to which broadcaster Phil Rizzuto then added, "Mel, this is just not your day." Doc did not, however, relish the game of 1971–73, when the Pittsburgh Pirates and Oakland A's won World Series, the American League adopted the designated hitter, a players' strike erased eighty-six games from the 1972 schedule, and Roberto Clemente proved that he was not just one of the four or five finest players of his time, but quite possibly the best. Baseball today, mourned the Doctor, was too dispassionate, too dull.

Instead, he preferred professional football, still enormously popular, which closeted most of Jones Hall in front of television sets Sunday afternoon and Monday night, leading to a blizzard of weekly pools. While Doc followed football, Mark Spitz won seven gold medals in the Summer Olympics, Bobby Fischer ousted Boris Spassky in the world chess championships—1972 saw interest surge in that cerebral and misinterpreted game—and Roger Angell's *The Summer Game* and Roger Kahn's *The Boys of Summer* were published, two of the most gifted books on any sport.

Doctor Erotica forswore these interests, as he did much of

the period's literature. *Chimera. The Best and the Brightest. Jonathan Livingston Seagull.* Eudora Welty's *The Optimist's Daughter. The Breast* by Philip Roth. And *Fear of Flying*, its pages dog-eared in Geneseo female dorms. "Figured I had enough reading in the classroom," he explained, adding, almost as if an afterthought, "but say, buddy, that doesn't mean we didn't get culture. We had movies, remember, and I went to a lot of them."

There were, as usual, a lot to choose among. *Cabaret. The Sting. The Exorcist. American Graffiti. Straw Dogs* and *A Clockwork Orange.* Diana Ross in *Lady Sings the Blues. Fritz the Cat*, the industry's first X-rated cartoon. Marlon Brando in *The Godfather* (as Don Vito Corleone, pledging "I'll make him an offer he can't refuse") and in *Last Tango in Paris*, art that was discreet and elegant, and which posed a dilemma that plagued the decade: Was it sensitive cinema about sexuality, or pornography masquerading as film?

"What did you think of that lineup?" asked Doctor Erotica, intently, sipping his drink.

"Oh, I suppose it's all right," I volunteered. "But I don't see any *The Days of Wine and Roses* or *On the Waterfront* in there. I don't even see *Ma and Pa Kettle on the Farm*."

A radio hummed in the next room. With Doc, as with me, as with Allegheny's Jeanne Braham, what mattered in the early 1970s was not Brando nor baseball nor Henry Kissinger—but music, and how its temper, almost subliminally, invoked a state of mind.

"I remember," Doug Brown told me, much earlier, "how in school, it sort of brought us together. At least it dealt with the attitudes and themes of the times." Slight and soft-voiced, he had entered graduate studies after Geneseo, soon to become a teacher. "Now, with disco and all that stuff, kids move back into their own separate worlds. There's not the ties between life and music."

Even at Geneseo, of course, the ties were variable. Like Allegheny's, the sounds of 1971–73 were tactile, their truths romantic. But their lens had changed from war and the environment and racial disease to the pain and glory of relationships and how others related to self.

Musically, said *Billboard* magazine, our time at Geneseo

was the 1970s most eminent; of the decade's twenty-one most
popular songs, five arose in our twenty-one months. Roberta
Flack smoldered with "Killing Me Softly" and "The First Time
Ever I Saw Your Face"; Bread unleashed "Diary," "If," "Sweet
Surrender," "Everything I Own," and "It Don't Matter to Me."
Nilsson gave us "Without You," Johnny Nash "I Can See
Clearly Now," Derek and the Dominos the scorching "Layla."
"Behind Blue Eyes" came from the Who. As Cat Stevens
bespoke "Morning Has Broken," Three Dog Night scored with
"Never Been to Spain," and Harry Chapin celebrated "Taxi,"
four hundred seconds long, written as "a theme-song [said the
Lamron] which enables him to examine and expound upon
such diverse themes as broken dreams, Greyhound buses, and
masochism."

The Doctor smiled, gusts of foam upon his tongue. "It's
probably no secret," he started, "that every generation thinks
its music is the best."

"And us?"

"We weren't any different. We thought ours was tops," he
recalled.

"Was it?"

"Who the hell knows what 'best' means? I only know that it
seemed so to some. I mean, you're never going to have the stars
we had back in the fifties—nothing's as good as when it first
surfaces, and that's when rock 'n roll began. Yeah, the music of
that time. It had . . . *feeling*.

"I remember listening in the fifties to the music of my
relatives. It had love. It had a message. And it had a
commitment. Just hear their lyrics sometime." Doc looked at
me, solemnly. "Back then, we used things and loved people.
Now it's all in reverse. Plastic, that's how everybody is. Even in
college it was starting to come apart—the willingness to relate.
Today everyone has their defenses up. Listen to the songs;
they're self-centered. 'Me, me, me.' Our last couple years at
Geneseo—it was like the last hurrah. When divorce still was a
plague, at least partially, and people tried, at least part of the
time, to work things out. And it was all there in the songs, true?
All there in the songs."

The Carpenters, one recalls, thrived at Geneseo. "Hurting
Each Other." "Good-bye to Love." "For All We Know."

"We've Only Just Begun." While Jackson Browne recorded "Doctor My Eyes," and Todd Rundgren "I Saw the Light," Neil Young shone with "Old Man" and "Heart of Gold," and America exalted "Horse With No Name."

One could hear the Chi-Lites' "Oh Girl," Seals and Croft with "Summer Breeze," Carole King's "Sweet Seasons," and "Let's Stay Together" by Al Green. In January 1973, Carly Simon released "Anticipation," followed that year by Maureen McGovern's "There's Got to be a Morning After" and the Carpenters' "Yesterday Once More." But no record moved Doctor Erotica, nor better sketched the era, more than the song already extolled by *TIME* in mid-1972 as "legendary," its lyrics mythic and impalpable. "American Pie" by Don McLean. A metaphor for loss.

"Doc just went berserk," Doug Brown reminisced. "Here you had this guy, almost the antithesis of his times, the black leather jacket, the tough, hard image. He's looking for meaning in an age he doesn't know. And when "American Pie" came out, when was it, the first part of 1972?"

"January," I said.

"He thought it was the greatest gig he'd ever seen. Doc, I. recall him saying, that it symbolized, maybe, life. It just dripped with a sense of—you know—a period being unrecoverable. Buddy Holly [killed in a plane crash in 1959]. We thought there was a passage in there about Kennedy ["I can't remember if I cried/When I read about his widowed bride"]. The Byrds. Woodstock. All the allusions were so cryptic, suggestive. It typified, I guess, a feeling of everything being gone ["But I knew I was out of luck/The day the music died"], and I think that while it meant a lot to you and me—Lord knows, it was big enough—for a guy like Doc, it must have left him blasted."

It is hard, now, to measure "American Pie"—what it meant to music in the early 1970s and, looking back, to us. It was not even 1972's largest-selling song (that honor graced a banality, "Alone Again Naturally"), yet it became a *national* song—the focus of radio and television and graduate seminars, debated by men and women less familiar with Alice Cooper than Alice Kramden, Ralph's wife.

On New Year's Eve, 1980, I attended a party in Georgetown, where at five minutes of midnight, a dozen young, mostly liberal couples saluted the 1970s by singing McLean's creation. "Doc should have made a house call," Brown said later. What Doctor Erotica sensed a decade earlier, many of us felt that night.

"Did I love that song?" Doc asked, ruminating my question. "I suppose so," he said. He puffed on a cigarette and sat wide-eyed. "You have to remember what those years were like for all of us. We didn't know each other—almost strangers—and here we're thrown together in a dorm. There are easier things in life to deal with, huh? I knew I was different. My background, I'd been through more. And when that song came along, it like to have described my life."

" 'Long, long time ago,' " I recollected.

"'I can still remember,'" he said, stealing McLean's balladry, "'how that music used to make me smile.'"

"And it..."

"A lot of you," said the Doctor, not entirely in pity, "you wouldn't have understood what he was saying or, maybe, even how I felt. Maybe you do now"—silence—"in time, but back then that song said everything. How you could just put on your socks, no pretense, and be around people who cared. Not like the disco glitter scene now, everybody whole-hog for himself. It talked about stages in your life. How like in high school and at Nassau, you could be nothing. And then how at Geneseo, you could be on a roll, God dammit, and redeem everything that had already happened. It shouted out in the headlines what we were trying to fill!"

"A void," I said.

"Yeah."

"And you filled it."

"At Geneseo?"

"I think so."

"Maybe," he confessed, more softly. Abrasive, Doc was not hard. "I know some guys thought I was a snake in the grass—hopping from girl to girl. But I never hurt anybody," he said, "and that's what matters. Not a one. Today I see these writers talking about great moments, times that count. Hell, that was what we had. Doctor Erotica, you know. The scoreboard. The fireside chats. We had it all," he muttered, "had it all."

The man of intuitive decisions reached for another beer.

"Sometimes when I think of Geneseo," he said, deliberately, "it seems like a million years ago."

"You can't go home again," I counseled.

"You can't go back, either."

Growing, maturing, debating, entertaining, Doc and I were changed by college but along divergent roads. After graduation, as we groped for our identity, such as it was, in writing (me) and quasi medicine (him), we looked upon Geneseo as the sunlight of our twenties. It was our union, the bond before the carnage.

Who could know then, the Doctor mused, that before the decade ended, America would lose a war, watch the resignation of a president, bow before an oil cartel? That a loaf of bread, priced at 27¢ in 1972, would cost 60¢ two years later? That by January 1975, more than 6.5 million Americans would be unemployed, the most since the Department of Labor first computed figures in 1948? Who could envision that fear of "another Viet Nam," so remote when peace in Southeast Asia appeared secure, would abet the Soviet Union's designs from Afghanistan to the Caribbean? Or that a "Decade of Entitlement," born of frustration with self-reliance, would imperil a dream as old as Ellis Island—the concept of the melting pot?

"A lot of those things hit home the first few years after graduation," Doctor Erotica said. "Even to somebody like me. It was one hell of a bad time. But we weren't alone, you know? The whole country was in a pit."

"But why did we feel it more?"

"Did we?" he challenged.

"You tell me."

"Man," Doc began, "no foolin'. But you gotta remember the difference. College is usually great. No exception for us, right? When we were there, the country had some direction too. I mean, even people who thought Nixon was crooked as hell—even before he proved it—thought he was strong. And then all of a sudden, we're gone from college and at the same time the country starts falling apart. Most people feel the loss one way. Leaving when we did, we got hit twice."

"Is that why you stuck around college?" I asked him.

"What are you getting at?"

"Well," I said, "you figured that this way you'd only lose once. You'd still have Geneseo to grab on to."

"After graduation, you're talking about," Doc said.

"Yes."

"No, I never thought that," Doc professed. He lowered his eyes and struck a match. "I was going with Lois," he said, finally. "We'd been together for seven years. We were going to be married. And then she broke it off. No reason to do it. We had so much going for us. Remember," he asked, "how I talked about life in stages?"

Shrugging, I concurred.

"All during college, people kept saying to me, 'He'll never get enough of it,' the sex, the drinking. But the funny thing is, I *did* get enough. All I wanted was to settle down, go on to the next phase. And then there was no one to do it with. When I was ready for another stage, she wasn't. And she wasn't mean or vindictive. It's just the times. Even good people, they don't have a chance."

Doctor Erotica lit a cigarette. "You know, when I said a ways back that college seems like a million years ago?"

I nodded.

"Well," he said, "sometimes it feels like yesterday."

Sifting through papers, I read a column by Erma Bombeck, circa 1979. "It hasn't happened yet, but it's inevitable," she wrote. "One night, Sandy Duncan will lean over the footlights of a Broadway theatre and in the childlike voice of Peter Pan ask, 'Will everyone who believes in Tinker Bell clap your hands?' And then the theatre will resound with silence. The silence will record the last Bastille of blind faith in America."

Peter Pan had never grown up. Neither, perhaps, had Doctor Erotica. But the 1970s had.

Was Geneseo our last Bastille, I wondered, or had our faith not been blind but timeless, and in the confused, disillusioned years after college, essential for us to see?

"I don't know. I only know you gotta believe," Doc bellowed, sounding like baseball's Tug McGraw. "I guess we didn't after leaving school. Believe, I mean. Looking for something we'd lost and not finding it, our faith fell apart. But after a while you accept the past—and the fact that it's gone— and when you do that you can live again. I don't trust people so much anymore. Maybe when I do—it's not going to happen tomorrow—I'll be able to look ahead. Maybe even grab a belch of hope."

"Sort of a renewal," I suggested.

Doctor Erotica half-smiled. "Renewal," he said. "You think there's a song in that?"

Doc vanquished a cigarette and entered the living room. He turned off his radio. The music died.

15
Household Word

WRITING ABOUT AMERICA'S PAST AND FUTURE, CARL SAND-
burg once preserved both in three words that became the title
for one of his most reverberant poems. "The People, Yes."

In 1969–73 no American, George Wallace excepted, spoke
more bluntly for *his* people than the vice president of the
United States, both calm and discordant, enlarging our vo-
cabulary and splitting the nation.

Variously admired and despised, thought by some to be
fit for the presidency—and others to be unfit for even his
present office—he occupied the vestibules of American power, hoping, one day, to preempt the inner sanctum. He was not
simply an elected official; he was a *presence*, taut and
uncompromising, one who disdained his critics and who
doubled as philosopher and scold.

Unknown, almost, before 1969, he had been forgotten,
virtually, since 1973. Word that he would not see me, nearly a
decade after his fall, arrived via telephone, its courier an aide
to the former vice president, Roy Goodearle, currently of
Houston. "I've talked to him," explained the ex-White House
assistant, "and it's nothing personal. He's just not talking to
anyone. Anywhere. Period."

"But I haven't had that problem with other bigwigs of the

seventies," I protested. "Does he understand what the book's about?"

"Sure," Goodearle answered, "but his reaction is just what it is about anything else concerning that period. 'What difference is it going to make?'"

Recalling Spiro T. Agnew, the starburst of the early 1970s reappeared. If I could not meet him, I must still write *about* him, wondering how the years had torn the former vice president and why, as public moralist, he had vanished as suddenly as he came.

His manner, I remembered, had been paternal, reassuring; his voice an incubative monotone. Subdued, he was not boyish; prideful, he was not immodest; formal, he was not unreceding. Spiro Theodore Agnew was not a major vice president, as Nixon and Walter Mondale had been or would become. Legislatively, he was not momentous: "I find up on the Congress, as I do in the executive branch, that I have no real power," he mourned in 1971. Unarguably, he was not honest. He was, in truth, not even a rousing stump orator; Agnew often refrained from street campaigning, preferring to talk before standing room-only audiences, which responded to his (frequently) well-reasoned arguments with (mostly) well-mannered applause. He was, at the same time, however, among the most memorable vice presidents in the history of the United States, the distinct, embodied image of an administration bent (evidently) upon the rule of law.

"Memorable?" jibed Goodearle. "Yes, that's a nice, safe term."

"The good thing about it," I said, "is that it leaves room for interpretation."

Often wintry, easily wounded, Spiro Agnew was both expansive (about his doctrine, self-made) and unyielding (toward those whose doctrines he opposed). By the early 1970s, when he proved that as an Episcopalian, he could be Calvinist too, he had become the most controversial man in America, more acclaimed/impugned than the president, a sheath of pride and rage and loyalty.

"A far piece," I proposed, "from Baltimore," where Agnew had lived, attended college, practiced law, and ultimately, in 1962, been elected county executive.

Goodearle laughed. *"Baltimore?"* he preached, half-mockingly. "It was a far piece even from 1968," when two years after ascending to governor of Maryland, Agnew was chosen by Nixon as the Republican nominee for vice president.

"I had been impressed [by Agnew]," the Nixon *Memoirs* read, "as a man who seemed to have a great deal of inner strength." As governor, Agnew had been moderate, understated; supportive of minority advancement, he denounced violent discontent; he "appeared to have presence, poise and dignity"; he would help deflect George Wallace's mid-southern flank. He would also, willfully, as the campaign of 1968 exposed, sacrifice his ex-self to the self of the moment, Agnew playing "Old Nixon" while the future president, above the battle, imitated a former president, Ike.

Not a household word when the Republican Convention ended, Agnew became so, spectacularly, as November neared—calling one reporter a "Fat Jap," dubbing Polish-Americans "Polacks," equating Hubert Humphrey with "being soft on communism," proclaiming that "if you've seen one slum, you've seen them all." In August, Nixon had said, "He's a tough, shrewd Greek. He can't give a speech worth a damn, but he's not going to fall apart," but as October supplanted September, and Agnew was likened to Caligula's horse, all encomiums seemed misplaced. At one rally, a placard contended, "Apologize now, Spiro. It will save time later."

"Not the best of times," I said to polite and diminutive Bryce Harlow, the Nixon aide Agnew most trusted, at his home in Harper's Ferry.

"The campaign of '68?" he inquired, two weeks after Goodearle's disclaimer.

"Well," I said, "Agnew came out of that election portrayed as the Village Idiot."

"Yes," said Harlow, grimly. "If the press likes you, you can commit rape in the Phoenix town square and it'll be hush-hush. If they don't, and with the vice president they didn't, mess up one syllable and they'll put you on a cross."

"In '68," I reminded him, "they were out buying the nails."

Absent from us for almost ten years, invisible, disjointed, he was still flesh and bones, not catchphrase or caricature. Thinking of him now, among the vivid tatters of the time, one thought of Agnew in the early 1970s, a man of sacrifice and anger, decrying his critics from afar, almost a mirror of Nixon's depiction of Leonid Brezhnev: "He prides himself on not being an intellectual. What [he has] is stamina, and a determination which can compensate for the lack of college and degrees and things of that sort."

Harlow looked out his window. I picked at salted nuts. "Agnew was not an insensitive man," I noted. "The ridicule he took in 1968—it must have hurt him."

"They were out to impair him, was the press, and Ted took it seriously," Harlow said. "I mean, he was being chastised in papers and TV and radio all over America—and this was his first exposure nationally—as a dope, a nincompoop, the Boor of the Year.

"Agnew made mistakes, but his muffs were so exaggerated, overdone, that the vendetta was ridiculous. And the press was trying to weaken Nixon—you remember, he was being very presidential that campaign—through Ted. Once he understood that, he could shrug it off and go ahead. But bitterness lingered."

"Like Nixon after '52," I said.

"You mean, when they accused him falsely of having a secret fund, then he had to go on network TV and defend himself?" Harlow asked.

"The Checkers Speech," I said. "He was under fire, like Agnew."

"I hadn't thought of that before," he said, slowly, evenly, "but I guess there was a residue of remembered hurt after both episodes that linked them." Harlow grinned. "At least they had that in common."

Surviving 1968, whose events were improbable, Agnew clasped the vice presidency, whose attributes rivaled fictive film. Inaugurated on January 20, 1969, his image molded, in Agnew's phrase, "in the role of the Neanderthal man," the laughingstock from Maryland (lauded mostly for his advocacy of the Baltimore Colts) found himself—astoundingly—transformed into one of the nation's most pivotal fixtures, a man Harlow would tab "Power-Pack Agnew," of whom the president would say, "He has made his office one of the most significant platforms for moral and political leadership in the

nation," and columnist John Osborne, censuring his abuse in
The New Republic, scorned "for his attacks on media liberals,
negative elitists, and the whole spectrum of anti-Nixon types
who somehow get identified as traitorous revolutionaries in the
familiar Agnew rhetoric." To his critics, he debased his
authority, engaging in Aquarius McCarthyism. To his admirers, he lent a continuity to the transient quality of life, a
normalcy amid the changing times that we urgently required,
lest change overwhelm us all. When I left college in 1973, the
word "Agnew," depending on one's allegiance, meant "divide
America" or "tell it like it is."

"And it all began in Des Moines, this evolution, on
November 13 of '69," Harlow told me. "There Ted Agnew was
born again.

"Remember, Agnew and Pat Buchanan put together a
speech blasting the news media. Not surprisingly, Nixon lent
his backing. Well, the networks got the advance copy, and they
were sure it was going to destroy Agnew, whom they hated. So
they televised the speech nationally, broadcast it live, turned
all their cameras on him, and it turned into a triumph for
Agnew, and to their absolute consternation," he said, "it almost
destroyed the *networks*.

"Agnew basked in the glory; the country actually backed
him. He blossomed; his petals unfurled. For a man to go from
what the media were calling a brainless bimbo to a folk-hero
overnight, one who would slug it out with the media, well,
Agnew was so excited, he could barely stand it. In a sense,
based on what had gone before, it was too much, too soon."

As Agnew sat in Rancho Mirage, California, right leg, I
imagined, habitually crossed over left, smiling in his self-
assured, imperturbable way, flashes from the fall of 1969, my
first in college, wreathed my memory—of blitzkriegs against
the "unelected elite of network television. A small group of
men, numbering perhaps no more than a dozen anchormen,
commentators, and executive producers, settle upon the film
and commentary that is to reach the public. They decide what
40 to 50 million Americans will learn of the day's events in the
nation and in the world," against the "spirit of national
masochism [that] prevails, encouraged by an effete corps of
impudent snobs who characterize themselves as intellectuals,"

against student protesters marching in Washington moratoriums who "are allowed to jeopardize peace efforts of the president of the United States. I say it's time to question the credentials of their leaders. And if in questioning, we disturb a few people, I say it's time for them to be disturbed. And if in challenging, we polarize the American people, I say it's time for a positive polarization"; and of the counterassault, urgent, vocal, of senators like Charles Goodell of New York, intoning, "There are some leaders today who instead of lowering their voices are raising strident calls to the flag, to patriotism, and against communism. They are even using the age-old device of imputing disloyalty to those in dissent. We say to them, 'You will not put us off with the divisive, clamorous, pointless rhetoric of yesteryear. We know that the best noisemakers are not necessarily the best peacemakers.'"

"Unbelievable," I said, halting between syllables, noting how Agnew once said of dissenters, "It is time to sweep that kind of garbage out of society."

"That fall? Hell, you might say it of every month," Victor Gold, Agnew's former press secretary turned author and consultant, had countered several months earlier. "Agnew felt someone had to speak out."

"About what?" I said.

"What he thought most Americans believed but no one would say. I remember once how enraged he got the time he saw on television a bunch of scruffy-looking students carrying a Viet Cong flag down Pennsylvania Avenue. All the while a national network commentator was running beside them with his microphone, all sweetness and light, extended toward them. Why? So they could make any statements they might choose to issue.

"To Agnew, it was incredible," Gold said. "Thousands of miles away you had this same flag being used by people in battle who were killing Americans—and here they were being interviewed. To the networks, of course, these occasions just marked the display of a mere difference of opinion."

"And to Agnew?"

"Hell, it was treason," Gold said.

"You know," I started, "perhaps..."

"It's no secret," Gold continued, "that I do not and have

not gotten along with Spiro Agnew for years. Due mostly, I suppose, to his Arab business connections and his attacks against Israel; there's some anti-Semitism there. I know his weaknesses; he has a great deal of insecurities; and he was not and is not what you'd call a nice person."

"Is that the whole picture?"

"No," Gold declared, "the flip side is what Agnew meant. Today you have more than two dozen books written in the last ten years about the power of the media. You have your token conservative columnists, opinion/editorial pages, a debate about the need for variety—and each is a byproduct of Agnew's rips against the media. All had never been discussed before. Today you go into the ghetto, or into southern cracker country, or in the New Left and labor unions and business corporations—and they're all complaining about the media having too much power. Its roots, well, they came from Agnew.

"He wasn't an ideologue," Gold reflected. "He *was* cerebral, but he also felt things viscerally. Too much so, in fact. It wasn't a case of having Nixon demand that he attack the media—he wanted to, felt a deep-seated bitterness against what it stood for, and against the so-called good guys—the Kennedys and student activists and the screamers in the streets—that they lionized."

"Agnew often spoke," I reminisced, "about the need to take irrevocable sides. And in that, didn't he symbolize the times—the need, I suppose, not to give in, not to compromise?"

Gold chuckled. "I remember getting off a plane in the early seventies and seeing a sign, 'Pat Sucks Dick.' This wasn't the type of thing conducive to rational discourse," he said, wryly. "And it worked both ways—I'll never forget having some college students over to my home for a visit and talking politics, and when they questioned administration policies, I overreacted, went sort of wild, and linked them in my mind with the Jane Fondas of the world. It was unfair, of course, because in retrospect, I realize there was some truth in both sides. But we couldn't see that then. It was the most bitter time of my life."

"And for Agnew?"

"He fit in well," Gold said, "because he didn't mind stands. That's why he would have been"—say what?—"a *great* president, because even with all his shortcomings, he had a feel for social issues and an opposition to big government. He came from a poor background, with ethnic ties, and he had an inner sense of decision, and a reserve and dignity that I respected. He could be very loose—I recall how on campaign trips, at the end of a day we'd all sit up in his hotel suite and order pizza and talk around political ideas—but publicly, he had a formality that befitted his office."

"But here you had the vice president of the United States," I argued, "obviously speaking for the president, with all the machinery of government behind him, and he was out blasting away. Where was the dignity there?"

"Who started the blasting?" Gold retorted. "The press and the media and the liberals and the academic community hated him, not because we were Republicans, necessarily, but because of what he represented, and even more," he said, his voice cutting the air, "because he had the backbone to speak out.

"And as he spoke out, he was applauded and vilified, and developed something of a reputation too"—the darling of Republican fund-raisers, the scourge of drugs and demonstrators and, supposedly, campus youth.

Emboldened by 1969, Agnew became, in Bryce Harlow's words, "a star with difficulty. A star because of what he stood for. With difficulty because now that he was a celebrity, and had a speechwriter—Buchanan—writing presidential-type speeches for him, Ted got the idea that he had real programs of his own; the veep was talking like the president. Well, we all know the vice president is powerless, does what the president tells him—and even though he did it well, he still was Richard Nixon's man.

"Once he calmed down and got that straight—and it wasn't easy," Harlow mused, "because he was a vastly, tremendously sensitive person beneath that tough exterior, and sometimes because his personal sensibilities became embroiled, it became difficult for him to perform, and he'd go off on a tangent—but after a while it got straightened out, and we were ready then for the Grand Event," the campaign of 1970, the

most memorably caustic off-year election of America's postwar epoch, an enterprise, said *TIME*, that propelled "Democrats scurrying to the center like frightened rabbits under
Agnew's tongue-lashings," with Harlow—traveling with the
vice president—acting as Nixon's emissary, and the vice
president serving as Nixon's mouthpiece, cutting edge, sword.

"You have to remember the backdrop," cautioned David
Parker, special assistant to the president. "The economy was in
a mess—inflation over 5 percent and rising. Ditto for unemployment. And the president couldn't go on the road and rip
away—it wouldn't befit the office. Besides, he was going to be
in Europe on a state visit until about three weeks before the
elections. So we decided to take the offensive where the
administration held the high ground, on the social issues,"
assailing crime and welfare and elitism and permissiveness,
"and guess who won the job of spreading the gospel by
default?" A short, tentative smile. "Agnew."

To those who loathed his foibles and saw only contention
in his wake, Agnew in 1970 reeked with the gloom and mucus
of the otherworld; to apostles, he meant delight.

"He was the most enjoyable campaigner I've ever traveled
with," said Harlow. "He loved to laugh, to joke with his staff.
Agnew didn't take himself too seriously at times. All of which,
naturally, goes against his image—like Nixon, he had internal
upsets, hangups if you will, that made him unable to let go in
public or even be continually happy. But he loved his message,
and he believed it and carried it out with relish—even though,
in being labeled as the Cave Man, he knew he was hurting his
long-range hopes for the presidency. But he was a marvelous
electioneerer, and what he did—putting Democrats on the
defensive, making them the softies on criminality and excessive violence, with the economy falling apart all the while—
was remarkable."

Visiting forty cities in thirty states, singularly changing the
election's referendum from wages and prices to law and order,
Agnew besieged America. We had become, he said, "a Spock-
marked generation"; we were weak, irresolute; we required
"demand feeding up to the age of thirty." Aided by an
unabridged dictionary—"it never left our plane," quipped
Harlow—and by Nixon writers Buchanan and William Safire,

Agnew patented the term *Radic-lib* (for radical liberal), berated "impudent snobs" and "rotten apples" and "pusillanimous pussy-footers" and "vicars of vacillation"; made of "nattering nabobs of negativism" and "hopeless, hysterical hypochondriacs of history" staples of Republican lore. His brusqueness, claimed friends, was an index of his honesty. He split the body politic and touched Americans and said what was on his mind.

"I'll never forget the night a bunch of us were in a hotel room, and Agnew came up with his line on Charles Goodell," his scheduler, John Damgard, would later say in Washington. "You remember, Goodell had been a very conservative Republican congressman from upstate New York, and then when Bobby Kennedy was killed in '68, Rockefeller appointed him as his replacement as senator. Well, all of a sudden Goodell became a born-again flaming liberal. So we're shooting the breeze and Agnew says, 'He's the Christine Jorgenson of the Republican Party,' the man, you remember, who had had a sex-change operation.

"Understandably, we roared. But Harlow was serious about it. 'You know, we laugh now but we can't use it,' he said. 'It'd be counterproductive.' And when we quieted down, we agreed. So Agnew put it off day after day; we were already coming under attack for going for the jugular. But finally, he couldn't resist—at a press conference, he used it, and as reporters were going berserk, scrambling for their telephones, Agnew comes up to Bryce and says, sheepishly, almost child-like, 'Sorry.' But it was that kind of campaign. We were the heavy artillery. We had our fun. And who knows?" he announced, laughing, "maybe we even sold some newspapers along the way."

Attacking my note pad, I heard Damgard's counsel. "I've been in politics for a long time," he told me, "and in all my years of watching elections, I never saw a vice president dominate an election the way he did that one."

From 1969 to 1973, urging decorum and (from his distance) moderation, Agnew did not act like the vice president of public relations for General Motors; nor imply, as John Connally would in his 1980 overture for the presidency, that "business is the heart of America; business is the heart of government." Nor did he focus on issues like productivity, business tax relief, and the genius of private enterprise—arenas reaffirming support among voters already committed to conservative views.

If now, unlike Chancellor, he seemed a dim, forsaken ornament; unlike Bond, without approbation; unlike Billy Graham, essentially used goods, he was not without conviction, and as he solemnized privacy (to be sure, only partly self-imposed), his life less a diatribe than a paean to what might have been, I found again, in this hard, disturbing man, a refusal to accommodate himself to prevailing public moods, and an instinctual rapport not with the NAACP, nor the Fortune 500 Club, but rather, the Great Middle Class.

"You know," I said to Bryce Harlow, "after all the turmoil of 1970, on Election Day you didn't do that well. Republicans lost eleven governorships, nine seats in the House, won only two more in the Senate. That may be better than the historical norm for the party in power, but you'd been swinging a verbal mace for two months. You expected more."

"Yes," he conceded, "but there were a couple reasons. First, Nixon got back from Europe and—after we'd succeeded far beyond our expectations in focusing people on social issues; we'd won that battle—he proceeded to hit the campaign trail, plow the same ground until it was barren, and do it harshly, so that he undid much of what we'd done. Second, the economy still was in a mess. And third, Democrats, surprisingly, can read too. They'd seen the tea leaves, seen the headway we were making with law and order—and they were scared. From October on, a lot of them campaigned like Marshal Dillon."

"So, in the end," I suggested, "the campaign really didn't amount to much."

"I disagree," Harlow said. "It marked the beginning of the forces, the swing toward us on traditional morality and values, that brought about the landslide of 1972." Silence and hesitation. "And I suppose, really," he said, quietly, "it summed up as well as anything the great battles of 1969–73 that we had in the country—over the war, the riots, over permissiveness, over radical youth."

"And that goes to prove?"

"You have to understand the Republican party," he stated.

"You know what I mean. They're not prone to talk about busing and pornography; they'd rather enunciate their views on balance of payments and business management. But in the period you're talking about, those issues didn't move people to vote Republican. Social issues did. That's what became apparent—in Agnew's campaign, and then against McGovern."

"Ten years later," I said, "what did it all signify?"

"What it meant," he nodded, solemnly, "was that a tide of conservatism began largely with Ted Agnew. It started, probably, in the fall of 1969—the swipes against protesters and the media, carried on through '70 and '72, and was interrupted by some of the things that happened afterward"—reliving resignation, Harlow's eyes tightened—"and then, because its force was so strong, and because it had been shown that, properly articulated, it was the country's majority voice, it came back with the Reagan landslide to the point where, now, liberalism is almost a dirty word."

So, though, ironically, was Spiro Agnew. In these, the early 1980s, in a conservative age, with a Republican president and the government increasingly bent upon right-leaning letters, the nation's once conservative eminence resided three thousand miles from Washington, an exile in his own country, abandoned, a virtual nonperson, his hopes and sensibilities spurned.

I had entered Allegheny less than two months before he first chastened "impudent snobs," the start of his beguilement of the "Silent Majority," of Agnew as folk spokesman and covenant. I fled Geneseo before evidence surfaced that as executive of Baltimore County, then as governor of Maryland, he extorted thousands of dollars from consulting engineers, granting, in return, government contracts. He resigned as vice president on October 10, 1973, one hundred and forty-two days after my graduation. For Spiro Agnew, my years in college were the most radiant of his life.

"You know, I go to other countries, and they treat me like royalty," I remembered Agnew telling a former associate. "Then I come home and I'm treated like a bum." He was a business consultant; he traveled frequently. Abroad, he was often remembered as past slogan—waving placards exhorted,

"Spiro's Our Hero," not as the haunted vice president who, to escape a prison sentence, pleaded *nolo contendre* to the charge of income-tax evasion.

More open than Nixon, more human than his image, more candid than, post-resignation, his clippings suggested, he had suffered "hell and injury," Agnew continued, since the dark bewitchment of late 1973. "It hasn't been easy. It all seemed so unjust."

Hearing his protestations ("The contributions I took," he wrote in his book, *Go Quietly or Else,* "were part of a long-established pattern of political fund-raising in Maryland"), and recalling Harlow's aside ("Unlike Nixon, charged with corruption of power, he was guilty of personal corruption, charged and held accountable. His was a different kind of problem than the president's, a sullied escutcheon, and that the American people find difficult to forgive"), I grasped Agnew's fear that the nation he knew had made him a pariah. Middle America had venerated Agnew's ordinariness, a quality of which he too was proud. What the public saw ultimately, though, and decidedly rebuffed, was his obstreperous arrogance, a belief that he could suspend legality, as if time could expunge his wrongs.

Before his golden age had passed, Agnew seemed steadfast, impervious; now, as in an epilogue, he was more vulnerable, perhaps, than any of the era's notables—more fragile than Mitchell, who found calm in silence; or Father Hesburgh, absorbed in the infinity of God; or Friedan, of the hale, conclusive assurances; or even the crippled Wallace, resigned to martyrdom and a chair.

Vulnerable? A strange epithet for Spiro Agnew, but among all his qualities, pride—or, as Greek-Americans termed it, *philotimo*—had been the most undaunted, and for nearly a decade, his pride had been defaced.

"Vulnerable?" Harlow repeated. "Oh, maybe. Sad, for sure. Yes, as you can imagine, I'm sure he thinks of what he otherwise could have done, how close he was to being president. Not so that he could rush on to some big ego trip, necessarily, but so he might have prevented some of the calamities to hit America in the seventies."

"Wasn't he one of those calamities?"

"Inadvertently, I suppose," he said, "but that's not the entirety of Ted Agnew."

"All right," I said, "how would America have been different if he'd survived?"

"Become president, you mean?"

I nodded.

"That's such an imponderable," he said. "His problem was that he too easily took offense because someone 'slighted me.' But a president gets heaped on every day—it's like a quarterback who is all the time getting sacked. You have to shake it off, take it impersonally. Ted had troubles there." Pause. "But he was tough too. He didn't flinch. He wasn't a toad. And Washington is full of them. So which would have won out? The toughness or the hurt? You know, we almost found out."

While vice president, as much as any of his contemporaries, Agnew made his age extraordinary—dispelling pluralistic ignorance, where the members of a majority felt somehow outnumbered; making an endearment of blundering candor; linking liberals with extremists and conservatism with the center; drawing praise from men like my father, who extolled his moralism, who lauded his intentional use of a new word every two or three days, employing it over and over again until it lingered, and who—with, literally, millions of Americans— thought of Agnew as their guy, a man who would say in 1971 of *his* father, "I am simply stating what America is all about. I guess it is a holdover from what he taught me. He had some very firm opinions on what was good and what was bad."

Tall and silver-peaked, the former vice president remained "always controversial," he allowed in early 1981. "People have always reacted strongly, not blandly, to what I had to say."

Yes, I found myself agreeing, and rising to leave Bryce Harlow, found self-doubt disappear about which Agnew one confronted—the Cro-Magnon of 1968; the master of homily of whom an enemy could write, "He is so relentlessly [huff] *middle-class*"; the social warrior once twitted (in *TIME*) as "Spurious Spiro, the smirking, spleenful spokesman of the sated, smug, self-satisfied society"; the vice president schooled to success and self-discipline; the phrasemaker dismissed as a buffoon, and later as a presumptive felon; during my college

years, thought of by partisans as a Cromwell or Judge
Brandeis, forthright and incorrupted, and a decade later, after
America's conservative groundswell, as a John the Baptist,
accursed, wronged.

He was all of these Agnews, I decided, at the mercy of his
past, without quite understanding it. Stiff, he was not unfeeling; brooding, not immune from slight. He cherished order and
called himself a patriarch. As president, he would have made
fathers of us all.

16
Born-Again (Again)

CELEBRATING EXTRAVAGANCE IN THE EARLY 1970S, SPIRO Agnew had decreed, "Yippies, Hippies, Yahoos, Black Panthers, lions, and tigers alike—I'd swap the whole damn zoo for a single platoon of the kind of young Americans I saw in Viet Nam."

A decade later, visiting New York, I recited another favored narrative. "There are only two lasting bequests we can hope to give our children," I said, quoting Henry Ward Beecher, to Jerry Rubin, age forty-two. "One of these is roots...the other wings."

His roots were palpable, I said to Rubin, still an instantaneous magnifico, wrapped in a gray wool jacket, residing in Manhattan, one coast and three time zones from the former vice president. But what about his wings?

"Wings?" he marveled, as we left the building that housed his new employer, the brokerage firm of John Muir and Company, and walked to a nearby restaurant, only Rubin's beard a relic of America's past counterculture clown. "Who in the hell do you think I am, Superman?"

"Truth, justice, and the American way," I answered.

"Yeah," he said, "but not *my* kind of way."

"Well, what if wings meant influence?"

"Oh, I've affected people," said the man who at age thirty-one, chorused, "Never trust anybody over thirty." "But why shouldn't I? I've always been an intellectual, an organizer. I've wanted to get things done. Today people say, especially those in the press, 'You've given up. You've joined the system. You've compromised.'

"It's all stupid rhetoric," stormed Rubin, shoving a door aside. "We were dreamers a decade ago. We had a vision. Now we have to be practical, find new solutions to better people's lives. And I just believe I can be more effective now, considering the way the country has changed, wearing a suit and tie."

"But don't a lot of people come up and say, 'Since I left college years ago, haven't you really sold out?'" I asked.

"Yes, and it's a lazy, empty question," Rubin said, opting for rebuttal. "They just see me as a projection of themselves and all the changes that affected them, and they think back, which I never do. And they're just spouting drivel. Let's just say I've always been adept at predicting trends."

From 1969 to 1973, Jerry Rubin deified revolt—against power and authority, institutions and politicians, against "the system." He pried apart generations; he sermonized the faithful; to Agnew, he was dirty, leprous; to cognoscenti, a leader, a reveler in absurdity, a court jester of the revolution.

Actor, ex-radical, a founder of the Youth International Party (the Yippie Agnew caged in his zoo), he had dawned upon us in 1968, convicted of rioting at the Democratic Convention. After the case was dismissed on appeal, Rubin adopted esalem and yoga, biogenetics and self-help, and by 1980—repudiating former melodies—corporate business as a securities analyst. "Welcome to Wall Street," he wrote then, his forum the opinion/editorial page of the *New York Times*. "Here I come. Let's make millions of dollars together supporting the little companies engaged in social, environmental positivity. Let's rescue American capitalism from overemphasis on large organizations. Let's make capitalism work for everybody." Jerry Rubin a capitalist? His manifesto exuded more of Harold Hill, Meredith Wilson's *The Music Man*—"But you've got to know the territory"—minstrel, extrovert, hustler.

"Does it bother you," I began, "when strangers say of Jerry

Rubin, 'He's flip-flopped. How can he have credibility? He's a hypocrite, you know, a phony'?"

Rubin laughed, nervously. His face—fine-featured, dark-haired—glowered. As he shook his head, a past proclamation embodied the conversion: "I'm not going to compromise about anything," he had vowed in 1969. "Don't you see, capitalism itself has to be destroyed."

"Bother me?" he said, finally, as we secured a booth, minute and informal, in a restaurant on lower Broadway. "Why should it? I think it's perfectly natural to end up working for a company that helps people speculate. You know, I've always been a risk-taker." He smiled, minus warmth.

"But you must wonder how you ended up on Wall Street?" I said. "Not exactly like the march on the Pentagon," which he organized, "or even Walnut Hill," where he grew up in Cincinnati and which he hated.

"No," he said curtly, staring past me. "I wouldn't have thought it possible ten years ago—but that doesn't make any difference. I used to think of myself as an outsider. Not now. And I've gone from someone who believed that capitalism was immoral to one who believes that capitalism has problems but can better everybody's lot." A chuckle dulled the air. "Information is power. Financial resources are power. The wealthy can afford financial information provided by lawyers and accountants. Maybe I can help even the score."

Whether he was mean and opportunistic, as Nixonians insisted, or prescient, as the antiwar movement claimed, Jerry Rubin was, by reputation, street-wise and caustic.

He was facile.

"I think my credibility is even greater than it used to be," he said. "I respond differently today, as everyone does, because these are different times. I don't follow fads. I lead them."

Practiced.

"I've known for a long time that the guy who writes the story, the play, the incident, *makes* the story. Everything's in his hands. And what is all that? Just marketing. I've always been involved with it. In the 1960s I was marketing antiwar consciousness, in the 1970s, growth of a personal nature, and now I'm marketing advertising, public relations."

Manipulative and fawned over and, ultimately, confident of life.

"Yes," he said, restating my reminder, "I used to say that my parents, for instance, they loved me so much, it was really total liberation. I knew if I yelled or misbehaved enough, I'd get my way."

"You knew," I said, "when push came to shove."

Rubin winked at my question. "Kids understand how to operate. And living in my house was a classic case of psychological conflict."

"Similar to what you undertook, say, a decade ago."

"It was hardly ungenuine," he injected quickly. "After all, we were the guiding spirit. America needed self-determination and an end to injustice, to the barbarism of southern whites and the jerks who ran the government. But my activity in that time, I think, without doubt, was a playing out on a national scale what I'd learned earlier."

"In your family."

"Yes," he responded. How to change America. How to "get my way."

He was, in short, not unlike other troubadours of guerrilla theatre, full of rectitude and clichés and repulsed by government sanctimony, who mixed intolerance with chants of "Ho Ho Ho-Chi-Minh, the NLF is going to win," and who spawned legions of imitators on college campuses—blunt and inplacable and, above all, sure.

"I've never met you before," I found myself saying, "but in the early 1970s, when I went to college, I knew a hundred people like you."

"How so?" Rubin asked.

"You were always so certain," I said. "Certain of yourself, of your ideas—at least at the time—so certain that what you said somehow meant something."

"What's so strange about that?" he said, yawning, his interest as elusive as his sincerity.

"Almost always, your friends were liberal, against the war," equating it with evasion and compromise. "Being rude came so naturally to them." I smiled. "I used to admire how they could be so abusive so quickly."

"And you weren't that way?"

"I used to be as adamant the other way," I conceded, "against people, I guess, like you. On the inside, scared; on the outside, certain. And I suppose people like me gave as good as we took. Still, it was an effort to be abrasive. But for the students I'm talking about, I always felt, to be abrasive was a breeze."

"You'd call it abrasive," he acknowledged, "I'd call it confident. We were awakening a nation—maybe that's why we didn't follow *Robert's Rules of Order.* We woke up America's id—the energy of the ghetto, the blacks, of Americans against the war. We attacked the status quo. Those on the offensive— like we were then—always seem to be more certain."

Among the liberal princelings of the early 1970s—from Bond to Ramsey Clark to George McGovern—I felt I knew Rubin better than any, yet understood him least of all. He was histrionic, at turns wild and cerebral; molding outrage, he valued shock. In him, I saw a beckoner of old, familiar remnants—classmates at Geneseo, like Allegheny, unsullied by reticence—who occupied buildings and praised Che Guevara and, miming war's atrocities, struck candles in the night.

Even his history was recognizable; like many of my classmates, Rubin offered escapism, not death. Though in the early 1970s, with Eldridge Cleaver, Mark Rudd, Abbie Hoffman, and Bernadine Dohrn, he became a fugitive, he did not, like them, confuse protest with terrorism or seem today—from a distance—an emotional dinosaur, their urgency as difficult to comprehend (or, looking back, to relate to) as the violence which marred their dogma.

I knew of Rubin's childhood—how he matured in Cincinnati, living with his parents and grandparents near the old Zoological Garden; how he idolized the baseball Redlegs, visited bandbox Crosley Field to cheer for Ted Kluszewski, and in high school, which he called a jail in 1969—"a place where the rich teach the rich to replace them"—was named the "busiest boy" in class; how, refused admission to Northwestern, he entered Oberlin College, and transferred to the University of Cincinnati, working forty hours a week at the *Cincinnati Post;* how, after graduation, "despising Cincinnati," he said, "and being bored, I had to get away from its provinciality so I could see the truth," he visited India, returned home when his father died, became legal guardian for his fourteen-year-old brother, traveled to Israel, and in 1964, seeking his Ph.D., enrolled as a special student at the University of California.

I knew how at Berkeley, he joined the Filthy Speech Movement ("The only profane word I know," he claimed in 1969, "is decency"), devoured drugs ("I love them," he said then. "My whole sense of politics changed. I began to find we had to create a movement that was an end in itself—not an external goal, but a living revolution each day"), met Hoffman and ran for mayor (his candidacy, luring 22 percent of the vote, urged police disarmament, legalization of pot and abortion, and free heroin for addicts); became, said Timothy Leary, "a grass Guevara"; oversaw the 1967 march on the Pentagon; and threw dollar bills from the visitors' gallery at the New York Stock Exchange, unleashing a wild scramble on the floor below.

I knew too how he helped form the Youth International Party, created on New Year's Eve of 1968, a year in which his nominee for president, Pigasus, fared dismally in November; how Rubin engaged in mayhem at the August Democratic Convention ("Kill the pigs. Kill the pigs," he cried); and how he was indicted by the Cook County grand jury for conspiracy to commit riot. "This is the greatest honor of my life," he said. "I hope I am worthy of . . . the Academy Award of Protest. It is the fulfillment of childhood dreams."

I knew of Rubin's cosmos, I told him presently, but I did not understand him.

"*No comprendé?*" he said, and for a long pause he eyed me. His voice was dulcet, soft-spoken; I could recall Rubin shouting, "One-two-three-four, we don't want your fucking war."

"Nope," I replied.

For a product of Caledonia, New York, the son of a Presbyterian Elder, whose mother washed his mouth out with soap because, at age eleven, he muttered the word *damn*, and who empathized with Julie Nixon's 1968 utterance (saying of her mother, the disciplinarian, and her father, who never spanked her), "but then, we never wanted to displease them; we wanted to be good," the sum of Jerry Rubin's ministry—and the response it lured in college among many students—was a phenomenon not without its mysteries.

"Yeah, I know what you mean," he acknowledged. "Like me with Nixon. His impact was so destructive, and he was around for so long, and yet how could I debate with him, or even know what he was talking about? He was unapproachable. He left no room for discussion. We were coming from opposite ends, different perspectives. It was like we came from two different poles."

"I wouldn't say that," I corrected. "How about two different planets?"

Rubin condoned Tito and derided the Shah of Iran and, in the 1960s, conceding, "I am a Communist," said of a trip to Cuba, "It just took me totally"; it was a "land of idealism"; "no trace of cynicism" existed, "or a 'what's in it for me' attitude."

Flaunting his evangelism, he unfurled the Viet Cong flag; waved assent as North Viet Nam Premier Pham Van Dong (speaking on October 14, 1969, the day before the first moratorium) told protesters, "May your fall offensive succeed brilliantly"; spawned applause by lashing federal officials: "What they say about marijuana, they used to say about masturbation"; said of his grandfather's heritage, "I have no cross to bear. If the Jews disappear tomorrow, it won't bother me at all."

Remembering, I wondered if concord was ever possible in 1969–73 between Rubin, who hung Castro's photograph in his apartment, and the descendants of Jimmy Stewart and Robert A. Taft, who would have opted for hanging. *Understanding?* We spoke at cross-purposes. We thought at cross-world. We talked at, not to. What we understood was hate.

"Understanding goes two ways," Rubin professed, his eyes narrowing. "It would have been nice if they'd tried to grasp *our* position. And anyway, the position of the administration was clear enough. You could see people getting killed on account of it every night on the news."

"And you were right? Always?" I said, recalling an early 1970s graffito at the University of Wisconsin: "Radicals are nothing more than excited moralists."

"Hey," he countered, shuffling his fingers. "You can't worry about that stuff. You had to move, act, do what your insides told you. And I didn't have to defend my position. I wanted social change, an end to the war, an integration of the races, and for America to be more open. I wanted this even though I think we live in what I call the Death of Christianity— then in the streets, now in the bedrooms. And while all of this was going on, you better make sure someone notices you."

"Or else?"

"Else why do it? P.R. It makes all the difference." Rubin's face softened. "Not always, of course, but you get my point. And besides, almost no one got hurt by what we did here at home. All the murders took place in Southeast Asia. And, you'll remember, that was hardly our doing."

Did he remember, then, I asked, the explosion in March 1970 that ripped a Weatherman bomb factory, killing three members of the group? "It happened here in Manhattan. It woke a lot of people up."

"Yes," he said, "and it made people in the movement aware that all terrorism did was turn public opinion against us."

"Remember what Kingman Brewster of Yale said about the incident?"

"No, tell me."

"'It is much more clearly recognized,'" I recalled, " 'that Weathermen beget Minutemen.'"

"Once people got it out of their minds that armed struggle was the only real revolutionary struggle, we could shift the battle from the bomb factories to the streets."

"The battle for P.R. again," I observed.

"How else were we going to win?"

As violence culminated, the antiwar movement turned from armaments to peaceful dissonance; from leaders bent partly on sabotage to the street soldiers of the workshops—and as its focus became more political, climaxing in the McGovern fiasco of 1972, many of its leaders vanished, resurfacing (dropping back in, not out) only after Nixon's political demise.

Cleaver, of the Black Panthers, forsook self-imposed exile in 1975. Weatherman founder Rudd surrendered in 1977; Hoffman three years later (a week before his autobiography, *Soon to be a Major Motion Picture*, assaulted bookstores, and after movie rights had netted $200,000). Dohrn, former leader of the Weathermen, now a mother of two, surrendered on the same day Walt Disney's Mouseketeers held their twenty-fifth reunion. Which cult fetish had proved more enduring, antiwar radicalism or Annette?

"I don't know," I said. "One's selling peanut butter, and it sticks to your mouth, so it can be around awhile."

Rubin paused, theatrically, and grinned. "Yes, but which side had the nuts?

"Look," he said, more intently, now. "The funny thing is that people were writing us off, and a lot of our leaders were underground, and despite all this going on, we never doubted that we were right."

"Not even in the early 1970s?" I said, when, in the aftermath of the riots of Chicago, and the diminution of the Students for a Democratic Society, and the abandonment— even by liberals—of groups like the Weather Underground, nine of the sixteen portraits on the FBI's expanded most wanted list belonged to political radicals.

"Sure, they were unsteady times," he agreed, reverting to his yawn. After his indictment, dismissed in 1969, Rubin was arrested for (and found not guilty of) possession of three ounces of marijuana. Freed, he marched on Washington; toured college campuses; proclaimed himself—clad in a Black Panther beret, Egyptian earrings, Viet Cong pajamas, American Indian headband, and a toy submachine gun clutched in his arms—"the revolutionary of the future"; and found, as Hoffman was forced to borrow $25,000 in 1971 to publish a book, *Steal This Book* (most bookstores would not sell it, nor newspapers publicize it), that even in the constellation of my last two college years, with the war still with us, the celebration of radicalism had waned.

"If you were writing this in the spring of 1973," said Rubin, obliging my premise, "yes, you'd believe that Nixon and his team had won. I mean, look how far we were then from the original manifestos of the 1960s, the exuberance, the thought that we could somehow do-in the government in Washington from Telegraph Avenue. All we saw then was repression."

"Of the Left, you mean?" I said.

"Campus activists were expelled, arrested. Or locked behind bars. Or facing financial ruination."

"What of the students?" I continued. "How had they changed, for example, from the mid-1960s to 1973?"

"Not much," he responded. "Young people were still

genuflected before. They were taken seriously. The media loved them. And they wanted to do good things—you know, play an important role. They thought that what they argued and fought over in college, they could bring to fruition in the world."

"And now?"

"Now those people are in the majority," Rubin stated. "They're in their thirties, and because there are so many of them, they rule. But in college, today, students are boring, listless. They have nothing to say. That's why I stopped hitting the college lecture tour—ended it a couple months ago. I used to go to colleges and I'd think 'Are you *alive*?' No protests, no emotions, nothing to show you're aware." He smiled, after a fashion. "The flip side, of course, is that in the outside world, you don't have the repression you did back then with Nixon, Agnew, Mitchell. Things that we fought for a decade back have become accepted into the culture."

"In college now," I said, "it's veered more toward what Nixon might have sponsored in the early 1970s—and in most of America, it's veered more back toward you."

"I don't believe that," he said sharply. "In college, they aren't cultural conservatives. They don't agree with what Nixon did. They have the same morals that your age did."

"But go back a decade," I urged, "and look at college campuses and American business. Look at the differences between them. Different languages, mores, manners, dress. And a no-man's land in between."

"Today there's not the dividing line," he said. "You have the Young Republicans on campus—ten years ago they would have been stoned"—and a Jerry Rubin in corporate finance, enshrining entrepreneurship, forging an allegiance to work.

"So around the country," I said, "attitudes are more similar, more homogeneous."

"The country has changed, not college," he retorted. "We have a spirit of toleration and permissiveness. There aren't any norms. No one knows what marriage means anymore. What work means. No one knows what femininity means, or masculinity either. Family relationships have lost their *raison d'être*. The country's in limbo. Some people want to bring back old principles. They're not going to. Those principles are dead.

But no one has defined what new principles are. So there are negative and positive things. The country has lost a sense of arrogance, but it's lost a sense of who it is and where it's going."

"And yourself?"

"I still have a strong sense of personal ethics," Rubin confided, "but I'm not sure how it applies anymore. I'm less judgmental, more willing to admit I'm wrong. I'm less sure of what kind of society I'd like to see."

Seated here, amid the pillars of capitalism, with Wall Street several blocks away, I found myself unwillingly appreciating Rubin's fluency, which I expected, and the growing perimeters of his insight, which I had not, and—for a moment—thought concord possible.

If the country was "in limbo," less "arrogant, less judgmental," the early 1970s had helped make it so. If we could agree on this, in itself a small, belated triumph, might commonality exist also in its scars and hidebound longings so that we could find, at last, long after the age had vanished, an age not bereft of trust?

"You mean, by looking back," he was saying, talking quickly, looking out the window, "we'll find some reasons for why the country has become what it's become?"

"Yes, and us too."

"Why take the time?" he rasped, turning stone-faced; and fastening a coat, he propelled the bill toward me. "There's no past. No future. I don't care about what's gone before. All that matters is now. Money, that's the poetry of the 1980s. I want to put my money where my mouth is, tell people about reform capitalism."

Fleeing the restaurant, Rubin talked of "visionary philosophy" and "cultural thinking" and of how "financial interest will capture the passions of the 1980s," and striding beside him back to John Muir and Company, I wondered if this man of bold, sunny simplicities had captured America's mainstream, or if the truth bespoke the reverse?

To Rubin, principles, like decades, were transient; he could as adroitly defend the rich (and aspire to expand their ranks) as he once had called them a four-letter word. If he saw himself as a financier—*venture banker* read his card—much as he once did a prophet, revolutionary, a patron of the perfect meritocracy, why should that surprise? Instead, what reverberated was not Rubin's fathering of private enterprise—how easy, for his soul of cardboard—but, rather, the measure to which his past dogma, the least substantive of all the era's notables, had *become* the mainstream.

What, after all, had Rubin asked? A nation unfazed by nuclear deterrents or military balance, unimpinged by such standards of conduct as self-restraint and authority, one devoid of shy goodness, a Fred MacMurray-type of geniality, and where children of the counterculture—freed to self-worship and absorb—might lose themselves in self-reverie, liberated from even secular morality, unable to assume its responsibilities, unwilling to discern what they were.

Rereading *The Greening of America* a decade after its publication, I sensed the enormity of Rubin's victory. Like nineteenth-century Chartists, who urged Great Britain, not unsuccessfully, to adopt much of their creed, the New Left in time made its agenda America's—insisting upon "no more Viet Nams"; on a defense posture that if frustrated and impotent, at least made warfare inglorious; on tolerance of drugs, abortion, and homosexuality, almost an ethical laissez-faire; on an undreamt-of "relativism" in television and cinema. One rainy, faceless Sunday afternoon in early 1981, watching the movie *Lassie's Disappearance,* (filmed only twelve years earlier), I felt as divorced from the present—and from the maelstrom of obscenity that inundated prime-time—as had Chiang Kai-shek, towering above the 1940s, from the fields and proletariat of China. "In the last decade," exulted Stewart Brand, publisher of the movement pamphlet, *The Whole Earth Catalogue,* "there has been an assimilation of practically our entire culture."

Andy Warhol, laboring to stimulate, once argued that before the second millennium, everyone would be "a celebrity for fifteen minutes." Among Rubin's convictions, were there any whose half-life was much longer? In truth, a truly ambitious prodigal, he shed precepts as shamelessly as he cradled them; here was a man of mirrors, a practitioner of the bumper-sticker mentality. Had martial pride tinged America in the early 1970s, as it would a decade later in the wake of the hostage release, when many—equally voguish—thought patriotism born again by the waving of yellow ribbons, would Rubin not have echoed it? Or mouthed platitudes, this time in *defense* of old decencies, as stupifyingly vacant as *make love, not war* and *kill the pigs* and *Nixon is a murderer?*

That he was still a celebrity, adjudged a folk-hero, not fraud, I conceded, spoke balefully of America's social wilderness; a singularly revealing nihilism. The court jester of the revolution? He should be laughing at *us*, I remember thinking. His triumph made shysters of us all.

Across the street, in a first-floor bar, surrounded by men who unearthed banalities, I read a beer-stained letter from a college classmate.

"At Geneseo, I learned to feel deeper, empathize with other people better, and to examine myself more closely," said Marty Shopes. "As young adults, we were exposed to many ideas and occurrences that we had no parallel experiences to relate to. So often we floundered while trying to integrate these experiences into our beings.

"What do I remember about college? How friends helped you to understand; they helped hold you together when you were unsteady; they were most always there and they always cared. It was OK to open up to people, and you could do so without fear of ridicule. For the next week that friend of yours might have to come back to open up to you."

Tall and lean and blond, a varsity swimmer, Marty Shopes wrote poetry in college, which moved him, and found meaning in relationships that alternately wrenched and illuminated. "I'm not married at this time," he continued, "and while it hasn't changed since college, it is a change in the sense that I was not supposed to be married in college whereas now I am *supposed* to be. I'm still an introspective person who can be an extrovert if the situation demands it. But basically, a loner.

"I'm older, wiser, calmer, and less idealistic, much like your typical 1973 graduates. I don't get as totally consumed by people or issues anymore. I thought I'd be married with two kids by now. I thought I'd be teaching. I never thought Ronald Reagan could be elected president—or that I would vote for him. I could never have conceived, back in college, all those electronic video games. I can't believe professional sports salaries.

"Mostly, I expected these to be settling-down years—wife,

kids, clubs years—and they haven't been. They've been more of the learning, growing, experiencing type of years I had at Geneseo. I get the impression at this point in my life that I am one of those people who will never settle down. I really don't know if I want to."

As undergraduates, both solitary, private men, Marty Shopes and I clashed on arms control and disobedience, ecology and Biafra, even on the worth and indomitability of major league baseball. Unlike Jerry Rubin, Shopes faltered. He misstepped. He was hesitant, unsure. But in searching, he was genuine, and because his sensitivity was tangible, his romanticism real, he understood—and could bring to the early 1970s—the humanity that Jerry Rubin could not.

I flushed my drink and hailed a taxicab. "Address?" I asked the driver. "It's not far from here." Waiting for Milhous, the quintessence of my years at Geneseo, I knew that from college I would never travel very far away.

17
Beyond Midnight

HIS HISTORY WAS OUR HISTORY. HE WAS LOVED BY MANY and hated by more. He was bitter and inscrutable, incisive and fascinating, and from his station, profoundly misunderstood. He was the thirty-seventh president of the United States. He was also the lodestar around whom our years in college turned.

"Before leaving," he confided frequently to aides, "I want to make a difference." In 1969–73, did Richard Nixon make a difference? Each autumn, do the Boston Red Sox fold?

Without this secretive, brilliant, and often disconcerting icon, college would have been different, out lives incalculably altered. His presence changed the nation. His actions changed the world.

"Nobody is going to remember an administration which manages things 10 percent better," I remembered Nixon saying in 1971. One decade later, rising in an elevator to the thirteenth floor of 26 Federal Plaza, New York, I sought to reassure him. Who could forget *his* administration? Five years after resignation, The *Washington Post* said of the shy, pugnacious ex-president, "He emerges as the one true superstar of the 1970s."

Until Watergate, one thought as the elevator opened, Richard Nixon was trusted by the American people—personally, perhaps, and professionally—to conduct his office as a president should.

Before I left college, the draft ended. The war ceased, "with honor," as it were. Doors were unlocked to the planet's most populous nation, freed by the man who, as a candidate for vice president, once reviled the "Red Devil," while in Moscow, the menace of nuclear arms ephemerally dimmed. Even in the Middle East, the president's oft-proclaimed goal, "a generation of peace," took root; a fragile truce, unsundered by ancient enmity, linked Egypt and Israel, and led, in time, to the Camp David Accords of 1978. Foreign affairs held Nixon's interest; it could be treated impersonally, shuffled through intermediaries; it lent itself to distance and deliberation. Here, where he felt most comfortable, Nixon proved superb, foreseeing a globe on which as America acknowledged the limits of its power, its adversaries respected the power of its will.

At home, his pulse was less distinct, attentive. Though, domestically, as it unfolded, the Nixon Doctrine sought to contain the Great Society, and supplant it with a decision-process dependent less on Washington than municipalities and states, many of its measures were frustrated—disarmed by Democrat dominance of the Senate and House of Representatives; by a philosophy which often seemed at cross-purposes— e.g. advocacy of welfare assistance and antibusing ordinances—and by a president who in midpassage of his first term reversed economic theory, fleeing Republican orthodoxy ("we must balance the federal budget so that the American housewife can balance the family budget") for the millennium of full employment. "We are all Keynesians," he declared in 1971.

As president, Nixon was intractably enigmatic—rough-hewn and delicate: the more we saw of him, the less we knew— but his record (and priorities) were clear. Would his legacy revolve around the role of peacemaker or the stain of criminality? Both were a part of his administration. Both made his presidency historic.

Leaving the elevator, I recalled recent counsel in *Esquire* magazine, like the *Post*, to Nixon, rabidly unbenign. "In the years since he had left office, it had become clear that he was the one political figure of our age who was bigger than life," it read. "There was no player in the national drama who came close to Nixon; the *idea* of Nixon was somehow central to the experience of being an American in the second half of this century."

The hallway was deserted. I turned to my right and found a door, number 1309. Entering the room, two Secret Service agents behind me, I fastened on huge color pictures that catapulted me back to college—of Nixon with Brezhnev; Nixon with Sadat; Nixon with Chou En-lai; Nixon embracing several Chinese youths; Nixon speaking, waving, deplaning; Nixon in a motorcade, with Pat, flinging high the V. I stopped, frowned in thought; such photos spoke of unforgotten years.

When I abandoned Geneseo, the shadow on these walls was a president seeking to reshape the earth, bold yet retiring, spurred by the panoply of his office. Now, if not an exile in his own country, he was strangely alone, removed from the pinnacle, standing there, slightly hunched, clad in a dark blue suit, beside an illuminated globe.

"Just fly in?" he asked, tanned, younger than one expected, settling in a moss-colored chair.

"Yes, this morning."

"Like New York?" he asked.

"Always have."

"Yeah," he said. "It has a ferment. It makes you feel alive." To Nixon's left loomed a large desk, its surface polished, uncluttered; to its rear, a patchwork of flags, one of the United States, a second bearing the presidential seal. "I've always said for years that you could be by yourself here easier than anyplace in the world."

"And that really means something to you, being by yourself."

"I've never felt you could afford to be undisciplined," he confided, the voice rich and disembodied. "That was especially true when I was president. You can't have a couple drinks, screw around with some friends; you have to live like a Spartan. Save yourself. Be mentally able to make hard decisions in an intelligent way." His eyes widened and went black. "Some people like to make decisions by committee, by consent, you know. Carter led by following polls, by giving people what they wanted, what was popular. Johnson too; he had Gallup and Harris Polls coming out of his underwear. But that's not leadership."

"What is?"

"Taking an unpopular course and making it popular," he said.

"But doesn't that negate a democracy?" I proposed. "What about the 'will of the people'?"

"Sometimes," he said, "you have to go against the grain."

"You had enough chance to do that."

"Yes," he replied, "I don't deny it. But people have the impression, mistakenly, I think," and unguardedly, he twirled reading glasses in his hands, "that a government is like a business. Hell, no. A president must have vision. I was reading a biography of Churchill by Isaiah Berlin—this was just a few weeks ago—and I saw this, 'Many leaders have judgment. Judgment is not unusual. But very few have vision.' Well, Churchill had it, a sixth sense, if you will."

"And you're suggesting, now," I said, "that you had it?"

"That's up to the historians," he conceded, not without a measure of self-deprecation. "I do know this. The decisions that are important," Nixon said, "are the decisions that must be made alone."

Listening, I stared at the former president. "The essence of this man," said Henry Kissinger, "is loneliness." With visitors, still tentative in their midst, he would often speak, mildly, gently, as he did today, of assortments like baseball and Central Park and fast-food and jogging, hoping, it seemed, that small talk, by itself, could abolish fear. He had always been among us; we knew him, or at least his caricature. He was a part of our lives. To me, unlike many classmates, hating Richard Nixon was not required study. But like them, I too belonged to what columnist Meg Greenfield called the "Nixon Generation," his orb a mirror, in ways we had yet to comprehend completely, of the trial and promise of the nuclear age.

"Longevity?" he said. "Oh, I suppose so. It probably seems an eternity, my life in the public arena, especially to someone your age."

"It does."

"Probably," he repeated, a half-smile pasted to his face. "But I didn't stay in politics for the glamour, the ego trips. Campaigns are a horrible, excruciating experience."

"Almost," I said, "like going to battle."

Nixon moved his palms outward and shrugged. "Yes," he laughed thinly, "but you know what I liked about it? Politics isn't a science. It's an art, a way to express yourself, and beyond that, a mystery."

"You used to tell Ray Price [Nixon's chief speechwriter] that politics was poetry, not prose."

"It *is*," he agreed, abruptly. "Prose is static, immobile. Poetry means potential, like going to China was poetry, the hope of the unknown, the possibility to think beyond immediate problems. It means taking the long view—having the backbone to ward off the screamers and the nuts. When you think of becoming president," he said, staring out the window at a row of buildings, "you know why I wanted it? The trappings? Hell, no. If I never had to review an honor guard, I'd have been delighted."

"Then why?"

"*Being* president is nothing compared to what you could *do* as president," I heard him saying. "What I liked about the job—why I sought it—is the chance that in the brief time I had, I could do something that someone else might not be able to. Limit nuclear proliferation. End the draft and the rest. That's what made it worthwhile. Why I could put up with the cries of 'murderer' and 'tyrant' and all that, and endure the abuse—nobody had a worse press than I did, both in the time you were in school," he said, recoiling from the memory, "and, of course, before."

As president, he made Americans listen—even Nixon-haters—in spite of themselves. So, though, had other presidents, I reminded him—Truman with the Marshall Plan, Ike amid his glorious somnolence, Kennedy in the primacy of Camelot. Why did *Nixon* polarize them? Was it the war alone, or the press, or the upbringing of his youth, or was there something in his being that made millions regard him as a hero, while others, echoing Irving Howe, thought of the White House and said of its occupant, "We know the nightmare is ours."

The former president stiffened; he leaned forward in his chair. "You know, I'm no good at this kind of talk," he said, his voice devoid, finally, after the reverent madness of the last ten years, of shame and sloganeering.

"I know this," Nixon added seconds later, looking me in the eye. "I'd be the first to admit I'm not a table-pounder. I never promised more than I could produce. And I don't put down my people the way, say, Johnson did. It's not my style. When I became president, I decided I wasn't going to change it. Even if I wanted to, of course, I couldn't."

"Why not? You might have been better off if you had."

"Oh, I know. Cold, removed, they say. They said it of Mrs. Nixon too. Well, I thought the president should retain a quality of dignity, remoteness," he said. "Sure, people want their president to be a nice guy, but not lewd. Not a bumbling slob." A brief, derisive laugh. "The press. How ridiculous. To them having dignity means being cold."

"But isn't that what you conveyed?"

"It wasn't a case of trying to be formal, of being something I'm not. I just *am*," he said. Pause. "But it's not just me. It's the whole cultural thing. These hypocrites, the little bastards, you know, the trash like the Abbie Hoffmans and the Jerry Rubins and so forth, and the Establishment liberals, they're always talking about the poor blacks, the poor Chicanos, the poor Third World. You'd think from their garbage that they love the world. But do you know 'em? You think they could choke up about their parents or the flag? Individually, they're insensitive, unfeeling, arrogant. They look down their noses at people— Humphrey, remember, was a rare exception to that rule—and they don't understand them. They adore humanity—they just hate people."

"And you," I said, wondering, "what do you adore?"

"You know," he continued, "they're the exact opposite of what you're taught in the Bible—the tenets of Christianity, where it says show respect and consideration for the individual. Oh sure, they may be informal, they may talk about their feelings and blow up a big smoke screen, and they may love people in blocs, but one on one, forget it. With me, I wear a coat and tie. I don't show feelings, though I have them. Does that mean I'm formal? Sure, but I can't change. It's just the way I am."

I hesitated slightly; Nixon on Nixon was rare, unfamiliar. If his rigidity was authentic ("If I had shown feelings," he contended, "I probably wouldn't have lasted"), was it not, I asked, also a mechanism for survival—a reality/rehearsal much like *Love Story*, that movie released during his presidency, where a college student told his girlfriend, "You put up this big wall to keep you from being hurt, but it also keeps you from being touched"?

"You mean, did I construct a facade?" Nixon asked.

"Yes."

"Possibly," he answered. "You know, politics is not very gentle," and as sunlight framed his profile, one heard again Nixon's 1970 admission, "I am an introvert in an extrovert's profession."

He discarded the reminiscence and rose from the chair. What mattered in the early 1970s, he said, liberated from self-scrutiny, were *issues*, "not charisma or what the sophisticates call style, all that mumbo-jumbo the trendies focus on and mutter about and which amounts to absolutely zero." Moving toward the window, calm, dispassionate, he talked about the rule of law, about the need for economy in government, about the creation of a volunteer army and the worth of nuclear parity, about past mistakes ("I'm an expert. We've been through a wrenching experience in the last decade—the war, the Watergate business, the feeling America couldn't do a damn thing right. And its cost.") and smoldering slander ("I used to think, 'Why do critics *hate* me so?'"), about the war in Southeast Asia and how it curdled campus youth. "I never bitched about it, and I didn't cause it, but the war plagued my presidency," he said, his manner turning urgent now, his fingers working in unrhythmic support.

"Yes, but you didn't stop it either," I said.

"I inherited the war. When I came in, five hundred thousand troops were in Southeast Asia, no hope for victory, no plans to bring them home. Actually," Nixon said, smiling wanly, "we were already very pregnant in Viet Nam by the time Johnson became president—it was Kennedy, you recall," the Ghost of 1960 reappearing, "who sent in sixteen thousand troops as advisers. Mel Laird [secretary of defense] and Bill Rogers [secretary of state], and some Republicans, they were screaming, 'Get out. Blame it on Kennedy. Or Johnson. It's a Democratic war.' But the point is, it was *America's* war."

"And you made it Nixon's war."

"No," he argued, "I made a decision early on to see it through to an honorable conclusion, not to be pushed around by the demonstrators and the rabble in the streets. You know, we're not like the British in the nineteenth century. They could lose one, blow a war, and they were still a world power."

"Well, we lost in Viet Nam," I said. "and we're still a power too."

"We'd never lost *before*," Nixon jousted. "And we're such

an isolationist people to begin with—just go back and read
Washington's Farewell Address. And I always felt the greatest
consequence of failing to leave Viet Nam honorably would be
to our morale—if we lost, we'd shrivel inward. We'd start
thinking of ourselves as in the grip of the damned."

"That hasn't happened," I said.

"Well, look at Ethiopia. South Yemen. Angola. Afghanistan. Iran," he challenged. "And Communists behind it all. And
we haven't kept our commitments, haven't done a thing to stop
them. None of this would have happened had Viet Nam not
ended the way it did."

"Looking back, was your conduct correct?" I asked.

"In Viet Nam?"

"Yes."

"Absolutely," he said.

"Despite the scars it left at home?"

"I think the proof is *in* Viet Nam. The bloodbath that's
taken place there is exactly what I said would happen if we
bugged out. And remember April of 1975, when Saigon fell?
Those refugees weren't leaving toward the North, toward
communism. They were heading *south*, toward what they
thought was us."

"Meaning what?"

"That like the boat people of four, five years later, when
people choose between democracy and tyranny, they'll choose
the former. What I regret is not our effort there. That was
worthwhile."

"Even with fifty-five thousand American deaths?" I reminded him.

"It was honorable," he said firmly, "and in light of
developments since then, with Communist endeavors all
around the globe, correct. What I regret is the cost here at
home, especially in college."

Nixon paused, reaching across artificiality, still one of the
most disciplined men in America, and the sensation announced
itself to me, as his silence awaited my response, that the former
president, in his seventh decade, having fallen and risen and
fallen again, had not so much triumphed over, as *outlasted*, the
sketchmarks and reservations of his opponents—a Nixon, they
said, nothing if not extravagantly phony, a man who could

ravage his own spirit as easily (and totally) as he canonized his mother a saint.

"I understand what you're saying," I said, finally, "but the war tore this country apart—not just its start, its continuation. We were at war here. Not with guns usually, but we got maimed anyway. And there are those who say the reason was you, your policies."

Turning, Nixon again sat in his chair. "Yes, you can make that charge," he allowed, "but I didn't get the troops in; I got them out."

"It took you four years to do so," I said.

"Sure," he responded, "but when I came in, the presidency was paralyzed, and even though I treated Johnson honorably," consulting with him after January 20, 1969; speaking of him publicly [as with Nixon, Jimmy Carter would not] as a well-intentioned, patriotic fixture, "the legacy he left me—the problems it caused trying to get out and not be humiliated—well, it's something that we were able to do what we did in foreign affairs, Viet Nam notwithstanding.

"But you're right," he said, "it made things so difficult, and nowhere more than with people of your age. Not so much with kids who didn't go to college—they understood what we were trying to do. They were waving American flags and marching with the hard hats and they weren't ashamed to say, 'I love this country.' They talk about your younger generation. Let me tell you—they were part of it too."

Nixon looked at the ceiling. I looked at his face. His countenance was pained, almost wistful, a prisoner, one gleaned, of an earlier milieu. "With college students," he said slowly, "I was so frustrated at times. It was hard for Julie; I couldn't even go to her graduation; there were threatened disruptions if I went. And Kent State, I can't think back upon that without a haunting sense of sadness, tragic, even though I don't blame the National Guard—they were just kids and they were provoked and they were no older, you know, than the students shot. But still," said the former president, staring at the carpet, "that picture of the girl kneeling above the dying student, it doesn't leave you."

"Nor other Americans, either," I concurred.

"And it's the students like that I'd hoped to have given a

vision of America, a reason to think of this as a great and good country."

"But the war went on, in part," I said, "because you wouldn't leave—it got in the way."

"I don't blame them, the students," he said, not hearing. "They were bright as hell. They wanted to learn. And who can doubt why they thought like they did? After all, 75 percent of the media against me, 90 percent television, 95 percent of the faculty," and now Nixon's head was rising, his eyes upon me. "Who needs to wonder why they fell for this stupid business about there being 'good wars' and 'bad wars,' as if it's bad to fight for freedom against communists and good to fight against the fascists? Or that they thought it was OK—May Day in '71— to go smashing windows and looting stores and try to bring the government to a halt? Why not? Why not get carried away by hate? They were being egged on constantly by teachers trying to ingratiate themselves with students—you know, they couldn't make a name any other way, couldn't butter a piece of toast—so they thought, 'I'll be a big wheel on campus and attack the war'—and because it became the thing to do, it snowballed.

"And these sanctimonious frauds on campus, they thought they were living in the real world. Hell, they don't understand the real world, that's why they didn't expect the Reagan landslide of '80. The responsibility for opposing America in the war falls on the leadership class. It was the faculty leaders and professional agitators and the pampered kids on campus who were out screaming, protesting, crowding around the White House." He smiled a small smile. "Sometimes it was so loud you couldn't even go to sleep at night."

"You'd have preferred to be out of town those week-ends," I said.

"Either that or buy a pair of earmuffs cheap."

Laughter washed the room. "I'll never forget," Nixon observed, "how a few weeks ago Abbie Hoffman was out at the University of Oregon, I think, getting $4,000 to make a speech, and he said, 'You know, we need a cause. We don't have one.' Well," he said, his arm sweeping across his thigh, "that says it all. These radicals, and their teachers, that's what the war was— a *cause*, something to feel altruistic about, and they always cloaked their opposition in such *high* and *mighty*, such *lofty*, *idealistic* terms," and speaking, Nixon mocked each syllable, implying in their idealism fraudulence, making their "lofty" low, "but what they really wanted was to avoid fighting, to keep from getting their asses shot off."

"What's unnatural about that?" I asked. "I mean, to live, is it bad?"

"No," he said, "but why didn't they just say so? Instead, all you heard about was their morality and their marvelous purpose and their desire for peace. What it really was—and this gets to their background—they really wanted their demands met. You look at the protesters—they were affluent kids—and they'd always been pampered rotten, spoiled."

"Not all of them," I said.

"No one had ever pointed out, 'You have a responsibility to your country.' No, it was always, 'Whatever you want, you get.' So when they found out they might have to fight for America, no wonder the trash went berserk." Nixon's face hardened. "It was always, 'Oh, look at our pollution. Look at our race problems. Look at how our parents gave us such a terrible country.' And the professors were always applauding. Well, when those same kids left America to travel abroad on trips— and, of course, they always had the money to do so—I didn't see many of 'em stay away from this 'terrible country.' They always came back."

Nixon shook his head and laughed scornfully. "We even had kids of our own cabinet members—they had the money, they were used to getting what they wanted—who were out marching in the streets. Not like those who were back in college working their own way through school."

"Like you did at Duke."

"Yeah, in law school," he said, halting, and then, "Did you work in college?"

"Yes," I answered.

"A lot?" Nixon asked.

"Four jobs."

"Not bad," he exclaimed. "You know, the worst thing that can happen is for parents to make life too easy for their kids. And another thing. You know, I can understand the signs and the chants and so forth by young people back then. But I could never understand the contempt some had for their parents. There's nothing more despicable than not giving your parents the respect they deserve. How can you justify it? How can you defend it?

"We once had a prayer service in the White House on Sunday, and this kid was going to Harvard through the good graces of his father, and he was at the service because his dad had been invited. Well, his old man was Greek, I think. He didn't have much education. Didn't speak good English. And his son laughed at him right there in the receiving line. Was ashamed of the way his father talked. And I saw so much of that. Who in the hell did they think they were?" he flared. "I was so mad, I could have hit him in the mouth."

Brooding, Nixon fell silent. "I remember my old man. He didn't have much education, never got through high school," he said, curiously pensive, almost inaudibly, "but he was a hell of a man."

He was sensitive, the former president; he valued privacy; his seclusion served as a defense. "You know," he said, "getting back to what we were talking about, I'm not well-educated either, but people *have* sort of thought of me as an intellectual—I enjoy the stimulation, the give and take, the debate. And I think without all the excesses from the war—I wonder if sometimes, some of the girls, especially, knew how beautiful they were and how ugly they turned when they spit things, screamed epithets, let hate destroy them—I think students and I might have found a lot in common. At least some of 'em," for antiwar radicals, in Nixon's parlance, indulged in "show biz ... empty gestures," playing to the television camera; the president engaged in substance.

Watching him reembellish time, still inward, with a fatalism surprising for a public official, I remembered the Nixon of September 16, 1970, cheered by students at the Kansas State University fieldhouse as they outflanked hecklers and he proclaimed, "Those who bomb universities, who ambush policemen, who hijack airplanes and hold their passengers hostage, all share in common not only a contempt for human life but also a contempt for those elemental decencies on which free society rests—and they deserve the contempt of every American who values those decencies."

The Nixon who later wrote the university's president, "Your students ... showed that there is a responsible majority, and that it too has a voice .... Their example will hasten the day when leaders in public life once more can routinely appear on college campuses, to meet with students, to discuss the great issues with them, to listen and be listened to—and when it will cease to be news that they are able to."

The Nixon of four months earlier (May 9), compassionate and troubled, unable to sleep, visiting the Lincoln Memorial before dawn, where, encountering protesters in the aftermath of Kent State, he talked of travel, pacifism, and "peace at the center." His trek was impromptu, unplanned; the president's dialogue was perverted by reporters (not present at the Memorial) who wrote, mistakenly, that he focused inanely on football and surfing. As a result, the sojourn was a "press opportunity debacle," as Ronald Zeigler might have named it. With proper advance work, Nixon confided to H.R. Haldeman, the incident could have been more accurately (and charitably) portrayed. "But I really wonder," the president continued, "in the long run, if that is all the legacy we want to leave. If it is—then perhaps we should do our job as easily as we can—as expeditiously as we can—and get out and leave the responsibilities of the government to the true materialists—the socialists and the totalitarians, who talk idealism but rule ruthlessly without any regard to the individual considerations—the respect for personality that I tried to emphasize in my dialogue with the students."

Or the Nixon, finally (in his dictated recollections), musing privately, deeply moved by his foray to the Lincoln Memorial. "What we all must think about is, why we are here. What are those elements of the spirit which really matter?...I said candidly that I didn't have the answer, but I knew that young people today were searching, as I was searching forty years ago, for an answer. I just wanted to be sure that all of them realized that ending the war, and cleaning up the streets and the air and the water, were not going to solve spiritual hunger—which all of us have and which, of course, has been the great mystery of life from the beginning of time."

A Nixon of distance and diffidence and much self-pity. A Nixon alternately timid, much-wounded, wary, deferential.

"At heart, a softie," Johnson's press secretary, George Christian, would call him. A Nixon, wrote Woodward and Bernstein, coauthors of *The Final Days*, of "almost demonic courage." A Nixon of many selves.

He was talking now, in a soft, thoughtful way, about Hangchow, Leningrad, and integration, and why he needed solitude ("I've always cherished time to contemplate, to write, think, and maybe," joked the old piano player, "even to draft some music someday"), and how his public image, stiff and fastidious, appalled those who despised him. "Today, remember," he said, "it's the decade to empty out your insides. You're supposed to confide and whimper and spill everything. Tell all, you know. 'Golly, I couldn't work yesterday because I was so upset...' and so forth. Well, I couldn't do that. Empty your insides? No. Not me. I wasn't brought up to ask people to comfort or do things for me. And now, I guess, that attitude is sort of out of style, sort of old-fashioned, passé."

Why, in 1969–73, I asked earlier, had America become polarized? Hearing Nixon, I knew. "You were born twenty years too late," a classmate once told me, striving to amuse, as singing with a band, I warbled "Wabash Cannonball." Need more be said of Nixon? His "many selves" were my (and others') selves, not personally, but culturally. The selves I respected, his opponents scorned.

Nixon was a folk hero/antihero, I suspected, not because of his politics (though they widened that gulf), nor because of his ideology (a conservative, he was loathed by the nation's tastemakers), but because of what he meant as a *person* and the emotions he upheld. His constituency lay among the stable and established, those who prized discipline and control—"good, decent, law-abiding, tax-paying citizens"—not Eric Goldman's "MetroAmerican," privileged by bearing and lineage to rule.

"He never knew who he was," critics, post-Watergate, nodded sagely, but as Richard Nixon conversed and afternoon faded, I sensed, strangely, as his manner spoke of propriety and a modesty, not newly formed, that was neither bogus nor offensive, that he knew himself too well.

Poor from childhood, determined to escape, Nixon realized how hardship could mangle life, leaving one naked, without money or prestige. Poverty made him leery, a man of lonely, hostile impulse. Savaged early by a foreboding world, he trusted himself and his instincts; seeking security, groping upward, driving, always driving, he found solace in tenacity. Blessed by later fortune, he was haunted, until the late 1970s, by the dread that someday, somehow, he might again be poor.

Nixon understood hardship. But he grasped self-reliance too, as did his wife—"I never had time to think about who I wanted to be, or who I admired, or to have ideas," she told Gloria Steinem in 1968. "I never had time to dream about being anyone else. I haven't just sat back and thought of myself or my ideas of what I wanted to do. I'm not like all of you . . . all those people who had it easy"—and knowing poverty and achievement, he became pridefully defiant, furious with leeches and loafers, a man who railed against "God-damned Ivy Leaguers" and "fucking academics," and whose mournful past, never forgotten, joined him with millions of kindred spirits, many among them in upstate New York.

To Nixon, self-control was essential; it was almost militantly protective; it could quiet rage. It also masked, in a way observers seldom realized, a quality which, unallayed, vulcanized vulnerability—his kindness, and thus his fear of being used, as if knowing of his prim and orderly heart, born of America's polite, decorous respectability, and regarding it as a weakness, he must compensate by divining strength.

"Most politicians waffle, waver, slink around on issues of substance. But individually, in public relations, they're outgoing, gregarious. Nixon was different," Bryce Harlow told me. "He had enormous courage. In decisions affecting war and peace, he was the bravest man in the world. But in a political world of 'hail fellow well met,' he was surprisingly mild and withdrawn.

"Nixon could be brutal—but in the mass, not one on one. Because with two people in the room, if Nixon was one, he'd inevitably give in. It made him easy to work for; Nixon wouldn't rip you to shreds like, for instance, Johnson would. The problem is, because he was aware most men in government weren't as sensitive as he, it made him insecure. And insecure, he retreated."

Nixon, said Harlow, drew back from confrontation; he used aides as a shield, his insurance against rebuff. "He could

cut your head off, but he'd always have somebody else do it."
Calculating, he was also considerate—writing notes of affection to his daughters ("it helps not to have to say things," said
Julie, "if you're shy"); asking at a dinner for returning POWs in
1973 that corsages be given wives; remembering birthdays
with roses; mailing private, handwritten letters to defeated
rivals; preferring, when a secretary made a typing error, to
redictate his memo, thus voiding her mistake.

He could be vengeful. But was Nixon mean-spirited, the
grimy monster of Herblock lore, or was his sense of past injury
("shafted," he put it) warranted, not imagined, and rooted in
hypocrisy?—a double standard which judged Watergate ab-
horrent (a Republican stigma) and indulged massive vote fraud
(by Democrats); which claimed for the Eastern Establishment
all trace of moral authority; and which condemned his administration as transparent, his deeds as president corrupt? Was he
cold or solicitous? He was both, I surmised, for his kindness
was often unreciprocated, his trust not infrequently abused.

"Well, anyway," he was saying now, "a thing I note, a
phenomenon, is that in recent years it's become the fad for
people to sit with someone and confess all their troubles and
their vices and their inner trials and get them to say, 'Gee, isn't it
great for you to be so candid. So forthright. Boy, do you have
my admiration and the rest.' And the press, of course, falls all
over themselves lapping it up, especially if they agree with
you."

"You say that," I said, "but some people would call it
concern."

Nixon whistled, again shaking his head. "What they really
want is the easy way out, for the person listening to say, 'Lord,
you have troubles. Isn't it so bad you have to fend for yourself.
Let me be your prop. Let me bail you out.' Well," he continued,
"what in the hell is admirable about that?"

"It's being compassionate," I suggested.

"It's being weak and even more, self-centered," he said. "I
prefer the Catholic way—go to a priest and confess your
frailties, but do it quietly, no flim-flam. I think you should be
responsible, keep your troubles to yourself."

Was Nixon incapable of asking for help? In "Us against
Them," among "us," he was not alone. He matured in an age (as

I did, in a home) where self-denial was right-minded, where self-aggrandizement meant selfishness, and where, no matter how desperate, one followed his wife's 1973 counsel: "I don't tell all."

In truth, neither satanic nor the dream to save the land, he was deemed, somehow, both—by my younger sister, who cried when he was elected, and my older sister, who cried when he resigned, and by my grandparents, who respected him, and my parents, who admired him, and my home town, which endorsed him, and by most of my girlfriends, who disliked him, and most of my classmates, who disdained him, and by the first three decades of my life—a figure so vilified and resilient and eclectic and voluminous that nearing the year 2000, only Franklin Roosevelt and Dwight Eisenhower eclipse him as firmaments of Henry Luce's American Century.

Nixon's sins, I saw as virtues. His virtues, critics saw as sins. His solitude, they called isolation; his solidity, arrogance; his propriety, aloofness; his sentimentality, corn. This schism— "this traumatic clash of cultures," Greenfield termed it— divided families, classmates, legislators, above all, generations, and as it lodged in the White House, in a man who was proud of the old culture, it underscored his rapport with America's great middle masses and then, after my graduation, helped bring about his fall.

He was unflamboyant, uncharismatic; decidedly not, in his pejorative phrase, a *glamour boy*. Few political signs were more miscast than the 1968 placards, "Nixon has soul," and "Nixon has that ooh-aah." But both at Allegheny and Geneseo State, as the Nixon presidency evolved, we did not feel, as Robert Lowell once said of the republic, that "the mausoleum [was] in her heart." America did not feel insecure. She did not feel diminished.

"So," said the former president, his voice rising, vigorous, "where do you go from here?"

"Back to school. Leave for Geneseo. Last chapter. Last stop."

"Yes," he replied. "I bet it'll bring back memories."

"Already has."

"Well, just remember this," he said. "You can't live in the past. Even with all that's gone before, you can't return. All the triumphs in the world, they don't matter if you don't go on, carve out new niches, give new meaning to life. And all the setbacks, they don't matter if you never give up. Never give up. Never. The key to life, it isn't winning, it's fighting. It isn't being vindicated, it's being right."

Addressing me, he was addressing himself. He had *endured*, he was telling me, endured the hate and malice and obscenities. Endured because, at sixty-eight, he was unsinkable; "like a bobbed cork," Harlow said. Endured because of his stoicism and refusal to change, his belief that, after Carter, Americans understood belatedly what vision in a president embraced. Endured so that, after what had visited him, scandal, disgrace, and for his wife, a stroke, the darkest midnight of life's experience, he might find dignity in survival, and survival in hope.

We shook hands. Nixon retired to his globe. One thought of Checkers and *Six Crises*, of Horatio Alger (whom he saw as Nixon) and Alger Hiss (whom he destroyed), of the Great Debates of 1960 (which cost him the presidency) and the Great Comeback of 1968 (in which, implausibly, he seized the grail), of Pat's cloth coat and the Nixon family, as straight and resolute as they came, of the Old Nixon turned New Nixon, the loser turned winner, of Viet Nam dissolving into Watergate and "bring us together," Nixon's cry of 1968, into the creed of four years later, "us against them." His presence had intruded upon college much as the World Series does October—defiled in the student union, acclaimed in a mathematics class, his words heard on radio as students hurried across campus, his fate dwelt upon in the evening news—a Nixon who invoked freedom and security and the nobility of work, and who, campaigning, spoke of law and order and "peace without surrender" and "the spiritual values of America," and who each election, as autumn crested, communed with rallies in the rain.

Leaving his office, I turned and saw, in the hued shadows of late afternoon, in a city he loved, in the nation he changed, the most remarkable American of our time.

18
Afterword

I HAD HOPED, SOMEHOW, TO PUT THE EARLY 1970S BEHIND me, for though I felt for them a loyalty and a love, their richness, I feared, ultimately meant infirmity, as if having lived the starburst of one's existence and known, like *Winesburg, Ohio,* how "one loves life so intensely that tears come into the eyes," what followed must bring sadness and cruelty and a yearning for a sense of time standing still.

My own decision, reached slowly, about that impossibility crested two weeks after meeting Nixon, when, revisiting Geneseo, where townspeople practiced the faith of their fathers, I found memories caught between puberty and adulthood, and understood—as I had not before—the permanence of their clasp.

They were too much with me, these years so proud and seething and straightforward; they had settled upon my consciousness. I could not discard them; I must accept them, and like all survivors of a winter of anxiety, use them to set me free.

Over the last decade, most people I knew had gained in certainty, yet among many of my classmates, the years since college an encircling debris, inner certitudes paled. Here, in walks amid Geneseo's pine cover or behind the wheel of my car, one could muse about such currents as "victory" and "defeat." Was there a difference between the two, and if there was, did it really matter? Was it better to have inflammation exalt my undergraduate years than, like most of my older friends—now serene and dutiful—never to have been affected at all?

I had supposed to find an answer, retreating to the college and enthusiasms of my past, but now, after leaving Washington for Atlanta, and South Bend for Lincoln Plaza, and Montgomery for the streams and locust trees of Montreat, I did not know. I knew only how the age had left us—inward yet combative, strident yet shy, qualities that brought one little in a new decade where compromise and conformity seemed to matter most. I knew only while absorbing this familiar soil, that even here at Geneseo—in this, the site of some of my warmest years, its land plain and rolling and unbroken, an expanse of haze and horizon, pleasant, almost golden—old verities had been supplanted, old landmarks struck down.

The early 1970s had been seared by colliding forces— right against left, hawk against dove, Main Street versus counterculture, hard hat versus hippie. And what had the clashes availed them? Who, in the end, had won? It seemed, in retrospect, that the turbulence that made the time electric later poisoned its causes and men. Those who opposed the Viet Nam War could not prevent its continuance; those who supported the war could not prevent its defeat. Apostles of law and order became entwined in massive scandal; proponents of "do your own thing" deteriorated into the generation of "Me."

Agnew had fallen, Ramsey Clark been humbled, and George Wallace shot; even Martha Mitchell died. Casualties *all*. For them, I realized, like those of us who, looking back, saw vulnerability and innocence, what the early 1970s uplifted, the late 1970s besmirched.

But was our pain without redemption? To age with courage, as Nixon and Chancellor and the Reverend Billy had, meant believing no. While our freshman class knew injury, it also radiated a breadth of experience, an empathy with an era, so sensual, so recognizable, so overwhelming, so kind, that a decade after college, enriched beyond other classes, enriched as much as scarred, I felt drawn, inexorably, more in hope than sorrow, to find what I loved and what I honored and what I thought would sustain the whole of life. College had been a magic place. Magic might come again.

Twilight dawned. The Genesee Valley glistened in the dusk. I passed the baseball field, its turf a swirl of emerald, and the student newspaper, where one felt bathed by consequence, and the campus center, dark and sullen. Entering a local restaurant, I ordered coffee at the same table where years before, black armbands mixed with tales of Richard Daley, and where naivete and promise merged.

How, an older teacher asked, would history judge the freshman class that controversy cradled? As a distant forerunner of some brave new world? Or, as "American Pie" phrased it, in a farewell song to youth, "There we were all in one place, a generation lost in space, with no time left to start again"?

Once upon a time, I answered quietly, the former—and perhaps by now the latter too.

Coffee arrived. The teacher departed, lured away by an inviting belle. And then I was alone, my anguished, exultant journey done, left to remember the lost America I once had cherished and still remained to mourn.

Index

About The Author

Curt Smith's first book, America's Dizzy Dean, *was called "a masterpiece" by the* Christian Science Monitor *and "remarkably eloquent" by NBC Network Radio. Chosen as a* Sports Illustrated Major Book of the Month Club *selection, the book focused largely on the values of small-town America—and the people associated with Dean's career as a baseball player and broadcaster.*

Formerly a feature writer with the Gannett Corporation's flagship newspaper, the Rochester, N.Y. Democrat & Chronicle, *and a public relations executive who has won numerous prizes for layout and design, Mr. Smith has also written for such publications as the* Washington Post, *the* Sporting News, *and the* New York Times.

The author of award-winning stories on subjects as varied as Floyd Patterson, Richard M. Nixon, and Roberto Clemente, he served as Chief Speechwriter for John B. Connally's 1980 Presidential campaign, then was appointed Senior Editor and National Affairs Editor of The Saturday Evening Post, *and is presently Senior Speechwriter for the Secretary of Health and Human Services.*

Mr. Smith was born in Caledonia, N.Y., and educated at Allegheny College in Meadville, Pa., and Geneseo State University, where he graduated with a degree in English. His interests include music, antiques, British History, and rooting— "usually in vain"—for the Boston Red Sox. Of Long Time Gone *he notes, "Ronald Reagan once said that 'Everyone has to have a place to go back to.' The early 1970s are that place for me."*